The Employer's Handbook 2015–16

The Institute of Directors is the professional body for business leaders and we have been representing our members for over 100 years.

The IoD is an influential network reflecting the full spectrum of international business leadership from the largest public corporation to the smallest family firm.

With such a diverse membership, a broad portfolio of benefits and services has been carefully designed to ensure that you and your business receive the practical support you need to successfully fulfil your role as a director.

IoD membership can add real value to your business. Benefits include free access to facilities offered by our prestigious premises in London, the UK and Europe, free business information and advice, professional development, training, conferences and publications to help you maximize your potential. This respected and influential organization works on your behalf, representing your concerns to government, and delivers you professional business support, wherever it is needed.

For more information about the IoD, visit www.iod.com.

Specialists in Employment Law

David Brook *"Takes a commercial view and is good at finding solutions to apparently impenetrable problems."*

"praised for his ability to assimilate the salient issues of a case in an instant."

(Chambers UK)

"Henderson Chambers' client care and management are second to none"

(Chambers UK)

"The set fields a cadre of silks and juniors few chambers can match"

(Chambers UK)

Personal Injury • Product Liability • Health & Safety • Business and Commercial • Group Actions • Information Technology • Finance and Consumer Credit • Public Inquiries • Environment • Property Litigation • Sports Law • Insurance • Clinical Negligence and Healthcare • Administrative and Public/Local Government • Employment • Public Procurement • Regulatory and Disciplinary • EU/Competition

Henderson Chambers
2 Harcourt Buildings
Temple
London EC4Y 9DB

goldmanbrook@hendersonchambers.co.uk
Telephone: 020 7583 9020
Fax: 020 7583 2686
DPA Clerk: Nick Bryant

www.hendersonchambers.co.uk

CAN I COME TO A BARRISTER DIRECT?

The short answer is yes. It is no longer necessary to come to a barrister through a solicitor. Companies and individuals can now come direct to a specialist barrister for advice and representation in all matters. A particularly useful resource in employment related matters.

But why bother?

Because it is usually more cost effective than going to a solicitor and you will be dealing direct with a specialist in the field. Solicitors routinely use barristers for specialist opinions in both contentious and non contentious matters and to represent their clients in litigation. There is no cost disadvantage in coming direct to a barrister. Court and Tribunal work underpins the practice of an employment barrister giving them a unique insight into how policies and procedures are best formulated to avoid litigation, or if unavoidable then to succeed on behalf of their client.

Benefits for Business

Small to medium sized enterprises ('SMEs') are greater in number than their larger counterparts and overall employ and engage more people both directly and indirectly. However the need to focus resources on productivity can mean that SMEs are under-resourced in human resource management and relevant legal support. Employment law underpins all working relationships, arguments concerning the same and, though it is usually best avoided, litigation. A basic understanding of what is required to sustain or terminate employment relationships can be acquired in advance of employment difficulties arising with brief in-house training. This too can be provided. Where difficulties do arise these can often can be resolved with the assistance of experienced practitioners. External assistance is all too often only engaged when an employment issue has become seemingly intractable. Often the absence of basic documentation and procedures lie at the root of the problem, the provision of which might have served to avoid the situation or at least render lawful the actions taken an employer. None of this need be the case.

Henderson Chambers

Barristers Linda Goldman and David Brook practise from Henderson Chambers and are specialists in employment law (for cases & citations see www/Henderson Chambers; Legal 500; Chambers & Partners). Each came to the law from a background in commerce and industry and each have sat part time as Employment Judges. Each primarily acts for industrial, local authority, commercial & professional clients in both contentious & non-contentious matters, regularly appearing before Employment Tribunals, the

County & High Courts, & the Appellant Courts. Linda has particular expertise in the drafting of employment contracts, internal procedures and employee handbooks. Each routinely negotiate exit packages, small and large scale redundancies, TUPE transfers, discrimination/whistle blowing claims, restructuring the workforce, short-time working, and across the board variations to salary and contractual benefits. They have practical experience in obtaining and resisting injunctions involving sensitive & confidential information, including those with cross border considerations, and the mediated resolution of employment disputes, as mediator or on behalf of a particular client.

Early Intervention

If possible litigation is to be avoided particularly in employment matters. It is disruptive, frequently expensive, and has uncertain outcomes. Early Intervention ™ ("EI") in employment disputes is intended to resolve matters at an early pre litigation stage or, if litigation has already begun, to bring the matter to a mediated conclusion. Intervention can be neutral, with a barrister acting as mediator, or with a barrister acting and negotiating on behalf of one of the parties. It can often help preserve and build upon existing working relationships or, where there is to be a parting of the ways, resolve matters with an agreed settlement thus avoiding litigation. When acting on behalf of a client negotiations are conducted with a view to achieving early resolution beneficial to that client and, if litigation becomes unavoidable, in a manner which will not compromise the client's position. If a matter is at too early a stage to engage in mediation then understanding the legal issues and access to draft scripts for use in discussions/investigations can help avoid an undesirable outcome, or at least help to move a matter in an acceptable direction. Instead of a de-briefing session after an employment tribunal case far better to avoid the case altogether. Early intervention can be an efficient and cost effective route to avoiding or resolving employment disputes before potentially expensive and inevitably disruptive litigation takes hold.

Litigation: Advice and Representation

Early Intervention is no guarantee of avoiding litigation. Where it does not succeed then there will be a conflict of interest in the mediator going on to provide advice or represent either party in subsequent litigation. The use of a solicitor mediator will generally preclude that firm from continuing to act. However other barristers within Henderson Chambers, otherwise unconnected with the matter to date, can accept instructions to take a litigated matter forward. If a solicitor is required, as can be the position when complex matters litigate, and a direct client has a favoured solicitor then David and Linda would be happy to work with them. If no favoured firm then they have tried and trusted relationships with established firms.

The legal landscape is changing and there is every reason to think that this will continue. Specialist expertise however remains a constant and the closer a client gets to that source then generally the better it is for all concerned. Direct access to specialist barristers provides that.

Contacting Henderson Chambers:

Email: **goldmanbrook@hendersonchmbers.co.uk**
Telephone: 0207 583 9020
Fax: 0207 583 2686
Clerk: Nick Bryant

Who is Zenith?

Zenith is a multi award-winning independent leasing and fleet management business. Our customer base includes many household brands and some of the biggest organisations in the UK.

We deliver innovative and intelligent vehicle solutions and have a strong focus on high quality service delivery and innovation.

Our products and services portfolio includes salary sacrifice car schemes, the full range of funding solutions, fleet management solutions, accident management, vehicle hire and tools such as Pulse, our award-winning online reporting platform.

Zenith has been providing salary sacrifice car schemes since 2008. We are experts in maximising employee engagement. You and your employees will get the advantage of advanced systems, our friendly and experienced teams and our culture of continuous improvement and innovation.

What is a salary sacrifice car scheme?

A salary sacrifice car scheme enables employees to drive a low cost, brand new car at no cost to your company. It is a great way to increase loyalty, motivation and productivity. And as the economy recovers there is more competition to attract and retain quality employees, which is making the provision of quality and innovative benefits even more important.

How does it work?

Employees exchange a fixed reduction to their gross salary and get to drive a brand new car with an all-inclusive package. As the employee's salary is reduced they pay less income tax and National Insurance. They also get access to corporate discounts which can enhance the savings achieved. The cars are subject to Benefit-in-Kind tax (BiK) as they are classed as a company car, however for low emission cars the savings that are made will more than offset the tax payable.

Salary sacrifice car schemes can be offered to a wide employee base, however in order to be eligible, employees must earn enough salary to ensure that the sacrifice does not take them below the national minimum wage.

Example Calculation

Audi A1

CO_2 Emissions	92g/km
Gross Salary Sacrifice	£328.52
Benefit-in-Kind Tax	£40.89
Income Tax Saving	−£65.70
National Insurance Saving	−£39.42
My Monthly All Inclusive Cost*	**£264.29***

*Price is indicative only for an Audi A1 3 Door 1.6 TDI 116 SE for a 36 month, 10,000 miles per annum selection. It is based on a 20% tax payer with no additional optional extras and may vary. Includes all maintenance and servicing, road tax, insurance, breakdown recovery, tyres, glass and accident management. Actual price may vary depending on the scheme structure, manufacturer prices, discounts, insurance and tax rates applicable at the time. Terms and conditions apply.

Benefits to your organisation

- A high value benefit at no cost to your company
- Attracts, retains and motivates employees
- Can replace a company car scheme or optimise cash allowance benefits
- Can open an additional income stream
- Improves your duty of care compliance
- Boosts your CSR objectives
- The scheme can be tailored to your company's specific needs

Benefits to your employees

- Fixed monthly payments
- No deposit and no hidden costs
- An all-inclusive package
- Significant cost savings compared to retail alternatives
- A wide range of choice
- Hassle-free motoring
- A dedicated team to help with any queries

Communication is crucial

Employers need to work closely with their salary sacrifice car scheme partner and ensure that communication channels are as open as possible. Marketing plans need to evolve and continue throughout the life of the scheme to increase take-up and engagement.

Some employers are concerned about over communicating schemes however a survey we carried out in 2014 showed that 85% of employees wanted more communication about them.

Digital communications are usually combined with other methods such as poster campaigns and roadshows at offices. You may be able to utilise employee newsletters and the intranet to ensure that employees are constantly reminded of the scheme and the latest offers available.

A provider should work with you to create a tailored marketing and communications plan. An employee survey can provide useful information to help market the scheme on launch in terms of types of cars to promote. Following scheme launch, data can be analysed on quoting and ordering patterns to provide a full and accurate picture of vehicle trends and price points.

How is a scheme implemented?

A scheme typically takes around 8–12 weeks to implement. Your provider should implement the scheme on your behalf and make the process as easy and simple as possible.

Lifestyle events

As the lease involved in a salary sacrifice car scheme is between your leasing provider and the employer, the company is potentially liable for any early termination. There are also cost implications that may arise from events such as maternity or paternity leave and long term sickness. However these can be fully offset through methods such as insurance and contingency funds. We can help you to put in place appropriate solutions to mitigate all risks.

ELEVENTH EDITION

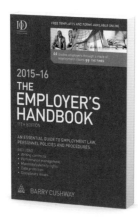

The Employer's Handbook 2015–16

An essential guide to employment law, personnel policies and procedures

Barry Cushway

KoganPage

LONDON PHILADELPHIA NEW DELHI

First published in Great Britain in 2002 by Kogan Page Limited
Second edition 2004
Third edition 2005
Fourth edition 2006
Fifth edition 2007
Revised fifth edition 2008
Sixth edition 2009
Seventh edition 2010
Eighth edition 2011
Ninth edition 2012
Tenth edition 2014
Eleventh edition 2015

Kogan Page Limited
2nd Floor, 45 Gee Street
London EC1V 3RS
United Kingdom
www.koganpage.com

ISBN   978 0 7494 7413 3
E-ISBN   978 0 7494 7414 0

British Library Cataloguing in Publication Data

A CIP record for this book is available from the British Library.

Typeset by Graphicraft Limited, Hong Kong
Print production managed by Jellyfish
Printed and bound in Great Britain by Ashford Colour Press Ltd

CONTENTS

It's time to put your pension through its paces

Given half a chance, your pension will sit around doing very little. But with our expert help, it can become a lean, mean, business-boosting machine.

While auto-enrolment may have taken over your agenda recently, it really is worth taking another look at your own pension arrangements. And if your eyes are already glazing over, allow us to explain what's on offer to you.

It's possible to free-up your pension savings to make investments that will assist your business. You can also take advantage of Capital Gains, Income and Corporation Tax efficiencies as well as a host of other benefits (see spotlight).

You could even use the funds to buy your own premises – it's simply a case of making the money you've already accumulated work harder for you. Even successful companies can be hampered by servicing their existing debts, and this strategy frees-up cash to make your expansion plans become a reality.

The Pension Solutions Group specialises in providing and managing Small Self Administered Schemes (SSASs) for small- and medium-sized business owners. These innovative schemes are regulated by the Pensions Regulator and tax registered with HMRC and have helped hundreds of entrepreneurs to take their business to the next level while saving for retirement.

● Spotlight: the interiors company

The Pension Solutions Group's Mike Baker explains how a clever approach to pensions investment has transformed the fortunes of a small business. "Dan and Alison own an interiors company and they had various pension arrangements with high street brands.

"We helped them consolidate their investments into one pot – a SSAS – which they could immediately begin using to help their business."

They then used their SSAS to buy the commercial premises they worked from so that it would be owned by their pension scheme and protected from creditors. They did this with additional funding from a mortgage lender.

"Having eliminated their personal bank loan and accessed available equity to use in their business, Dan and Alison are able to pay back their pension scheme mortgage quicker than they would have done had they or their company borrowed the money, because they can do so from income that is not subject to tax. Plus they now effectively rent the place from themselves which grows their pension pot."

So, if your business could do with a financial shot in the arm, look no further than your own pension. The Pension Solutions Group specialise in crafting innovative, ingenious financial strategies that really make the most of opportunities that are already available. And while the legislation and the thinking behind our solutions are complex, you'll find the process seamless and straightforward.

● At a glance: five valuable benefits of a small self-administered scheme

1 Inject working capital into the business, e.g. in the form of a loan from the pension scheme to the company

2 Unlock and access equity in commercial property assets

3 Eliminate expensive personal or corporate debt

4 Eradicate future Capital, Income and Corporation Taxes

5 Grow pension scheme with tax free rental income or with loan interest income

● Free consultation! PLUS £200 off your set-up fees!

Come and see us, or we'll come to you, and find out how we can boost your business. Bring your professional adviser or accountant and we'll explain how we can turn your pension in to a lean, mean fighting machine.

Make an appointment today on:

call **01249 280020**
email **info@tpsg.eu**
web **www.tpsg.eu**

the
pension
solutions
group

Employee Incentive Arrangements
Genevieve Moore and Nimesh Shah, Blick Rothenberg LLP

Recruiting and retaining key personnel is an important issue for all businesses. Many employees are looking for more than just a cash reward and a stake in the future growth of the company can be a great motivator as well as being tax efficient for both the employee and the company.

Share incentive schemes are typically "approved" (by HM Revenue and Customs (HMRC)) or "unapproved". Approved schemes are generally more tax efficient but unapproved schemes can be extremely flexible and if structured correctly can also be very effective ways of rewarding employees.

Enterprise Management Incentive (EMI) Scheme

An EMI scheme is generally considered to be the most tax advantageous share scheme available. It is targeted at the smaller, growing companies.

An employee is granted an option to acquire shares in his employer company up to an unrestricted market value at the date of grant of £250,000. The exercise price is fixed at the date of the grant and agreed with HMRC. At some point in the future, generally when the company is sold or listed, an employee exercises his option and acquires shares at the price fixed at grant.

Provided the exercise price is at least equal to the market value of the shares at the grant date, the employee will have no income tax or National Insurance Contributions (NIC) to pay when he exercises his option, but the company may obtain a tax deduction for the increase in value.

When the employee subsequently disposes of the shares, he will pay capital gains tax (CGT) on the difference between the sales proceeds and his exercise price. Most shares acquired under EMI should qualify for entrepreneurs' relief, reducing the rate of CGT to 10%.

Company Share Option Plan (CSOP)

The CSOP is the tax advantaged scheme which has traditionally been favoured by UK groups. The company must self-certify that the share scheme meets the necessary requirements to qualify as tax advantaged. Employees may be granted options to buy company shares worth up to £30,000, valued on the date of the grant. Provided the options are exercised more than three years after the date of the grant, there should be no income tax or NIC on exercise but any ultimate gain is subject to CGT. However, unlike EMI, entrepreneurs' relief is not automatically available and an employee will need to own at least 5% of the ordinary share capital and keep his shares for 12 months before selling them if he is to benefit from the 10% rate of CGT.

Employee Shareholder Status

"Employee shareholder" is an employment status introduced in September 2013. An employee who accepts this new employment status will receive shares in exchange for abandoning certain employment rights. The employee must be awarded at least £2,000 worth of shares in his employer or parent company.

There is no income tax or NIC due on the first £2,000 of share value received by the employee shareholder. However, the value of any shares awarded above the £2,000 threshold is subject to income tax and NIC.

On the disposal of the shares, there is an exemption from CGT for the first £50,000 of shares sold (valued at the date of acquisition).

Share Incentive Plans (SIPS)

A SIP is an approved share scheme and all employees with a minimum length of service must be offered the chance to participate.

SIPs can provide three different types of share award: £3,600 of "free shares" (given by the employer); £1,800 of "partnership shares" (bought by the employee); and "matching shares" (where the employer can match the partnership shares bought by the employee).

The shares issued are retained in a trust for the employee until they leave or decide to take shares from the plan. In order for the award of the shares to be free of income tax and NIC, the shares must be held in the trust for five years.

If the shares are retained in the plan until sale, any gain on disposal is not subject to CGT. If the shares are taken from the plan and then sold, any growth in value is subject to CGT.

Unapproved share options

Whilst unapproved share schemes do not have specific tax advantages, they can offer flexible alternatives for companies and employees.

The most common form of unapproved share scheme is an unapproved share option. On the exercise of the option, income tax and NIC is payable on the difference between the market value of the shares at the date of exercise and the price paid for the shares.

On a future sale of the shares, the growth in value is subject to CGT.

Growth shares

Growth shares may be used as an alternative to an unapproved share option scheme. Unlike an approved share option, a growth share gives an employee real equity in the company at the outset.

Growth shares are carefully structured to have a low market value on acquisition whilst enabling the employee to participate in the future growth in value of the company.

Provided the employee pays market value for the growth shares on acquisition, there is no income tax or NIC. On the disposal of the growth shares, the growth in value is subject to CGT.

Partly Paid Shares

Partly paid shares provide an employee the opportunity to own shares in their employing company without a large upfront acquisition cost or income tax charge.

The employee purchases shares for a small initial deposit, with the balance unpaid until a defined event, such as a sale or listing of the company.

As the individual commits to paying the full market value for the shares (albeit an amount is unpaid), there is no income tax or NIC on the acquisition of the shares and all future growth in value is subject to CGT.

For tax purposes, the amount unpaid is treated as a beneficial loan to the employee and the employee is assessed to income tax on the benefit. However, the actual income tax charge can be relatively small, if not nil.

This type of arrangement carries greater commercial risk for the employee, as in the event of liquidation of the company, the employee may be required to pay the unpaid share capital.

Conclusion

An EMI share scheme is often the most tax efficient way of providing an equity reward to employees, but there are strict conditions which have to be satisfied by the company and the employees. Alternative arrangements are available to companies and when structured correctly, these can be a tax efficient and effective way to recruit key personnel.

Genevieve Moore, Partner
+44 20 7544 8815
Genevieve.moore@blickrothenberg.com

Nimesh Shah, Partner
+44 20 7544 8746
Nimesh.shah@blickrothenberg.com

Blick Rothenberg LLP
16 Great Queen Street
Covent Garden
London
WC2B 5AH

AUTO-ENROLMENT IS HERE TO STAY AND IS GETTING CLOSER FOR US ALL

Carey Corporate Pensions UK

Christine Hallett, CEO,
Carey Corporate Pensions UK,
discusses the main issues for
Small to Medium size companies,
offering support and assistance.

Is your staging date fast approaching?
Are you prepared?
Do you know what you need to do?

The Auto-enrolment journey has started for many and will be beginning for many more in the coming months. In 2015, we will see in excess of 150,000 firms reaching their staging dates, and this increases steeply in 2016 with over 600,000 firms staging and a further 500,000 in 2017 *(Source: The Pensions Regulator Report Sept 2014).*

Employer attitudes are positive according to various recent surveys, with opt-out rates being much lower than expected, so getting workers to start saving for their retirement has begun.

In the next 12 to 18 months, the SME marketplace will have started or will be commencing their journey. The process begins 12 months from the company's staging date, when they will receive their formal communication from The Pensions Regulator (TPR). This introduces the SME's to their duties as employers and what they need to be doing, to become compliant. The communication is critical and should be the start of the journey for each and every company.

Have you had your communication?
What have you done about it?

Your journey starts here today, so don't delay, take positive action and make that call.

Information from various industry surveys within the SME marketplace indicates that the smaller firms coming up to their staging dates are assuming that their Accountant will deal with Auto-enrolment for them and they wont have to worry. The reality of the situation is that many Accountants have not yet made enough preparation themselves in order to support their clients through the process and reality is now sinking in fast.

If you don't yet have a plan, then you need to start TODAY in determining your position and be proactive, because it's you, the company, that must comply. There is help and support out there. However, the capacity is reducing for professional providers of services as more and more companies are seeking their help and guidance.

6 months prior to the staging date The Pensions Regulator states:

"By now a firm should have chosen their scheme and have the auto-enrolment process for all workers in place"

Have you?

At staging date, every SME must be compliant and have started assessing and communicating with their workforce.

How many of you have started your journey?

If you haven't, make sure you don't leave it too late as the choices will reduce.

Auto-enrolment is all about Compliance and making sure all companies avoid regulatory sanctions.

Do you know what the impact to you is of not being compliant?

TPR have already started to sanction companies who have not complied and you certainly don't want to be the one receiving a letter from TPR advising you that you are not compliant and may be subject to a sanction. The cost to you in terms of financials and time would be significantly more than getting compliant in good time.

The reality is that TPR are reasonable and helpful to both the adviser community and the firms themselves, and as long as progress is being made and the intention is to get it right, they are willing to support advisers and firms and indeed pension providers, to get companies into a compliant position.

So practically what does this mean for SMEs?

1 Know your firm's staging date. If you don't, you can find it by going to TPR website.
2 Work with a provider partner to ensure you have a qualifying workplace pension scheme in place to which you will automatically enrol your eligible workers. The provider partner will understand all the moving parts and help you avoid the pitfalls they have already seen.

3 Establish processes to monitor and to continually assess the workforce – this doesn't ever stop it is an on-going obligation, so make sure the mechanisms are in place.

4 Communicate with employees.

5 Make the declarations of compliance to TPR.

6 Make contributions for all eligible workers who are auto enrolled and maintain these payments (you may have to make contributions for those non-eligible that opt in too).

EASY!

Sounds it and it can be if you plan in advance and work with a provider partner that has been through it with many other companies.

REMEMBER:

- Keep it simple and own it
- Be clear in your communications
- Understand your obligations and ensure you understand everyone's roles and responsibilities
- Make the right choices for your employees
- Plan ahead, early engagement is key

This doesn't have to be a headache, so make sure you make a plan and prepare for it and if you need a helping hand, call in a professional that can help you.

Make auto enrolment a positive experience for you and your employees.

Carey Corporate Pensions, an independent pension specialist, can provide an end to end auto-enrolment solution that provides auto-enrolment compliance and a qualifying workplace pension, so you don't have to go too far.

How do you engage?

We are running a series of FREE webinars for employers. You can register to find out more about the Carey Auto-enrolment and Workplace Pension proposition.

Registration details:
https://attendee.gotowebinar.com/rt/7222829684903340801

What about the people?

It is important that you have people to support you and make the service you provide to your employees, seamless and valued.

Carey Corporate Pensions have a specialist auto-enrolment and corporate pension team that are here to help. Call us to discuss how we can assist and provide you with an end to end solution, and become your pension partner.

Carey Corporate Pensions is an independent pensions Provider and Trustee and can provide a Qualifying Workplace Pension for you. They can assist with auto enrolment compliance with the use of their auto enrolment portal, and they can support the implementation program.

Carey Corporate Pensions provides direct access to auto enrolment solutions and works in a co-operative way with all the companies they engage with. They have an operational team of 50 in their Head Office in Milton Keynes and you will have direct access to dedicated Client Account Administrators for your employees.

Call us: 01908 336010
Email us: **autoenrolment@careypensions.co.uk**

Introduction

Aim of this book

A key stage in the growth of any business comes when employees are appointed for the first time. With employees, however, comes a range of complications. Many of these arise from the complex legal framework that now governs UK employment law. Others arise from the sheer complexity of trying to manage and motivate people from diverse backgrounds with widely different attitudes and aspirations.

This book attempts to identify those aspects of employing staff that any employer must know to be able to manage this complexity successfully. These can be divided broadly into legal essentials (what employers are legally required to do) and non-legal essentials (those actions that, although not legal requirements, are fundamental for effective people management and are consequently critical to the success of any business).

The Employer's Handbook is not intended to be a comprehensive guide to UK employment law, but rather to point you in the direction of the actions you may need to take to deal with a variety of employment issues. A large number of letters, policy documents and flow diagrams have been included to help you to deal with many of the topics covered. Employment law can be complex and many small employers can sometimes be nervous of taking decisions that might result in them ending up on the wrong end of an employment tribunal decision. However, it needs to be borne in mind that, though it may not feel like it at times, legislators do not deliberately set out to try and make life difficult for employers. The complexity usually arises from the varied interpretations placed on the legislation by lawyers. It is also the case that many professional advisers have a vested interest in retaining an air of mystique about their specialism.

There are times when you will need to seek advice. Generally, however, as long as you treat your employees fairly, as you yourself would wish to be treated, follow your own procedures and try to be consistent in your decisions, most of the time you should keep out of trouble. It should also be remembered that failure to take action when it is required could end up being more costly to the company anyway. As always it is a question of balancing the risks associated with taking action with those of doing nothing.

What's new in this edition

The main changes described in this edition of *The Employer's Handbook* are as follows:

1 The new provisions operative from 1 January 2014 relating to the employment of Bulgarian and Romanian nationals;

2 A new section relating to the employment of interns;

3 Information about Equal Pay Audits which can now be ordered by employment tribunals where an employer has been found guilty of gender discrimination on pay;

4 The new National Minimum Wage rate;

5 The new guarantee payments rate;

6 The new earnings trigger for pensions auto-enrolment;

7 Changes to rules relating to the taxation of benefits;

8 Information about The Reserve Forces (Payments to Employers and Partners) Regulations 2014;

9 The abolition from the 2014/15 tax year of the Percentage Threshold Scheme under which some employers could reclaim SSP payments;

10 The right from 1 October 2014 for fathers and partners to attend ante-natal appointments subject to certain conditions;

11 The New Statutory Maternity Pay, Statutory Paternity Pay and Statutory Adoption Pay rates;

12 Information about the introduction of shared parental leave from December 2014;

13 Information about changes to adoption leave and pay from April 2015;

14 Changes affecting the calculation of holiday pay;

15 The new rules relating to flexible working;

16 The implications of BYOD (Bring Your Own Device) for flexible working;

17 Changes to TUPE arising from the Collective Redundancies and Transfer of Undertakings (Protection of Employment) (Amendment) Regulations 2014;

18 A suggested procedural change when conducting a disciplinary hearing;

19 A suggested procedural change when seeking volunteers for redundancy;

20 Updating of the average awards made by employment tribunals;

21 Updating of the compensation figures for unfair dismissal;

22 The new requirements of the Reporting of Injuries, Diseases and Dangerous Occurrences Regulations 2013.

Style and conventions

The main aim has been to make this a user-friendly handbook with the emphasis on what you need to do as an employer or a manager to avoid people problems, rather than describing employment rights in detail. A certain amount of such description is unavoidable, as you need to know what you might be letting yourself in for when taking specific actions. However, you will not find separate chapters covering topics such as employment rights and discrimination, as these are covered when describing the actions you need to take at different stages of the employment relationship. Wherever possible, legalistic language and case references have been avoided.

He and she

One of the problems any author has is that of dealing with gender. The use of 'he' exclusively throughout the book would offend some people, as no doubt would the similar use of 'she'. The use of the phrase 'he or she' throughout the text can lead to complex and clumsy sentences. Equally, the use of the plural 'they' can often be inappropriate or ungrammatical in a particular context. Consequently the convention adopted in this book has been to use 'he' or 'she' in alternate chapters, except where the subject relates specifically to one gender, such as maternity rights.

Employees and workers

There has been a tendency in recent legislation to refer to 'workers' rather than 'employees'. This is the case, for example, with the Working Time Regulations and pensions auto-enrolment. The intention, where this applies, is that the legislation should apply not just to direct employees but also to those in a slightly different employment relationship, such as agency workers. Therefore, where the legislation specifically refers to 'workers' rather than 'employees' this has been reflected in the text.

Employment rights

Although the rights of employees at different stages of the employment relationship have been covered under each chapter heading, for convenience the main employment rights are set out in Table 0.1. These do not apply to all employees at all times and you should refer to the specific chapters relating to them for more information.

Company size

When considering the employment issues that affect you, a relevant factor is the number of people you employ. This is because certain rules only apply to companies of a certain size. Table 0.2 shows the stages at which different aspects of employment law begin to apply. Employment rights in general, set out in Table 0.1, apply to all employees with the required length of service.

TABLE 0.1 The main employment rights

Employment right	Required period of employment
Written statement of employment particulars	One month
Itemized pay statement	None
Equal pay	None
Not to be discriminated against on grounds of sex, sexual orientation, race, religion or belief, age, or disability	None
Medical suspension pay	One month
Not to be discriminated against because of trade union membership or non-membership	None
Not to be unreasonably excluded or expelled from a trade union	None
Time off work with pay for trade union duties	None
Time off work without pay for trade union activities	None
Time off work without pay for public duties	None
Time off work with pay to look for work or training if under notice of redundancy	Two years
Time off work with pay for antenatal care	None
Parental leave without pay	One year
Time off work to care for dependants	None
Time off work with pay for safety representatives	None
Time off work with pay for employee representatives	None
Statutory sick pay (SSP)	None
Statutory maternity pay (SMP)	26 weeks
Maternity leave (52 weeks)	None
Written statement of reasons for dismissal	Two years

TABLE 0.1 *continued*

Employment right	Required period of employment
To bring a claim for unfair dismissal	Two years
Not to be dismissed or disadvantaged in any way because of pregnancy or parental or maternity leave	None
Paternity leave	26 weeks (by 15th week before EWC)
Statutory paternity pay (SPP)	26 weeks
Adoption leave	26 weeks
Statutory adoption pay (SAP)	26 weeks
Not to be dismissed or disadvantaged in any way for asserting certain legal rights	None
Not to be dismissed or disadvantaged in any way for whistle-blowing	None
Not to be dismissed or disadvantaged in any way for taking action on health and safety matters	None
Redundancy pay	Two years
To be consulted about proposed redundancies	None
Guarantee payments	One month
To apply to Secretary of State for redundancy pay on insolvency of employer	Two years
To apply to Secretary of State for arrears of pay, holiday pay, notice, etc, on insolvency of employer	None
Minimum period of notice	None
National Minimum Wage	None
Not to have to work more than 48 hours per week, except by choice, and to receive 5.6 weeks annual holiday	None
To make a request to work flexibly	26 weeks

TABLE 0.2   Stages at which additional employment rules apply

Number of employees	Additional employment rules
Five or more	Written safety policy Safety committee, if requested Consultation on health and safety
21 or more	Recognition of a trade union mandatory where a majority votes in favour
50 or more	Required to inform and consult employees on organizational changes

Further information

The following can provide useful guidance on general employment issues:

Armstrong, M (2014) *Armstrong's Handbook of Human Resource Management Practice*, 13th edn, Kogan Page, London
Butterworth's Employment Law Handbook (2014) 22nd edn, Butterworth, London
Department for Business, Innovation and Skills (BIS): (www.bis.gov.uk)

Why is Automatic Enrolment
a challenge for many Employers?

Automatic Enrolment began in October 2012 and two years into this project, the Government's view is that to date it has been a great success with low numbers opting out (around 9%). Having started with the largest employers, as we move into 2015 and beyond it is the medium small and micro employers that are now being faced with this challenge. These employers have far less resources so it remains to be seen how the picture will change.

But Automatic Enrolment is easy isn't it? In theory the answer to this question is yes. The employer must enrol the majority of their employees into a "qualifying workplace pension arrangement", deduct the employee's contribution from their pay, and pass this and the employer contribution over to the pension provider. These funds are then invested and build a fund to provide the employee with an income in their retirement. Simple!

The Pensions Regulator guidance does however run to 418 pages! As an employer have you read and digested all of this material? Do you understand what "qualifying earnings", "entitled workers" "eligible jobholders" and "non-eligible jobholders" are and how this impacts what needs to be offered? Once all these definitions are understood, you need to determine your "pay reference period" for each employee, identify what is payable in that period and compare this with the qualifying earnings for automatic enrolment. The amount "payable" is not necessarily the amount that is actually paid! For those who are paid a regular non fluctuating amount this is reasonably straightforward but becomes more complex for those with fluctuating payments. Other issues such as payment of holiday pay or bringing forward payments at Christmas time or other periods of factory shut down all add to the complications. If you have employees from overseas, are they "seconded" and therefore exempt from these requirements, or effectively on UK contracts and therefore need to be included. Your definition of "seconded" may not match with the one the Pensions Regulator uses. If you pay weekly then you will need to assess your workforce every week.

The Pensions Minister, Steve Webb, has stated that employers should not need help to deal with Automatic Enrolment. At the simplest level this may be true. However, it has been estimated that there are some 33 administrative tasks that need to be completed prior to staging date possibly involving over 100 days of work. Few businesses will find it easy to make available this level of resource as their effort, energy and focus quite correctly is on running their own business. Automatic enrolment also requires continual ongoing assessment of your employees, and unless suitable software is in place, this process could take 3 days a month or more to administer.

The cost of this needs to be factored into budgeting alongside the requirement for employer contributions.

In theory for those with reasonable spreadsheet skills, the processes can be dealt with using several templates taking data from payroll providers and sorting this to produce the data required for Automatic Enrolment. However not only must all this work be done, sufficient audit records must be held to demonstrate that it has been done correctly. The Pensions Regulator may ask to see these records. Software to automate this process is available, but at a cost. The software providers are finding ways to provide support on a basis that is affordable to the smaller employers. Engaging with professional advisers who can provide advice and access to suitable systems to reduce the burden of administration and help demonstrate compliance will help significantly reduce the administration costs and increase accuracy. The word "automatic" is important. Only with automation can the time involved both initially and ongoing be kept to a minimum. Many organisations are keen to work together to ensure the success of the Automatic Enrolment project leading to the formation of Friends of Automatic Enrolment and the development of an industry standard (the Pensions and Payroll Data Interface Standard or PAPDIS) for systems given the need to enable smooth transitions from payroll systems to pension provider systems. With the right system the whole process from end to end can be managed efficiently and effectively, ensuring that full records are maintained to keep the Pensions Regulator happy and any potential fines at bay.

The Pensions Regulator suggests a planning time of 12 to 18 months. It need not take this long but time is required for deciding on strategy and ensuring that budgets allow for the contributions and other costs of automatic enrolment. There are heavy fines for non compliance starting at a fixed penalty of £400 but then rising to daily penalties of up to £500 a day for companies with 5 to 49 employees and £2,500 a day for companies with 50 to 249 employees and rising further for larger employers.

Help is at hand from employee benefit consultants and financial advisers with assistance from accountants, solicitors, payroll providers and pension providers. However with the increasing number of companies reaching their staging dates (110,000 between October 2015 and December 2015 and 101,000 between January 2016 and March 2016 and 215,000 in the last quarter of 2016) resources will become stretched. The development of industry standards for systems will help to alleviate this.

Pension providers are beginning to restrict the type of scheme they will assist employers with – often insisting on an average contribution above a certain level, and introducing scheme fees they have not previously charged. This is a function of supply and demand, and we are likely to see terms harden as more employers reach their staging date. At present, there are choices available with a range of new and traditional pension companies in the market. NEST is the only provider with a statutory duty to make a Workplace Pension Scheme available to every employer.

The selection of the appropriate qualifying workplace pension arrangement is important but only a small part. For the project to be successful finance, human resources, payroll and senior management must all work together. There is a real project management aspect to ensure that the right people are available to make decisions at the right time, to keep the automatic enrolment project on track.

Internal communications to staff is a key part of this exercise. The way in which the communication process is handled can make this process a human resources triumph or complete failure. The same approach will not be appropriate for all groups of employees so you will need to consider the most appropriate communication methods for your employees. Experienced employee benefits consultants will be able to assist. All of this is likely to also impact on your terms and conditions of employment and potentially require amendments to staff contracts and employee handbooks.

As an employer, particularly if you do not have any form of existing pension arrangement, automatic enrolment may represent an additional and possibly unwelcomed financial outlay but it can not be avoided. You therefore need to gain something from this and good communication materials can play a big part. It is important that your employees understand the value of their new pension arrangement. It may be an opportunity to also consider other employee benefits such as group risk arrangements as such cover against death can be provided at far lower cost on a group basis then employees seeking this individually. This would be another cost to the employer but could be repaid many times over if well appreciated by staff. The use of good systems can then lead onto offering other benefits and providing total reward statements so that employees understand the full value of their employment package.

In summary, automatic enrolment will not go away. Use the tool on the Pensions Regulator website to find out your staging date and begin planning or ask us to find this for you. Seek suitable professional help as this will save you significant amounts of time and overall should save you money. Given the number of employers who will be approaching their staging dates over the next 18 months, now is the time to engage with advisers and secure their support.

Robert J Young BSc FIA

Consulting Actuary

Gordon Dadds Consulting LLP

0207 518 0251 | **robertyoung@gordondadds.com**

advertisement feature

elementlaw
employment law

Straight Talking Employment Law and HR Advice

If Employment Law, HR concerns or employee disputes are your headache

we are your aspirin.

Unchained from the constraints of cumbersome law firms, we respond to help you and your business resolve your Employment Law and HR challenges rapidly and effectively.

We also provide essential and dynamic HR and Management Training, and Workplace Mediation.

Employment law may be a minefield, but choosing your legal expert shouldn't be.

What we can provide for you:

1 Solution-driven practical advice.

2 A pro-active and approachable partner for your business.

3 Strong and broad commercial and technical legal experience.

4 Transparency on costs and reasonable fees, including fixed-fee and retainer arrangements.

Kate Lawson
Director

"We are very impressed with Element Law's commitment, professionalism and their proactive, practical approach to all human resource matters, it is great to work with someone who acts as your partner on issues and who delivers great value to our human resource area."
Abi Holland, Stratton Street Capital LLP

"Kate understands the dilemmas faced by us an employer and provides clear advice. She is very quick to respond to queries and thorough in her approach. I have found her a great help when dealing with tricky employment problems. I would wholeheartedly recommend her."
Semra O'Reilly, GirlGuiding UK

Contact Kate Lawson on 07825 687015
or email **katelawson@elementlaw.co.uk**
Website: **www.elementlaw.co.uk**
Twitter: **@elementlaw**

The Making of Middle Management

As an indication of improved performance and growth, a good proportion of SME's have in the last 2 to 3 years created a new level of middle management to allow for wider delegation of responsibilities and to ensure more effective day to day management of an increasing headcount.

This decision to create this new tier of management has many potential benefits, but undeniably brings with it its own challenges. Thorough planning and preparation is key to the successful introduction of the new middle management arrangement.

The Appointment

It is important to spend some time defining what you want to achieve with the creation of a middle management tier, as well as the skills and experience that are needed for the roles. Technical expertise is important; communication and people skills are usually key.

You must also decide whether to advertise internally only, or internally and externally at the same time, or externally only. Unless it is clear in any one team that there are simply no internal candidates with the appropriate skills and experience, it is wise first to advertise internally only. If you then proceed not to promote from within, you need to be clear as to why this is the case and ensure clear and encouraging communication with those internal candidates who have not been successful. Bear in mind that the appointment of an external candidate is likely to lead to resentment, at least until the new appointee has achieved some successes and started to win respect.

Appointing an internal candidate can in itself be fraught with difficulties, as many may think they should get the job, while the relevant director or directors may be clear in their minds that there is only one employee with the appropriate leadership potential. Therefore unless there is one clear "winner" whose colleagues acknowledge that, and in my experience this is unusual, there will be some bitterness from peers on the appointment of an internal candidate. It will be important to give clear feedback to other applicants in a careful and fair manner.

The selection process can also be a useful tool in weeding out those who overrate their value to the business: the decision may make them walk. The downside is some valuable employees who are however not appointed due to a better candidate may also leave as a result. This often results from the fact that the best worker or even highest revenue earner may not be the employee with the best leadership potential or management skills. It would be wise to head off this possibility with careful communication of the appointment decision, including discussions about what career progression opportunities may better suit the skills and/or experience of any unsuccessful applicants. This communication is likely to involve a wider sharing of the longer terms plans and objectives of the company, so these employees can see their part in the company's future. Such sharing is to be highly encouraged in any event across the board.

Also bear in mind the clear legal issues involved in the promotion, meaning that the usual recruitment procedures on interview of new applicants should be followed in the same way, albeit that you may be interviewing internal candidates only. Even if you know whom you want to appoint, and indeed even if rightly or wrongly, consciously or subconsciously you have created the role largely for that internal promotion, you must make clear records of interviews or assessments with all applicants. You should if possible avoid simply promoting without an open forum for application, although there are indeed times when this is appropriate. In all cases, make sure you have a clear note as to the reasons you have appointed the successful individual, to avoid any allegations of unlawful discrimination or constructive dismissal. If you do not follow an interview or assessment process at all, at least link the appointment to recent appraisals and make sure the appointment process is explained to the whole team well before you simply go ahead and announce it.

The format of the process will depend on the circumstances of each situation. In some cases an interview may seem ridiculous if it means general discursive interviews are conducted by directors who work closely day to day with the applicants. It is not advisable to use this selection method only, if this is the case, as this can give the process an air of insincerity and pure box-ticking. It would be best to focus very specifically on the distinctly new aspects of the new role in the interviews, by asking interviewees to explain their vision of the team and the role and their proposed plans for the future of the team. Business plan explanations may also be appropriate. It is often depending on the role good practice to include an assessment exercise focussing on the particularly significant skills required. All candidates should of course be put through the same assessment or asked the same questions, and their answers noted on an interview template.

Ongoing Training and Support

Following the appointment, be aware that the internally promoted employee will now be managing their peer group. This can be fraught with emotion and resentment in any team and particularly where this person is very much first among equals. It will be important to ensure the new manager is trained sensitively in both soft and hard skills, and has someone they can share concerns with in an open environment. Middle managers usually find some practical management training very helpful, around topics such as managing difficult situations and diversity issues including bullying and harassment. The training is best delivered on a small group basis with no more than 5 middle managers in attendance. This group session also allows newly promoted managers to get together and share what are often similar challenges in their new role. Depending on finances, it would be worth appointing a coach or mentor, internal or external, to provide at least initial support to each newly promoted manager.

Something that needs to be tackled head on is that the new manager may well have one or two favourites in the team: their particular friends. Even if they do not treat these individuals more favourably, there is likely to be a perception amongst the team that they will, or do. Similarly, they must be seen to deal fairly with people with whom they may previously have clashed. Part of the training of these new managers will be to highlight the extreme importance of fairness in management style, both for the sake of harmony and progress for the team and more narrowly in order to protect the company from grievances and complaints of discrimination. New middle managers may not have fully considered the issue of the perceptions of their team and the possible impact on morale. They will also need to be supported in having to pull up "friends" on performance and conduct issues, and in appreciating the importance of maintaining some distance and ensuring they lead by example. This can be difficult and may make them feel isolated but it is important they see that if handled well these initial teething problems can be overcome, and the relationship will be positive.

Delegation from the Top

Also be aware that directors may have trouble letting go of their entire domain; this is a common problem with delegation in an expanding company. Directors need to be confident to delegate, and to show their new managers they have belief in them. Mistakes will be made by the new managers but one mistake means more support, mentoring and/or coaching is needed, and is not a reason to pull back from all or most delegation or to delegate mundane tasks only. Directors can also benefit from having an external coach or mentor to support them in developing the skills to deal with the new structure. It is important that the directors keep the job descriptions for the new roles in mind and also avoid undermining the authority of the new manager. The directors need to take account of and involve the new manager before implementing changes. It is important to be patient, not to expect too much too soon and to encourage the newly appointed manager.

Creation of a new tier of management is a positive step for any SME. This level of management provides structure and opportunities for all employees, making the environment more positively competitive and the organisation more attractive for recruitment and retention purposes. It is also a key step in growth, allowing executive directors and other more senior managers to be freed from day to day management in order to concentrate on strategic planning and growth.

Kate Lawson, Element Law Employment Law

For HR, Employment Law Advice, HR and Management Training or Workplace Mediation, please contact me on 01892 516 216 or 07825 687 015 or by email **katelawson@elementlaw.co.uk**

Please see legal updates at
www.elementlaw.co.uk and on **twitter@elementlaw**

Recruiting Staff

01

This chapter describes the recruitment and selection process and the legal implications of that process. A summary is set out in Figure 1.1, although you may need to modify this to reflect your particular requirements.

Deciding whether to recruit

Before recruiting any new or additional staff you should consider whether there really is a need to do so. Not only do additional staff add to the organization's overheads but they will also increase the complexity of managing it. In some cases increases in staff numbers might trigger additional employment regulations.

Options that might avoid the need for an increase in permanent staff include:

- using contractors for certain activities;
- outsourcing or developing shared services arrangements;

FIGURE 1.1 The recruitment process

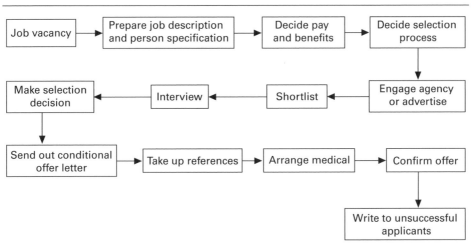

- introducing more flexible working arrangements such as job-sharing, shift working or part-time working;
- redesigning jobs or changing the company's organization structure and/or processes;
- increasing working hours or introducing or increasing overtime;
- improving productivity;
- using temporary staff;
- redeveloping and retraining existing staff.

Preparing a job description

Uses of a job description

Although there is no legal requirement for a full job description, it makes sense to prepare one, as this will:

- clarify the responsibilities of the jobholder;
- aid the recruitment process;
- provide a basis for assessing training needs;
- help in appraising performance;
- help in assessing future staffing needs or in changing responsibilities;
- provide a valuable tool in analysing or changing the organization;
- be an essential requirement for any job evaluation process;
- be useful information in the event of any disciplinary action relating to job performance.

Content of a job description

There is no one formula for what should go into a job description but it should generally include the following:

- job title;
- name of jobholder;
- main purpose of the job, which should describe succinctly, in one or two sentences, the key role of the job in the company;
- reporting line – the title of the job to which this one reports;
- subordinates – the jobs reporting to this one;
- main tasks or accountabilities – some jobs will be routine in nature, in which case the main tasks should be listed (see the job description extract for a secretary, below), whereas others will be relatively complex with the emphasis more on the achievement of objectives, in which case the main

accountabilities or responsibilities should be described in terms of end results (see the job description extract for a finance director, below);

- relevant statistics, such as budgets managed, sales targets and caseloads;
- main contacts and the reason for these;
- signature of jobholder and immediate line manager;
- date;
- generic accountabilities – many job descriptions now contain obligations which apply to all jobs whatever their nature eg 'be responsible for your own continuing professional development' and 'follow the company's safety policies and procedures and take all necessary actions to ensure the health, safety and welfare of yourself, your colleagues and third parties'.

Job description (extract) for secretary

Job purpose:

To provide a full secretarial support service to a director.

Main activities:

- Type letters, reports and other documents, as required.
- Draft routine correspondence.
- Screen telephone calls, take messages and respond to routine enquiries.
- Respond to emails.
- Maintain a diary of appointments.
- Arrange meetings, travel and accommodation as required.
- Act as receptionist for visitors.
- Open and deal with post.
- Take minutes of meetings.
- Order stationery and office supplies.
- Maintain the office filing system and records.

Job description (extract) for finance director

Main purpose of job:

Contribute to the attainment of the company's business objectives by providing strategic and financial guidance and by ensuring that the company's financial commitments are met.

Main accountabilities:

- Direct and control finance staff to ensure that they are appropriately motivated and developed and so that they carry out their responsibilities to the required standard.

- Contribute to the achievement of the company's business objectives by providing advice and guidance on financial strategy.

- Provide financial advice and guidance to the company's managers and staff to enable them to achieve their objectives.

- Oversee the preparation of the company's financial accounts to ensure that these are presented accurately and on time.

- Develop and implement an internal audit programme to ensure that the company complies with financial procedures and regulations.

- Develop and maintain all necessary systems, policies and procedures to ensure effective and efficient financial management within the company.

- Monitor external contracts and services provided by suppliers to ensure that these are operating effectively and provide the best value to the company.

- Carry out all necessary actions to ensure that the company meets its financial and legal obligations.

Preparing a person specification

A person specification is complementary to a job description. A job description describes the content of the job while a person specification describes the desired characteristics of the person required to do that job. Like a job description it is not a legal requirement, but is very useful for recruitment and in determining training needs (see sample person specification below).

Sample person specification

| **Job:** | Secretary/PA |
| **Reporting to:** | Managing director |

	Essential	*Desirable*
Qualifications:	Educated to GCE 'A' Level	Degree
	GCSE English	GCSE Maths
	Secretarial training	
Experience:	Previous office experience covering a range of activities similar to those required in this role.	
Skills/competencies:	Keyboard skills including word processing and familiarity with Word, Excel and PowerPoint, report writing skills	Web publishing skills, including HTML, DTP
	Tact and discretion	
	Good team worker	
	Good written and verbal communication skills	
	Highly organized	
	Conscientious with a desire to do the job to a high standard	
	Able to exercise initiative	
Physical requirements:	Good health and smart appearance	
Circumstances:	Living within commuting distance of London	
	Able to work overtime on occasions	

Two long-standing approaches used in the preparation of person specifications are Alec Rodger's seven-point plan and Munro-Fraser's five-fold grading system. Both of these suggest headings under which the attributes of an ideal candidate can be classified. Although these are now somewhat dated most of the criteria are still relevant, provided they are applied with discretion and you remember to take full account of the diversity of job applicants. For example, in assessing manual dexterity you would need to take account of any relevant disability, and verbal fluency might be affected by an applicant's country of origin.

The seven-point plan

The seven points (from Rodger, A, 1952, *The Seven Point Plan*, NIIP, London) are as follows:

1 Physical make-up – appearance, bearing and speech.
2 Attainments – education, qualifications, experience.
3 General intelligence – intellectual capacity.
4 Special aptitudes – mechanical, manual dexterity, facility in use of words or figures.
5 Interests – intellectual, practical, constructional, physically active, social, artistic.
6 Disposition – acceptability, influence over others, steadiness, dependability, self-reliance.
7 Circumstances – any special demands of the job, such as ability to work unsociable hours, or travel abroad.

The five-fold grading system

This (from Munro-Fraser, J, 1954, *Handbook of Employment Interviewing*, Macdonald & Evans, London) involves the following five considerations:

1 Impact on others – physical make-up, appearance, speech and manner.
2 Acquired qualifications – education, vocational training, work experience.
3 Innate abilities – quickness of comprehension and aptitude for learning.
4 Motivation – individual goals, consistency and determination in following them up, success rate.
5 Adjustment – emotional stability, ability to stand up to stress and ability to get on with people.

The majority of organizations would also add competencies to any person specification. Essentially these are the characteristics and behaviours required of an individual for effective or superior job performance.

It should be borne in mind that only factors relevant to the job should be taken into account. Including any that may not be necessary for effective job performance, eg requiring a high level of physical fitness for a sedentary job, could leave you open to claims of discrimination in selection. Equally, physical appearance might be relevant for customer-facing roles but not for those in research or back-office jobs.

You should describe the characteristics required for a particular job, determined by reference to the job description, against the various headings used. It is a common practice to enter two levels – the ideal and the minimum acceptable requirements to do the job. Job applicants can then be compared against these headings, although making the necessary assessments can be a complex and unreliable process.

Role profiles

Many organizations use role profiles rather than job descriptions. The essential difference is that these will typically include not just a description of the job's responsibilities and tasks but will also incorporate the knowledge, experience, skills and competenices required in the role. This means that a single document can replace the separate job description and person specification. Role profiles are often written in more generic and less specific terms than job descriptions and are commonly part of a job family approach which groups roles with similar characteristics eg sales, administration, production, finance, research etc.

How to recruit

The first step when filling a vacancy should be to consider whether there is anyone internally who might be suitable, perhaps after a period of retraining. Where you take the decision to recruit externally the main ways of attracting applicants are:

- word of mouth;
- advertising;
- using recruitment agencies and selection consultants;
- using executive search firms ('headhunters');
- recruitment fairs;
- through the internet (see 'E-recruitment' below).

Word of mouth

Recruiting staff by encouraging existing employees to tell their friends and relatives about vacancies is very common and some companies even offer financial incentives to staff who persuade someone else to join. Probably the main advantage of using this approach is that you may know more about the employee's background and there is likely to be a certain amount of peer pressure to do a good job. The main danger is that recruiting from a limited pool in this way could be discriminatory if all the recruits come from one section of the community and this does not reflect the mix in your catchment area.

Advertising

The aim of an advertisement is to encourage applications from suitable candidates for the job and also to promote the image of the company. The wording and layout should attract a sufficient number of candidates of the right quality but it should also discourage applications from those who would be unsuited to the job.

The basic content of the advertisement should be:

- the job title;
- the location;
- salary and main benefits;
- a brief description of the key responsibilities or duties;
- the qualifications, skills and experience required;
- the advantages of the job;
- how and to whom application should be made and any deadline date.

Information about salary is sometimes omitted from advertisements, for various reasons, but experience shows that this generally reduces the number of applications. You can usually obtain assistance with the design and wording of job advertisements from newspapers and professional journals, although it is clearly in their interests to sell as much advertising space as possible. An alternative approach would be to place the whole matter in the hands of an advertising or recruitment agency.

If you are preparing a job advertisement yourself you need to ensure that it is not discriminatory by implying that the job is open only to people of a particular race or sex, or that marital status, sexual orientation, religion or belief, age, disability or any protected condition as defined by the Equality Act 2010 will exclude applicants, unless there are compelling reasons for any such exclusion. For example, some disabilities will prevent a person from effectively carrying out certain types of work. Words that are one-sex specific, such as 'salesman', should be avoided. You cannot insist that an applicant must, or must not, join a trade union.

Avoiding age discrimination

The Employment Equality (Age) Regulations 2006 came into effect on 1 October 2006 and are incorporated within the Equality Act 2010. The position is that, with some rare exceptions, you cannot discriminate on grounds of age when recruiting an employee (or during employment generally). When advertising you should:

- not specify a particular age or age range or use terminology that implies that you are looking for someone of a certain age, eg 'dynamic young graduate', 'mature person';
- avoid asking for a specific number of years of experience but instead describe the type of experience required;
- make clear that where certain qualifications are required an equivalent level will be acceptable; older candidates, for example, may not have taken GCSE examinations;

- use advertising media that can include a wide field of candidates rather than advertising only in publications that might appeal to a specific age range;
- review advertising and publicity information about the organization to ensure that there are no hidden messages about the age of applicants you are seeking to recruit.

Most organizations include an equality statement in their advertisements and an example is provided below (reproduced with the kind permission of the National Council for Voluntary Organisations – NCVO).

Equal opportunities – statement of policy

[insert company name] is an equal opportunities employer and will apply objective criteria to assess potential suitability for jobs.

We aim to ensure that no job applicant or employee receives less favourable treatment on the ground of race, colour, nationality, religion, ethnic or national origins, age, gender, marital status, sexual orientation or disability.

Selection criteria and procedures are reviewed to ensure that individuals are selected, promoted and treated on the basis of their relevant merits and abilities.

All employees will be given equality of opportunity and, where appropriate and possible, special training to enable them to progress both within and outside the organization.

[insert company name] is committed to a continuing programme of action to make this policy effective and bring it to the attention of all employees.

Recruitment agencies and selection consultants

One of the main advantages of using a recruitment agency or a selection consultant is that they can bring considerable expertise to the selection process and can frequently give advice on the kinds of reward and benefits package likely to attract suitable candidates. They can take many aspects of the recruitment process out of your hands including, for example, advertising vacancies, interviewing and shortlisting candidates and providing assistance with the final selection. They can also allow you to remain anonymous until the final stages, if desired.

The greatest drawback is probably cost, fees usually being based on a percentage of salary and ranging from about 15 to 30 per cent. The service will usually be provided on a no-result-no-fee basis and it may also be possible to recoup the fee if the candidate leaves within a certain period.

Executive search consultants ('headhunters')

This approach is more appropriate for the most senior vacancies where the company has very specific requirements. In this case the consultants will conduct a market search, often targeting people in senior positions in other companies or referring to their own database of candidates. This is a very useful way of approaching individuals who are known to be suitable but without revealing the name of the company.

The main drawbacks are that it can be costly and will automatically exclude those outside the headhunter's network who may nevertheless be very able but with a low profile. One other possible drawback is that there is an assumption that those who are currently occupying comparable positions would be suitable candidates, but this may take no account of how well they might be performing in those positions.

Recruitment fairs

Recruitment fairs provide an opportunity for the employer to give information about the organization and job vacancies in an informal setting. Candidates are able to see what opportunities are available without having to attend a formal interview. The fairs have the added advantage that they might attract applicants who possibly would not otherwise respond to job advertisements.

These fairs are generally professionally organized, with employers having stands to display information about their organizations. In the past these have proved particularly popular for recruiting graduates. To avoid infringing age discrimination legislation you must be careful to use other selection methods as well and also not to debar older candidates who may still be graduates, even if not recent ones.

Application form or curriculum vitae (CV)?

One of the decisions you will have to make when recruiting staff is whether to ask candidates simply to submit a CV or to require them to complete an application form. The more appropriate approach will depend primarily on the seniority of the job and the number of vacancies to be filled. Where you are filling a senior job it is more common to ask for a CV and experience shows that asking for application forms in such cases can reduce the number of applicants. However, where you expect to receive a large number of applications, forms can be very useful in screening applicants, primarily because you are asking everyone for the same information in a structured way, which makes comparison easier.

Some of the relative advantages and disadvantages of application forms and CVs are set out in Table 1.1. An age bias-free application form can be downloaded from the Employers Forum on Age; website at **www.efa.org.uk**.

TABLE 1.1   Advantages and disadvantages of CVs and application forms

CVs	
Advantages	**Disadvantages**
Speed – most applicants will have a prepared CV.	Many CVs are professionally prepared and may not accurately reflect the applicant's true presentation skills.
The standard of presentation can give information about the applicant.	The applicant can conceal or leave out vital information.
Some applicants may be deterred by having to complete an application form.	Varied content and presentation can make comparison of different applicants complex.
It is simpler to ask for a CV than to design and issue an application form.	They may not give the information you actually require.
	They do not give applicants the opportunity to highlight the aspects of their career they consider the most relevant.

Application forms	
Advantages	**Disadvantages**
They can be designed to provide the information you require.	One form may not be suitable for all jobs.
Because the information is structured it is easier to compare applicants.	Forms put some people off.
Gaps in information can easily be seen.	They are not as fast and convenient as CVs.
The form can be used as a template for the interview.	Poorly designed forms may not obtain all the information you require and often do not provide sufficient space for certain answers (online application forms can overcome this by providing expandable sections).
Information from a form can easily be transferred to a personnel database.	There is a cost involved in producing and dispatching forms.
The standard of completion gives an indication of a candidate's ability to follow instructions.	

E-recruitment

The growth of the internet means that a significant amount of recruitment is now carried out online. E-recruitment, or online recruitment, is defined as 'the use of technology to attract candidates and aid the recruitment process'.

According to a 2005 survey conducted by the Chartered Institute of Personnel and Development, 77 per cent of organizations used some form of human resources information system and 51 per cent reported that their use of technology systems was for recruitment and selection purposes. There is little doubt that this use of technology for recruitment will have increased in the intervening years. Research by the British Market Research Bureau has suggested that an internet search is the preferred job hunting method for one in four adults.

Technology can be used to:

- advertise vacancies on your company's website, on commercial job sites or job boards, or on social networking sites;
- track and process applications;
- select candidates through the use of online testing and by gathering applicant details.

Company website

The company website can be used to give as much or as little information about jobs as you wish. At a minimum you could just provide details of any vacancies, or the website could be used to provide a more comprehensive recruitment service giving full details about the company, supplying job descriptions and person specifications, and providing an online application form.

Job sites or job boards

These are databases of vacancies that are similar to the recruitment advertising section of a newspaper or magazine, but on a much larger scale. They will generally carry several different jobs from a variety of employers although there may also be a focus on a specific profession or industry, level of seniority or geographical location. They can include questionnaires or tests to enable applicants to improve their job-hunting skills. There is usually a reference back to the company's website. In using this approach the key considerations will be the cost of the service and the popularity of the site with the target audience.

Applicant tracking

Applicant tracking is the process that enables you to keep track of the progress of candidates in respect of any vacancies applied for and to assist in managing the process.

Online testing

Online testing involves the evaluation of candidates over the internet through psychometric or aptitude tests. Enabling tests to be conducted in this way reduces the considerable administrative burden of distributing and collecting written test papers.

Advantages of using e-recruitment

The main advantages of using e-recruitment are:

- it can speed up the recruitment process and reduce administration;
- it can improve the efficiency of the recruitment process;
- it has the potential to reduce costs;
- the ability to reach a wide pool of applicants;
- the ability to focus on a target applicant pool;
- the ability to advertise vacancies widely internally through the use of the company intranet;
- it promotes the image of the company as a modern, up-to-date employer;
- it offers 24-hour, seven-days-a-week access;
- it can reach a global audience;
- it makes handling high volumes of applications easier;
- it provides a databank of applicant information;
- it can be used to provide more information about the company and the job;
- it makes it easier for the applicant to apply for a job.

Disadvantages of using e-recruitment

The main disadvantages of using e-recruitment are:

- not everyone has access to the internet or would use it to conduct a job search and this can limit the field of applicants;
- ease of applying for jobs might attract a greater number of unsuitable applicants;
- it could limit applications from groups who cannot fully use the technology, eg certain disabled groups;
- if not carefully designed the process could discourage some applicants or give an unfavourable impression of the company;
- some tests could potentially give rise to allegations of discrimination;
- the process may be seen as impersonal, and put off some candidates.

E-recruitment is something that cannot be ignored but the process should conform to all the criteria of more traditional approaches and should be regularly monitored to ensure that it is delivering the required results. It should be fully integrated with other recruitment methods. It is also important to ensure that websites are kept up to date and that there is a contact number for those having technical difficulties.

Interviewing

General rules

Probably the most common way of selecting a person for a job is through the face-to-face interview. The most important points to bear in mind when you conduct an interview are:

- Ensure that the interview is free from interruptions and outside noise and that the location is suitable for the purpose.
- Ensure that enough time is set aside for each interview.
- Ensure that all parties involved have been told the date, time and venue for the interview.
- Read all CVs and/or application forms in advance.
- Prepare questions in advance (see example questions below).
- Avoid any questions that might appear to be discriminatory on grounds of sex, race, religion or belief, age or disability etc, such as, 'Do you intend to start a family in the near future?' or, 'Are you likely to want to take long holidays in your own country?' or, 'Will your disability mean that you have to have time off for hospital visits?' or, 'Do you think you would be able to work in a team of younger people?' These all suggest that factors other than ability to do the job are likely to be taken into account.
- Ensure that you ask a large number of open questions, ie questions that encourage discussion, rather than closed questions that elicit a 'yes' or 'no' answer. For example, it is better to ask, 'What do you like about your present job?' than, 'Do you like your present job?'
- If disabled people are attending the interview ensure that appropriate facilities are provided.
- If more than one person is involved in conducting the interview ensure that it is clear who will ask which questions.
- Keep notes of decisions reached and the reasons for them, as these will be important in the event of any candidate querying the selection decision. Remember, though, that candidates can have access to such notes through the Data Protection Acts.

Using the following checklist will help you ensure that you have covered all relevant points when you are about to conduct a selection interview.

Preparation for interview – checklist

Consider the following factors when preparing for an interview:

- Do you have all relevant information about the candidates, including:
  - application forms/CVs;
  - all other correspondence with the candidates;
  - references if obtained;
  - results of any tests carried out;
  - personnel files of any internal candidates;
  - other relevant information?
- Have you identified important issues to be discussed at the interview?
- Do you have the job description?
- Do you have the person specification?
- Have the candidates been told the date, time and venue of the interview?
- Have you taken account of their travelling or work constraints?
- Have reception and security staff been told who to expect and at what times?
- Have the other members of any interview panel been told of the time and place of the interviews?
- Have the other panel members all been given the above information about the job to be filled and the candidates?
- Have the panel members been fully briefed about their roles in the interview?
- Have arrangements been made to pay any travelling expenses?
- Do you have all necessary information about the salary and terms and conditions relating to the job in question?
- Have you decided on the information you require and prepared a list of relevant questions (see below)?
- Have you considered the questions that candidates are likely to ask and your responses to these?
- Has a suitable interview room been prepared?
- Have you arranged to divert telephone calls and avoid interruptions?
- Have waiting and cloakroom facilities been provided for the candidates?
- Have candidate assessment forms been prepared and made available to the panel members (see example below)?
- Has the decision-making process been agreed?
- Has the process for notifying candidates of the result of the interview been agreed?
- Have the candidates been told about the stages in the interview process?

Interview structure

When carrying out an interview you should have a structure in mind. This should comprise an opening, a middle and an end, and you need to take specific actions at each stage.

When opening the interview:

- Try to stick to the timetable; interviews too frequently overrun.
- Start by welcoming the candidate and try to establish rapport, perhaps by chatting about something inconsequential.
- Introduce yourself and any other interviewers.
- State the purpose of the interview and describe how it is to be conducted.

In the middle stage:

- Try to ask questions that are open-ended and encourage discussion – basically questions that begin with who, what, where, when, why and how, or phrases such as, 'Tell us what you think about …'.
- Ask questions that relate to required job competencies and the applicant's previous experience, eg, 'Describe a time when …' and, 'What did you learn from this?'
- Ensure that you avoid questions that could be construed as discriminatory.
- Avoid just going back over the application form or CV, repeating the information that is already there, but do clarify anything that is not clear.
- Do not hesitate to probe if the need arises; it is better to get any doubts out into the open than to wonder about them afterwards.
- Listen carefully to the replies, remembering that the candidate should do most of the talking, and try to read between the lines.
- Ask the interviewee to supply examples of the kinds of things he has done to get a clear idea of current and past experience.
- Keep notes of what is said, and if a number of candidates are being interviewed it is a good idea, in the absence of a photograph, to write a short pen-portrait of each of them; it is surprisingly easy to become confused after interviewing, say, six people in one day.

At the end of the interview:

- Invite the candidate to ask any questions about the job or the company.
- Tell the candidate what will happen next and when he can expect to hear the outcome.
- Ask the candidate if he has any expenses and explain how these can be claimed.

After the interview:

- Discuss and record your conclusions.
- Notify the candidates of the outcome as soon as possible; you may wish to delay telling any reserve candidate until the first choice has accepted but this delay should not be too long.

● Negotiate the salary and terms of employment with the successful candidate and prepare a contract of employment.

Note: It is important to retain a note of your reasons for appointing a particular candidate in case you receive any complaints of discrimination from those who were unsuccessful.

Example interview questions

Some examples of the kinds of questions that can usefully be asked at interviews are set out below. However, you should remember that these are only examples and will need to be modified to meet your own precise requirements and in relation to the information provided by the candidate:

● Tell me about yourself and your career to date.

● What interests you about this job?

● What do you know about this company?

● What contribution can you make to this company?

● Why did you (why are you planning to) leave your last job?

● What do you consider to be your main strengths?

● What areas do you think you need to improve?

● Describe your current responsibilities.

● What have been your major achievements in your career to date?

● Looking back over your career, what would you have done differently?

● What have been the biggest problems in your current (or previous) job?

● What experience do you have of managing staff?

● Can you give examples of the types of people problems you have had to deal with?

● What experience do you have of managing budgets?

● Where do you see yourself in, say, five years' time?

● What other jobs have you applied for?

● What salary and benefits are you looking for?

● If offered this job, when could you start?

● Why should we appoint you in preference to any other candidate?

● Can you give an example of a time when you have had to:

  – make an important decision;

  – deal with a sensitive issue at work;

  – introduce a new system or process;

  – work as part of a team to achieve an important objective?

Candidate assessment form

Name:
Job applied for:
Interviewer(s):
Date:

Rate the candidate as follows on the criteria below:
1 = Exceeds minimum requirements
2 = Meets minimum requirements
3 = Does not meet minimum requirements

		Rating		Comments
Qualifications	1	2	3	
Relevant experience	1	2	3	
Skills/competencies	1	2	3	
Team fit	1	2	3	
Personality	1	2	3	
Analytical ability	1	2	3	
Organizational skills	1	2	3	
Presentation skills	1	2	3	
Decision making	1	2	3	
Management skills	1	2	3	
Business acumen	1	2	3	
Drive/enthusiasm	1	2	3	
Health record	1	2	3	

Overall conclusion:

Other selection methods

A detailed discussion of other selection methods is beyond the scope of this book. However, some other techniques that might be appropriate in certain circumstances are described below.

Psychometric tests

Psychometric tests provide an analytical and quantifiable way of measuring personality traits and abilities, intelligence and aptitudes that are likely to be relevant to the job.

Such tests should satisfy six criteria. Any test should be:

1 a sensitive measuring instrument that discriminates between subjects;
2 standardized, so that an individual score can be related to others;
3 reliable, in that it always measures the same thing;
4 valid, in that the test measures what it is designed to measure;
5 acceptable to the candidate;
6 non-discriminatory.

There are a number of different types of psychometric test that, for selection purposes, may be classified as intelligence tests, aptitude and attainment tests, and personality tests.

Intelligence tests

Intelligence tests are the oldest kind of psychometric test, having been designed in 1905. However, they are rarely, if ever, used for selection purposes these days. The main problem with intelligence tests is that they are attempting to measure something that is very complex and about which there is much disagreement. It is possible that intelligence tests only measure an ability to do intelligence tests. In any case, they have limited application in the selection context and their use in the wrong circumstances could provoke resentment if candidates feel that they have already proved their intellectual capacity through their qualifications and experience.

Aptitude and attainment tests

These are designed to test particular aptitudes or abilities and can therefore be made very relevant to the job in question. Aptitude tests measure an individual's potential to develop, whereas attainment tests measure skills that have already been acquired. Aptitude tests can examine such things as verbal and numerical reasoning skills, spatial ability and manual dexterity. Some of the most common attainment tests are keyboard skills tests, which are widely used and accepted. The most important aspect in designing all such tests is to ensure that they are properly validated.

Personality tests

Personality is an even vaguer concept than intelligence and this is probably the biggest problem with personality tests. What exactly are they measuring? There are a number of different theories about personality and a number of different definitions, with some people taking the view that it cannot be defined and measured.

Personality tests can take a number of different forms, testing, for example, individual traits or characteristics, interests or values. Others may concentrate on specific workplace behaviour.

Some of the more common tests include the 16PF, Myers Briggs Type Indicator (MBTI), the FIRO-B and SHL's OPQ. There has been much debate about the validity of personality tests and studies have given variable results, but they are generally found to be more valid than the standard interview, especially when used in combination with other techniques.

Using tests

Whatever tests are used, they should:

- ideally, be used as part of an integrated process with the selection procedure and supported by other approaches;
- be rigorously designed and validated;
- be administered by, or supported by advice from, someone trained to the standards of the British Psychological Society.

Assessment centres

An assessment centre is not a single building or place, as the name might imply, but a range of tests and exercises, such as in-tray exercises, group discussions or presentations, given to a group of candidates who are evaluated by a number of assessors. They can last for several hours or several days. Because of their duration, the complexity of designing them and the associated costs, they are unlikely to be appropriate for small companies. However, they have generally been shown to be good predictors of job performance.

Outdoor selection

Outdoor selection involves using a series of outdoor activities as part of the selection process. Participants are put into challenging situations requiring them to demonstrate how they interact with others, for example by working with an appointed leader to solve a complex problem such as crossing a river by making the best use of their collective skills and materials provided, or by undertaking a physical challenge. This type of approach is most appropriate for large organizations with groups of applicants moving into new roles, and will not generally be suitable for small companies.

Work samples

A work sample is an approach that requires applicants to perform the kinds of tasks they would carry out in the job. Although in the past this approach was confined to jobs requiring practical skills, such as skilled craft work, it is now often used for office jobs. Examples of work samples for such jobs include getting an applicant to carry out a role play, such as conducting a disciplinary interview, if that is likely to be part of the job, or writing a report about some aspect of the company. A common technique is the in-tray exercise, which requires applicants to show how they would deal with a typical range of internal problems and correspondence.

Biodata

Biodata selection involves selection on the basis of biographical information including age, qualifications and jobs held. It is based on the assumption that past experience and attainments are likely to be a good predictor of job performance. Biodata questionnaires vary in the number and types of question asked but will typically seek information such as number of jobs, length of employment, hobbies and interests. Their main drawbacks are that they can be discriminatory because of the nature of the questions asked, they need to be individually designed for different organizations and they can quickly become out of date.

Avoiding discrimination in selection

Under the Equality Act 2010 it is unlawful to discriminate in selection because of a 'protected characteristic' relating to an individual. These 'protected characteristics' are sex, sexual orientation, gender reassignment, marriage or civil partnership, race, religion or belief, age, disability, pregnancy and maternity. Discrimination can arise even if it is not the applicant who has the protected characteristic but the selection decision is affected by their association with a person who does, eg where an applicant is rejected because he has to care for someone with a disability. It is also unlawful to discriminate on grounds of trade union membership or non-membership.

An exception to the rules on discrimination is where there is what is called an 'occupational requirement' that can be justified as a proportionate means of achieving a legitimate aim. However, this must be crucial to the job in question, for example in dramatic performances where the role calls for a specific race or sex, where a social worker is required to deal with a particular ethnic group or where the work is of such an intimate nature that members of the public might object to a member of the opposite sex carrying it out.

Section 159 of the Equality Act also allows the employer to take a protected characteristic into account when recruiting or promoting where people with that characteristic are at a disadvantage or are under-represented. For example, if you have two equally qualified candidates, one man and one woman, but women are under-represented in the company, it would be legal to appoint the woman in preference to the man. In practice, there are usually very few occasions when there is a dead heat between two candidates and there are usually clear reasons for selecting the best person for the job.

Discrimination may be direct or indirect. Direct discrimination arises when one applicant is treated less favourably than another because of a protected characteristic. An example would be restricting certain jobs to members of one sex or a particular race. Indirect discrimination arises when the selection criteria are such that a smaller proportion of people with a particular protected characteristic can comply with them and the criteria are not justified by the requirements of the job. An example would be requiring applicants to take tests not relevant to the job and which would have the effect of putting certain groups of people at a disadvantage – for instance, physical lifting tests, which would discriminate against women or those with certain types of disability.

Avoiding discrimination against disabled people

The legislation relating to disability discrimination is now contained within the Equality Act 2010, which has repealed and replaced the Disability Discrimination Act 1995 and applies to all companies, regardless of size. This means that it is unlawful to refuse to offer employment for a reason connected with disability unless this can be shown to be 'a proportionate means of achieving a legitimate aim'. A legitimate aim would be where a physical disability prevented someone from carrying out a job to the required standard.

When considering applications from disabled people you should:

- consider what adjustments you can reasonably make to the job or the workplace to enable the disabled person to meet the requirements of the job – failure to make a 'reasonable adjustment' amounts to unlawful disability discrimination;
- emphasize the essential elements of a job in the person specification and job description so that any disabled person who can meet these requirements can be considered seriously;
- modify the recruitment process where necessary, for example by adapting tests;
- adapt physical arrangements if practical, for example by providing wheelchair ramps;
- consider allowing a disabled candidate to be accompanied, if appropriate;
- train managers and staff in their responsibilities in relation to the law.

Avoiding age discrimination

The Department for Work and Pensions suggests that you should:

1 Remove the date of birth section from any application form and instead put this information on a separate monitoring form that interviewers will not see.

2 Remove any other age-related questions. You can still ask applicants to describe their experience and jobs held.

3 Ensure that any special recruitment programmes for graduates or managers are open to all ages.

4 If you use a recruitment agency, check that it does not exclude people because of their age.

5 Focus on skills held and avoid preconceptions such as wondering whether an older person will be able to work with the latest technology or at a particular speed.

6 Train interviewing staff in all aspects of avoiding discrimination, including age discrimination.

7 Use people of different ages on an interview panel (where possible) to avoid any accusations that judgements were based on age.

8 Ask job-related questions.

9 Use selection criteria to assess candidates.

10 Monitor the ages of the candidates who applied, those who were shortlisted and the age of the person appointed.

Much of this advice amounts to no more than good selection practice, so it should not present a problem for most employers.

Making a job offer

Once you have made the selection decision your next action should be to write to the successful and unsuccessful candidates. You can make an unconditional job offer but it is more usual to make any offer subject to the candidate meeting certain criteria, such as providing satisfactory references or passing a medical examination. At this stage it is better to defer writing to other shortlisted but unsuccessful candidates because your first choice may decline the offer.

The job offer should contain, as a minimum:

- the title of the job being offered;
- any conditions attaching to the offer;
- the location of the job;
- details of salary or wage, payment intervals and the annual review date;
- any significant benefits;
- the starting date;
- the hours of work;
- holiday entitlement;
- to whom the new employee should report;
- what the employee should do next.

Examples of offer letters are shown below.

You may also wish to consider making any appointment subject to a probationary period. If you do so this should be clearly stated in the offer letter, as should any special conditions attaching to this period. It is important to remember that what goes into the offer letter forms part of the contract of employment.

Example offer letter 1

Dear

Following your recent interview at these offices I am pleased to be able to offer you the job of [insert job title] with this company.

This is subject to:

(a)   the receipt of satisfactory references;

(b)   a medical report from the company's medical adviser;

(c)   [insert any other conditions attaching to the appointment, such as the completion of a satisfactory probationary period].

If in the opinion of the company your references and/or medical report are not satisfactory, the company will withdraw this offer, or if your employment has already commenced, terminate your employment without notice.

The full details of this offer are as follows:

Job title. You will be employed as a [insert job title], although you will be expected from time to time to carry out other duties appropriate to a job at this level. You will report to [insert job title].

Place of work. Your place of work is [insert location], although you may be required to work at any of the company's premises on a permanent or temporary basis.

Salary and benefits. Your starting salary will be £ [insert amount] per annum [or insert any other agreed period] and this will be paid on the last day of each month by bank credit transfer [or insert any other method agreed]. Your salary will be reviewed annually on 1 January [or insert any other review date]. In addition to your basic salary you will also be entitled to the following benefits [set out details of any bonus, company car, medical insurance or other fringe benefits].

Hours of work. Your normal hours of work will be from [insert start time] to [insert finish time], Monday to Friday [or other working days] with a paid one-hour break for lunch each day [or other appropriate wording]. The nature of your role means that you may be required to work overtime without additional payment. [Any requirement to work more than 48 hours on average and any need for the employee to sign an opt-out under the Working Time Regulations should be mentioned.]

Holidays. You will be entitled to [insert number] days' holiday per annum in addition to all public holidays. The company's holiday year runs from [insert date] to [insert date] and holidays cannot be carried over from one year to the next. During your first year of employment you will accrue holiday at the rate of [insert accrual rate] for each completed month of employment.

Sick pay. Your entitlement to sick pay and the procedure for reporting absences are set out in the staff handbook.

Pension. The company operates a pension scheme which you will be enrolled into on appointment and details will be sent to you separately.

Notice period. The company will give you [insert notice period] weeks/months' notice of the termination of your employment (on grounds other than gross misconduct), or any longer period required by statute. You are required to give the company [insert notice period] weeks/months' notice if you decide to terminate your employment.

   Further information about the detailed terms and conditions applying to your employment can be found in the staff handbook.

Acceptance. I would be grateful if you would confirm your acceptance of this offer on the terms and conditions set out above by signing and returning the attached copy of this letter to me. I would also be grateful if you could contact me to confirm your likely start date.

   I look forward to you joining us and hope that this is the start of a long and happy association with this company. If you require any further information or would like clarification of any aspect of this offer please let me know.

Yours sincerely,

Example offer letter 2 (for larger companies)

Dear

Further to your recent interview I am pleased to offer you a job at this company based at [insert location] with a start date of [insert date].

   This letter of appointment, together with the terms and conditions outlined in the enclosed staff handbook, which should be read in conjunction with this offer letter, constitutes the basis of your continuous employment with the company.

Job title and grade

Your initial job title and grade will be [insert title and grade]. Further details are given in the section on grades in the handbook. As a term of your employment, you may be required to undertake, from time to time, such other duties as may be commensurate with your position in the company.

Pay

With effect from [insert date] your remuneration will be at a rate of £ [insert amount] per annum and comprises a basic pensionable salary of £ [insert amount] per annum plus a non-pensionable regional allowance of £ [insert amount] per annum. Your non-pensionable car allowance will be at a rate of £ [insert amount] per annum. Payment, which is subject in all cases to statutory deductions of Income Tax and National Insurance Contributions, will be made into your bank account in 12 monthly instalments on or around the [insert date] of each month. You will receive a monthly pay statement detailing gross pay and deductions and any subsequent changes to your salary will be highlighted on that statement.

Salary arrangements

The company operates a performance-related pay policy and individual managers are rewarded according to their objectively assessed performance. Each year the amount of money available for distribution is expressed as a percentage of the basic salary bill for managers.

An individual manager's performance is reviewed against his or her annual objectives at the end of each year and a performance rating determined. The performance rating influences the pay award but comparisons with peers or peer groups within the company and market information of similar jobs outside the company will also be taken into account. Any awards are normally made in [insert date]. Full details of the company's performance-related pay policy will be available at your place of work.

Healthcare plan

You will be eligible for private health cover during your employment in accordance with the rules of the company scheme. The scheme operates on terms and conditions that are in force from time to time. The company reserves the right at any time to vary the scale or level of benefits in force.

Details and registration documents will be sent to you from head office. Full cover under the scheme will commence from the date of acceptance of your signed application for scheme membership.

Car scheme

You are eligible to participate in the company's car scheme subject to the rules of the scheme, which may change from time to time. For full details of the scheme please contact [insert appropriate person]. Alternatively, you may elect to take a cash option.

Hours of work

The normal working week is 35 hours and this is normally for seven hours per day (excluding a one-hour unpaid lunch break) Monday to Friday inclusive. Your initial start and finish times will be 9.00 am to 5.00 pm Monday to Friday inclusive unless you have been advised otherwise.

Leave

Annual leave. The holiday year runs from [insert date] to [insert date]. For further details including the entitlement for one completed year of service and above, refer to the handbook.

You are required to take a minimum of two working weeks of your annual leave as consecutive weeks. Further information on arrangements for taking annual leave will be available at your place of work.

Public and bank holidays. In addition to annual leave you are entitled to paid leave on public and bank holidays. Different arrangements may apply to shift workers and details are available at the relevant work location.

Absence from work

No salary will be paid for periods of unauthorized absence. Subject to you following the absence rules laid down by the company, normal pay will be continued during periods of authorized absence due to sickness, subject to any service criteria that may exist from time to time. Any statutory sick pay entitlement will be included within this pay. Further details are given in the section on sickness in the staff handbook.

Place of work and mobility

Your initial location will be [insert location]; however, you may be required from time to time to work at or from any company location. Full details are set out in the staff handbook.

Pension

Details of the company pension scheme are available from the company secretary.

Data protection

It is important that our confidential personnel records are maintained as accurately as possible and under the Data Protection Acts 1984 and 1998 the company and employees have a mutual responsibility in this regard. You must notify the company in writing of any change in your personal circumstances, such as your address, marital status, birth of children, attainment of professional qualifications, and so forth. For further details refer to the 'data protection' section in the staff handbook.

No smoking

A 'no smoking' policy operates in all company premises. Staff who smoke on these premises may be subject to formal disciplinary procedures, which may ultimately lead to dismissal.

Disciplinary rules

Contravention of any disciplinary rules, misconduct or a failure to achieve the required standards of performance is likely to result in action being taken under our disciplinary procedures, which could include dismissal. General disciplinary rules are set out in the staff handbook.

Grievance procedure

If you have a grievance related to your employment, you have a right to apply for redress. Details of the procedure are set out in the staff handbook.

Termination of your employment by the company

You are entitled to [insert notice period] notice from the company to terminate your employment, or by such notice as may be required by statute, unless your employment is terminated on the grounds of gross misconduct. For further details please refer to the 'notice period' section in the staff handbook.

Termination of employment by you

You are required at any time to give the company [insert notice period] notice in writing.

Acceptance

I should be grateful if you would kindly sign and return the attached copy of this letter to your line manager to confirm your acceptance of this offer.

Yours sincerely

I hereby accept the offer and the terms and conditions with the company as set out in this document, together with the other conditions contained in the staff handbook, which I have read in conjunction with this offer letter.

Signed:
Name:
Date:

Taking up references

Although there is generally no legal obligation on an employer to give a reference (apart from certain jobs regulated by the Financial Conduct Authority), many are happy to do so. Any reference you are given must be fair, honest and accurate. However, there is nothing to stop an employer from providing a neutral reference – one that confirms that the employee was employed in a particular job with that company for a particular period, but makes no other comment about performance or attitude. Fear of possible litigation means that increasing numbers of employers now provide such references.

To ensure that you obtain all the required information about a prospective employee, the safest course of action is to provide a reference form, such as that set out below or, better still, to obtain references by telephone. Previous employers may be willing to disclose information about a prospective candidate over the telephone that they would be reluctant to put in writing, and it may also be possible to judge attitudes by the tone of voice used. However, for a telephone reference to be of real value, you need to ensure that you ask the right questions. Using the reference form will help ensure this. In addition, you may want to confirm impressions gained at the interview or clarify any doubts you may have.

Most employers ask for two references: one from the last employer and one from another person who knows the candidate. In practice, it is only the reference from the candidate's last employer that is of real value because the other will generally be from a personal friend.

You should always get the candidate's permission to take up any references. A common practice is to take up references from previous employers at the offer stage, and to make the job offer subject to a satisfactory reference from the current employer. This allows the candidate time to give notice before the company is approached. An example letter and form asking for a reference are set out below.

Letter applying for reference

Dear

Re: [applicant's name]

The above-named person has applied for a job as a [insert job title] with this company and has given your name as a referee.

We would be grateful if you would give us your opinion of his suitability for the job described by completing the enclosed form. We would also appreciate any other information you can give us that you feel might help us in making our decision, and which has not been covered adequately on the form.

Any information given will be treated as confidential. If a subject access enquiry is received from the applicant, under the terms of the Data Protection Act, we would be obliged to disclose the content of the reference, but the source of the information will be kept confidential.

Thank you for your cooperation.

Yours sincerely,

Application for reference

Name of prospective employee:
Company name:
Company address:
Name of person requesting reference:

Information required:

Date employee began employment with your company:
Job title:
Main responsibilities:

Number of days sickness in last year of employment:
Has the employee been subject to any disciplinary proceedings? YES/NO*
If YES, please give details.

In your opinion is the employee:

Honest? YES/NO*

Reliable? YES/NO*

Punctual? YES/NO*

A satisfactory performer? YES/NO*

Would you re-employ him/her? YES/NO*

Do you know of any reason why we should not employ him/her? If so, please specify.

Please give any further information that you feel might be relevant.

Would you be prepared to discuss this further over the telephone? YES/NO*

Signature:
Name:
Date:
Position:
Telephone number:

* Delete as appropriate.

Medical reports

You can make an appointment subject to a satisfactory medical report from the company's medical adviser or the candidate's own doctor following any job offer. It is preferable to employ a company medical adviser because that person will have the company's interests at heart and the employee will have no right of access to the report. Where the report is prepared by the person's own doctor he has the right to see it and to amend it or to withhold information (Access to Medical Reports Act 1988).

Under the Equality Act 2010 it is unlawful to ask an applicant health-related questions before making any job offer except to:

- determine whether or not a reasonable adjustment needs to be made to the recruitment process;
- determine whether or not an applicant is able to carry out a function intrinsic to the role;
- monitor diversity;
- ensure that a disabled applicant benefits from any positive action measures in place;
- determine whether or not the applicant has a disability where this is an occupational requirement of the job; and
- vet applicants for national security purposes.

Checking qualifications

There is ample evidence that a significant minority of applicants lie about, or exaggerate, their qualifications in job applications. You should make a point of checking qualifications by reference to professional yearbooks, by asking the applicants to bring any certificates along for verification or by direct reference to the examining body. Alternatively, there are a number of companies that are able to provide this service.

Rejecting candidates

When rejecting job applicants the general rule is that you should try to notify them speedily but avoid entering into detailed explanations of the reasons for their lack of success. While it may be good practice to offer a verbal explanation if this is likely to help the candidate in any subsequent application you must be careful to ensure that you do not imply that rejection was for any other reason than suitability for the job compared to other candidates. An example of a rejection letter is set out below.

Example rejection letter

Dear

Job of:

Thank you for [attending the interview for the above job at these offices on date]/ [applying for the above job].*
    I regret that, after careful consideration, we will not be [taking your application any further]/[making you an offer]* as there were a number of other candidates whose qualifications and experience more closely matched our requirements.
    I would like to thank you for your interest in the company and to take this opportunity to wish you every success in your job search.

Yours sincerely,

*Delete as appropriate

You should also retain the notes relating to any selection or shortlisting decision so that in the event of any complaint about your decision you can produce evidence in support of it. There have been a number of cases where members of ethnic minorities have been able to show that just putting a different name on an application can affect whether a person is invited for interview.

Withdrawing a job offer

You might sometimes have to withdraw a job offer that has already been made. Where this is not because of any fault of the candidate, such as failure to provide a satisfactory reference where that was a condition of the appointment, you should give the candidate pay in lieu of the notice period set out in the contract.

Special cases

Employment of offenders

Under the Rehabilitation of Offenders Act 1974 an offender does not need to give the employer details of any past offence for which he is now considered to be rehabilitated.

Equally the employer must not take into account any such offences. These periods of rehabilitation vary depending on the nature of the offence and some, such as a sentence of custody for life, are excluded completely. The practical effect of the Act is that not only does the applicant not have to mention any 'spent' conviction, but could effectively lie about having committed an offence if asked directly whether he had any convictions. The relevant offences and time periods for rehabilitation are set out in the Act.

Exceptions

There are some jobs for which people are required to declare their convictions regardless of whether they might otherwise be spent under the provisions of the Act. These include:

- appointment to any post providing accommodation, care, leisure and recreational facilities, schooling, social services, supervision or training to people aged under 18 (including teachers, school caretakers, youth and social workers, and child minders);
- employment providing social services to elderly people, mentally or physically disabled people, alcohol or drug misusers, or the chronically sick;
- appointment to any office or employment involving the administration of justice, including police officers, probation officers, traffic wardens, etc;
- admission to certain professions that have legal protection, including lawyers, doctors, dentists, nurses, chemists, accountants, etc;
- appointment to certain jobs regulated by the Financial Services Authority;
- appointment to jobs where national security may be at risk (eg certain posts in the civil service and defence contractors).

A full list of these exceptions is contained in the Rehabilitation of Offenders Act 1974 (Exceptions) Order 1975.

Where appointments are to be made to jobs that are excepted from the Act you should make it clear to the applicant that checks about any previous convictions will be made and that the appointment is conditional on these.

Working with children or vulnerable adults

For many jobs, such as those involving work with vulnerable adults or children, there may be a need to check whether the employee has any criminal convictions which would bar that person from the job in question. These checks are now carried out by the Disclosure and Barring Service and are consequently now known as DBS (formerly CRB) checks. You would firstly need to decide whether the job met the eligibility criteria for such a check and further information on this can be obtained from the DBS website at **https://www.gov.uk/disclosure-barring-service-check**.

You can only arrange a DBS check on a successful job applicant but can withdraw the offer if anything is disclosed which would make the applicant unsuitable. If you carry out more than 100 checks per year you should register with the DBS otherwise you can use an umbrella body to carry out checks on your behalf. You should ask the employee to complete an application form obtained from the DBS or umbrella body and then return the completed form to that body. The certificate will be sent direct to the employee and you would need to ask to see this.

You should tell the employee whether you require a standard check, which sets out spent and unspent convictions, cautions, reprimands and final warnings (cost £26) or an enhanced check (cost £44) which includes the foregoing plus any additional information held locally by police forces that's reasonably considered relevant to the post applied for.

You must not apply for a check unless the job role is eligible for one and you must tell the applicant why they are being checked and where they can get independent advice.

Restrictions on employing children

There are certain restrictions on the employment of children. These are:

- no children may be employed under the age of 14, except on 'light work', information about which should be available from the local council;
- children aged 15 may only work for up to eight hours on a non-school day;
- children under 15 may only work for up to five hours on a non-school day;
- children must not work for more than two hours on school days and Sundays;
- they must not work for more than 35 hours in any week in the school holidays if over 15, or for more than 25 hours if under 15;
- they must not work for more than four hours in any day without a rest break of one hour;
- they must not be employed for more than 12 hours in any week in which they are required to attend school;
- there must be at least two consecutive weeks in the school holidays without employment.

Employment of overseas nationals

All European Economic Area (EEA) nationals, citizens of Switzerland and Commonwealth citizens with the right to abode have the right to work in the United Kingdom. Other nationalities will generally need a work permit, although there are a number of exceptions to this general rule. Further information can be obtained from **www.ukba.homeoffice.gov.uk**.

The EEA includes the following countries:

Austria	Germany	Malta
Belgium	Greece	Netherlands
Bulgaria	Hungary	Norway
Croatia	Iceland	Poland
Cyprus	Ireland	Portugal
Czech Republic	Italy	Romania
Denmark	Latvia	Slovakia
Estonia	Liechtenstein	Slovenia
Finland	Lithuania	Spain
France	Luxembourg	Sweden

Since February 2008 a points-based system has been in place to assess people wanting to come to work in the UK. There are five tiers within the points-based system:

Tier 1: Highly skilled

Tier 2: Skilled

Tier 3: Low skilled

Tier 4: Students

Tier 5: Temporary workers (including holiday workers)

Sponsorship by an employer is essential for Tiers 2–5. Those in Tier 1 who meet the points requirement are allowed to come to the UK to seek work or to pursue self-employment opportunities.

The criteria applying to these categories are kept under constant review and as the coalition government sets limits on the number of migrant workers it is essential to check the latest information on one of the relevant websites mentioned below.

Previous restrictions on the employment of Bulgarian and Romanian nationals were removed from 1 January 2014.

More information is available from **www.ukba.homeoffice.gov.uk**.

Employment of Croatian nationals

From 1 July 2013 Croatia joined the EEA giving Croation nationals the right to live and work in any EU member state. However, member states are allowed to apply transitional arrangements restricting access to the labour market and the UK is applying such restrictions. This means that any Croatian, with some exceptions, wishing to work in the UK must obtain an accession worker authorisation document before he can be employed. This is normally a Purple Registration Certificate issued by the UK Border Agency. You will need to check, validate and keep copies of this document unless the employee falls within an exempted category as described in the Home Office Guide 'Guidance for employers on preventing illegal working in the UK: Croatian nationals', dated July 2013.

Immigration, Asylum and Nationality Act 2006

Under the Immigration, Asylum and Nationality Act 2006 it is a criminal offence to employ overseas nationals aged 16 or over without authorization from the immigration authorities. This means that you must check to ensure that any potential employee can provide evidence of his entitlement to work in the United Kingdom. Any employer who knowingly employs an illegal immigrant is liable to a penalty of £20,000 per illegal worker.

There are two lists of documents that can be used as evidence of the right to work in the UK. Documents provided from List A establish that the person has an ongoing entitlement to work in the UK. Documents from List B indicate that he only has limited leave to be in the UK, so the checks should be repeated on that employee at least once every 12 months, until he produces documents from List A or leaves your employment.

List A documents are:

- UK passport;
- EEA or Swiss passport or national identity card;
- UK residency permit issued by the Home Office or UK Border Agency;
- Biometric Residence Permit issued by the UK Border Agency indicating that the person can stay indefinitely in the UK;
- passport or travel document showing a right of abode in the UK;
- immigration status document issued by the Home Office or UK Border Agency giving a right to stay in the UK indefinitely if produced with an official document showing that person's name and National Insurance number;
- birth certificate issued in the UK, Channel Islands, Isle of Man or Ireland if produced with an official document showing that person's name and National Insurance number;
- adoption certificate issued in the UK, Channel Islands, Isle of Man or Ireland if produced with an official document showing that person's name and National Insurance number;

- naturalization certificate if produced with an official document showing that person's name and National Insurance number;
- letter from the Home Office or UK Border Agency indicating that the person is allowed to stay indefinitely in the UK if produced with an official document showing that person's name and National Insurance number.

List B documents are:

- passport or travel document indicating that the person is allowed to work in the UK;
- Biometric Residence Permit issued by the UK Border Agency indicating that the person named in it can stay in the UK and is allowed to do the work in question;
- work permit, letter or other approval to take employment issued by the Home Office or UK Border Agency when produced with either a passport or another travel document showing that the holder is allowed to stay in the UK and do the work in question;
- Application Registration Card issued by the Home Office or UK Border Agency stating that the holder is permitted to take employment, when produced with evidence of verification by the UK Border Agency Employer Checking Service;
- Immigration Status Document issued by the Home Office or UK Border Agency indicating that the holder can stay in the UK and do the work in question, when produced with an official document giving the person's name and National Insurance number;
- letter issued by the Home Office or UK Border Agency to the holder or the employer indicating that the person named can stay in the UK and is allowed to do the work in question when produced with an official document giving the person's name and National Insurance number.

Further information is available from **www.ukba.homeoffice.gov.uk/employingmigrants** and **www.ukba.homeoffice.gov.uk/employers**. You should ensure that you check the latest rules before employing overseas workers.

Further information

Access to Medical Reports Act 1988
Accession of Croatia (Immigration and Worker Authorization) Regulations 2013
Asylum and Immigration Act 1996
Chartered Institute of Personnel and Development (2005) *People Management and Technology: Progress and Potential*, CIPD, London, online: http:www.cipd.co.uk/surveys
Data Protection Act 1998
Edenborough, R (2002) *Effective Interviewing – A Handbook*, 2nd edn, Kogan Page, London
Employment Act 1989
Equality Act 2010

http://www.askgrapevine.com/
http://www.direct.gov.uk/en/campaigns/Vetting/DG_183218
http://www.homeoffice.gov.uk
http://www.ind.homeoffice.gov.uk
http://www.ukba.homeoffice.gov.uk
Immigration, Asylum and Nationality Act 2006
Rehabilitation of Offenders Act 1974
The Children (Protection at Work) Regulations 1998 and 2000
The Executive Grapevine, Executive Grapevine International Ltd
The Safeguarding Vulnerable Groups Act 2006

Writing Employment Contracts

02

Deciding whether someone is an employee

A key decision you have to make at the outset of any employment relationship is whether the person being employed is actually an employee and therefore subject to a whole range of employment protection measures, or whether that person is self-employed with any contract being a contract for services rather than a contract of employment.

A person is likely to be self-employed if some or all of the following conditions are met:

- she is in business on her own account and carries all the financial risk;
- she also works for other companies;
- no guarantee of work is given by the company;
- she provides her own tools and equipment;
- she is not under the control of the company's management;
- she can hire others to do the work or provide additional help at her own expense;
- she can decline work.

There is an increasing tendency in legislation to refer to 'workers' rather than employees, such as in the Working Time Regulations, but although this definition would include people such as those providing domestic services or working for an agency, it would not apply to the genuinely self-employed.

Agency workers

Under the Agency Workers Regulations 2010 temporary agency workers are entitled to equal treatment to comparable permanent employees after 12 weeks in a job. This means that they are entitled to the same working conditions and employment terms as permanent staff. This excludes certain payments such as sick pay, redundancy pay, and pension and benefits in kind. Full guidance on this is available in the Agency Workers Regulations Guidance at **www.bis.gov.uk/.../a/11-949-agency-workers-regulations-guidance.pdf**.

The contract of employment

The contract of employment between you and the employee is not one single document but comprises the contents of any offer letter, any verbal promises made by you to the employee that are intended to be part of the contract, and any other written terms and conditions applying to this type of job in the company, such as those that might be contained in any staff handbook. There may be customary practices in the company that would also form part of the contract. For example, if you customarily pay a Christmas bonus to all staff this would be likely to be equally applicable to any new employee, unless there were conditions attached to the payment such as a minimum length of employment.

There are also aspects of the employment contract that are not written anywhere, but are implied. For example, it is to be expected that any employee will follow any reasonable instructions given by an authorized manager and, equally, that you as the employer will provide all the necessary facilities to enable an employee to be able to do her job effectively.

Where the company has collective agreements, ie agreements negotiated between the employer and any unions or employees' representatives, these will also be part of the employee's contract although they may not actually be contained in a staff handbook.

Statement of employment particulars

What is written into a contract is a matter for agreement between the employee and you and is not specified by law. However, it is a legal requirement that you issue any employee with a written statement of employment particulars within two months of commencing employment. The content of this statement is specified by statute (Employment Rights Act 1996) and must include the following information:

- the parties to the agreement – the name of the employer and the employee;
- the date employment began (in this job);
- the date continuous employment began, including service with any predecessor organization;
- the rate of pay, the method of calculating it and the intervals at which it will be paid;
- terms and conditions relating to hours of work;
- holiday entitlement and holiday pay;
- the title of the job or a brief description;
- the place of work and any mobility requirements.

You must also give the employee other information as part of the written statement, but this does not have to be set out in a single document and may be given in instalments, provided it is given within the two months' time limit. This additional information includes:

- where the employment is temporary, the date it is to end;
- any terms and conditions relating to sickness or injury, including sick pay provisions;
- terms and conditions relating to pensions;
- whether a contracting-out certificate for pensions is in force;
- the length of notice required from both parties;
- details of any collective agreements that might affect the employee;
- information about the conditions attaching to any requirement to work outside the United Kingdom;
- the procedure for dealing with grievances (or where it can be found);
- the disciplinary procedure and any disciplinary rules (or where they can be found).

If there are no details to be entered under one of the above headings, that fact should be clearly stated at the appropriate point in the statement.

As indicated above, the statement of employment particulars is only part of the contract of employment, but it is strong evidence of the intentions of both parties. Two copies of the statement should be sent to the employee for signature, with one being retained for your records.

An example of a statement of employment particulars for a management job is set out below. A statement for clerical and other jobs should contain the same headings but the details might need to be modified. You should note that there is no legal requirement for the contract to be signed, and it still applies if the employee declines to sign it. However, a signature does indicate that the employee has read the contract and is hopefully aware of the content.

Example statement of employment particulars for a manager

This statement is a legal requirement of the Employment Rights Act 1996 and forms part of your contract of employment. It sets out the main particulars of the terms and conditions of employment between:

[Name of company] and
[Name of employee]

Date on which employment commenced: _____

Continuous employment

Your period of continuous employment began on [the same date] OR on ...
[taking into account any employment with previous employers which counts
towards continuous service].

Job title: _____
You should note that the company may require you to undertake other duties and
responsibilities appropriate to a job at this level. You must carry out your work
diligently and faithfully and comply with any general or specific instructions given
to you by the company.

Reporting to: _____

Confidentiality

You must not at any time during your employment, or after it has ended, make or
permit any unauthorized disclosure of any information that is confidential to the
company or any customer of the company. Confidential information includes
information relating to the transactions, finances, business or affairs of the
company or customers of the company.

Place of work

Your main place of work is [insert location], although you may be required to work
at other company locations on a temporary basis.

Work outside the United Kingdom

If you are required to work outside the United Kingdom for a period of time of more
than one month you will receive separate particulars of the relevant terms and
conditions applicable to that work and to your return.

Normal hours of work

Your normal working hours are 35 hours per week, plus a one-hour lunch break
each day. However, you will be expected to work the hours necessary to reach your
targets. [As this may occasionally require you to work more than the maximum of
48 hours per week specified in the Working Time Regulations you will be required to
sign an agreement opting out of this provision in the Regulations. You can terminate
this agreement at any time by giving the company three months' notice.]
   Overtime is not paid.

Pay

Your salary is £ [insert amount] per annum. Your salary is payable by equal monthly
instalments in arrears on the last working day of each calendar month. Payment will

be made by cheque or by credit transfer to your bank account. Your salary will be reviewed annually on [insert date].

Expenses

The company will reimburse all travelling and other out-of-pocket expenses properly incurred by you in the performance of your duties, subject to the production of invoices, vouchers or other reasonable evidence of expenditure.

Deductions from your pay

The company shall be entitled to recover any debt owed by you to the company or any other sums lawfully due from you to the company by deduction from your remuneration, including holiday pay and pay in lieu of notice, or any other payment on termination of employment.

You are not entitled to any remuneration or other payment from the company during any period of unauthorized absence from work.

Holiday entitlement

You are entitled to [insert number] working days' holiday per annum with full salary in addition to public holidays. During your first year of employment your holiday entitlement will be in proportion to the number of complete months worked based on the accrual rate described below. All holidays must be approved in advance by the company. [Unused holiday cannot be carried over from one holiday year to the next.]

On the termination of your employment for any reason (except misconduct) you will be entitled to holiday pay for each day that may remain after deducting from your accrued holiday entitlement the amount of holiday already taken in the holiday year in which your employment ceases. Accrued holiday entitlement is calculated by taking, for each completed calendar month of employment during the holiday year in which your employment ceases, one-twelfth of your annual holiday entitlement for that holiday year to the nearest whole day. The daily rate of holiday pay will be your annual salary at the date of termination of your employment divided by [insert agreed figure].

If you have taken holidays in excess of your accrued holiday entitlement the company may deduct from your final salary or any other payment due to you on the termination of your employment the amount overpaid to you for the excess holiday, calculated on the same basis as for holiday pay.

Sickness absence

If you are unable to attend work because of sickness you must notify your manager as soon as possible on the first day of absence and at least within one hour of your normal start time. You must complete a company self-certification form for the first seven days and give this to your manager on your return. For illnesses of more than seven days, a doctor's certificate must also be produced on the eighth day and weekly thereafter.

If you realize that your sickness will last for more than the working week, you should contact the company and ask us to send a certificate to you at home, which you should complete and return by post.

Your certificates should show all the actual days of sickness even if they are not days you would normally work, such as weekends and public holidays.

If you do not comply with this requirement the company may take disciplinary action against you and you may forfeit your right to sick pay.

Company sick pay

Company sick pay will be at the discretion of management but will not be unreasonably withheld. To qualify, you must have had six months' service with the company and have complied with the requirements on notification of absence and the provision of medical certificates. The entitlement increases with length of service as follows:

- six months to two years – one month's full pay, one month's half pay;
- two years to five years – two months' full pay, two months' half pay;
- over five years – three months' full pay, three months' half pay.

Company sick pay includes any entitlement to statutory sick pay (SSP) but the total of company pay and SSP will not be greater than your normal basic salary. If you are not entitled to company sick pay, you may still be entitled to SSP, which will be paid in accordance with the regulations for the time being in force. The rules relating to the payment of sick pay and SSP are set out in the staff handbook.

The company can at any time require you to submit to an independent medical examination, by a medical practitioner nominated by the company, which we will pay for.

Pensions

By signing this section of the contract, you agree that [company name] will act on your behalf in taking the steps necessary to enrol you in [the company's group personal pension scheme/group stakeholder pension scheme] (the Scheme). You hereby declare that you wish [company name] to take those steps on your behalf. The company undertakes not to enrol you into the Scheme before you have received the essential terms of the contract, including in particular the name of the supplier of the Scheme, details of your right to opt out of membership of the Scheme by a specified date, and details of the amount, or date by which you will be informed of the amount of contributions that you would pay to the supplier by way of deductions from your wages under the Scheme.

Termination of employment

You are required to give not less than [insert period of weeks or months] notice to terminate your employment.

You are entitled to receive not less than [insert period of weeks or months] notice if the company terminates your employment, for any reason other than gross misconduct, or any longer period required by statute.

The company reserves the right to give you pay in lieu of notice.

On the termination of your employment for any reason you must return all documents, equipment or other property belonging to the company or relating to the company's business which are in your possession or control and you must not make or retain any copy, extract or duplicate of any such document OR [where the period of employment is for a fixed term] you are employed on a fixed-term contract which will expire on [insert date].

Disciplinary rules and disciplinary procedure

The disciplinary rules and procedure which apply to you are attached as an appendix to this contract. They do not form part of your contract of employment.

Grievance procedure

If you are dissatisfied with a disciplinary decision or if you have any grievance relating to your employment you should apply in the first instance to [insert name of supervisor or line manager], either orally or in writing. If the matter is not resolved you should follow the following procedure [set out grievance and disciplinary appeals procedures or refer to other documents such as staff handbook].

Collective agreements

Your terms and conditions of employment are affected by the following collective agreements between the company and [insert name of union/employer's association/staff association, etc]: [list relevant agreements]. OR no collective agreements directly affect the terms and conditions of your employment.

Personal information

You must notify the company of your current address and any changes, your bank account to which salary payments are made, details of the person(s) to contact in an emergency, and other information that is needed by the company to maintain accurate records and to ensure compliance with its statutory obligations.

You agree to give the company permission to collect, retain and process relevant personal information about you. The company will keep such information confidential and will make every effort to ensure that it is accurate and kept up to date.

Signed: _____for the Company

Date: _____

Signed: _____Employee

Date: _____

Specific contractual clauses

In addition to the employment particulars contained in the written statement, employment contracts will usually contain a number of other clauses or variations on standard clauses. Some of the more common ones are described below.

Probationary period

Employers sometimes wish to apply a probationary period before offering an employee permanent employment. An example of this type of clause is as follows:

> The first six months of your employment with the company are probationary. During this period the company may terminate your employment by giving you one week's notice. At the end of the probationary period your employment with the company will be reviewed.

Non-competition clause

A non-competition clause or restrictive covenant is put into a contract to prevent the employee from competing with the company, or revealing trade secrets, once that person has left. Any such clause must be worded to give the company only the protection that may be considered reasonable to protect its business interests, and should therefore be limited in time and scope. If the clause is too widely drawn it may not be enforceable. An example is:

> For the protection of the company, its business, its employees and its customers, you agree that: you shall not, during the 12-month period starting with the date of termination of your employment, either on your own account or with or on behalf of any other person, solicit or entice away or try to solicit or entice away from the company, any individual who is an employee of the company; you shall not, during the six-month period after the date of termination of your employment, either on your own account or with or on behalf of any other person, solicit or entice away or attempt to solicit or entice away, any company customer; and you shall not, during the six-month period after the date of termination of your employment, either on your own account or on behalf of any other person, have dealings, directly or indirectly, with any company customer. However, you are not prohibited by any of these restrictions from seeking or doing business with a company customer who is not in direct or indirect competition with the company.
>
> You agree that these restrictions are reasonable and necessary for the protection of the company and that if any of these are found by any court to go beyond what is reasonable to protect the company's interests that the remainder of the contract will still apply as modified.

Benefits

You may wish to refer in the written statement to some of the main benefits applicable to the job. These might include for example:

- a discretionary bonus (be careful to ensure that you do not word this in such a way as to create a contractual entitlement, unless you intend to do so);
- a company car;
- medical insurance;
- season ticket loan;
- life assurance.

The full range of benefits that might apply to any job is covered in Chapter 4.

Termination of employment

The period of notice you give to the employee or require from her will depend on the type of job. For monthly paid staff, one month on either side is typical. For more senior jobs or those where the employee has to continue providing a service to a client or customer, longer periods may be required. There is also a statutory right to notice, which is one week for anyone with more than one week's but less than two years' service, rising by one week for every year of service thereafter up to a maximum of 12 weeks after 12 years.

It is a good idea to insert into the contract a clause that gives you the right to give the employee pay instead of requiring that her notice be worked out. Adding such a clause removes the danger of your being in breach of contract in these circumstances. See also the section below relating to garden leave.

An example of a termination of employment clause is:

> Your employment may be terminated by either party on the giving of one month's written notice and the company reserves the right to pay salary in lieu of notice during the notice period.
>
> When you have completed five years' employment with the company you are entitled to one week's notice for every year of employment, up to a maximum of 12 weeks after 12 years.
>
> Notwithstanding the other provisions of this contract, the company shall be entitled to terminate your employment without notice or payment in lieu of notice for dishonesty or gross or persistent misconduct, whether in connection with your employment or not.
>
> On termination of your employment for whatever reason you shall return to the company all books, documents, papers, computer data, materials, credit cards and other property relating to the business or belonging to the company, which may then be in your possession or under your power or control.

Garden leave

When an employee leaves the company, either through resignation or dismissal, that person has the right to continue attending the place of work during the notice period. However, this is not always desirable because she might continue to have access to commercially sensitive information or might be a disruptive presence. To prevent attendance during the notice period you should insert a provision into the employment contract giving you the right to require the employee not to report for work. You can attach conditions to this 'garden leave', such as not permitting the employee to work for another company, but these should be clearly spelt out in the contract.

An example of a garden leave clause is as follows:

> The company shall have the right during the period of notice, or any part of that period, to place you on leave, paying the basic salary and benefits to which you are entitled. During this period you are not to visit company premises, other than at our request.

Exclusive employment

You may wish to ensure that an employee devotes all her energies to her job and is not distracted by external activities. For example, someone who works late evenings and early mornings in a nightclub may not be on top form during the day. Also, you could fall foul of the Working Time Regulations (see below and Chapter 8) if an employee works more than 48 hours a week in total because she has another job. It may therefore be advisable to insert a clause in the contract similar to this:

> Employees are not permitted to take second jobs, for example in the evening, without written company agreement. Any person in breach of this requirement will be subject to disciplinary action and may be dismissed.

Confidentiality

It is an implied term of the contract of employment that an employee should remain loyal to the employer and act in good faith, which clearly includes not giving confidential information to competitors, but you may wish, nevertheless, to protect such information with a confidentiality clause, such as the following:

> Except for information already in the public domain, you will not disclose any confidential information concerning the business or affairs of the company, or any associated company, or our customers or suppliers, to any other person or organization. This also applies after you have left the company.
>
> Any information relating to the company, our customers or suppliers remains the property of the company, and when you leave any such information must be handed back to the company.

Working Time Regulations opt-out

Where a member of staff may be required regularly to work more than 48 hours per week you should ask that person to sign an opt-out similar to the one in the following extract.

Agreement to opt-out of the 48-hour working week

Company:
Name of employee:

I understand that under the provisions of the Working Time Regulations I am not required to work more than 48 hours per week on average.

I agree that I may work more than an average of 48 hours a week. If I change my mind, I will give you [insert period of notice – up to three months] notice in writing to end this agreement.

Signed: _____

Date: _____

Other clauses

In addition to the clauses set out above there are a number of other employment terms and conditions that are usually contained within a staff handbook, as set out in Chapter 9, but that could, if desired, be incorporated into the written statement. The main problem is that this can tend to make the statement a long, complex and possibly off-putting document. On the other hand, it does mean that all the key terms and conditions can be found in one place.

Types of contract

Open-ended and fixed-term contracts

Most employment contracts are for an indefinite period of time and only end when the employee leaves. However, it is also common to have a fixed-term contract when the employment is for a specified period of time, such as one year, and automatically ends when that period has elapsed. To avoid any doubt such a contract should specify a definite end date. You should bear in mind that non-renewal of a fixed-term contract is a dismissal and is subject to the normal rules applying to any dismissal. If the principal reason for the dismissal is that the contract has expired and no further work is available then the dismissal is likely to be fair (see Chapter 14). Anyone employed for four years on successive fixed-term contracts automatically becomes a permanent employee.

Joint contracts

In a joint contract it is a condition of the job that two people are employed jointly to carry out the work. An example of a joint contract would be where a husband and wife are employed to run a hostel. In this type of contract, ending the employment of one party to the contract will result in the automatic ending of the employment of the other person.

Directors' service agreements

A director's service agreement is very similar to any other employment contract and should contain everything required in the statement of particulars of employment. However, such contracts usually contain a number of other provisions that may only be appropriate for company directors. These typically include:

- longer notice periods, six months or a year being common;
- a non-competition clause, requiring the director not to enter into competition with the employer, nor to solicit the employer's customers or staff, for a period following termination of employment;
- a garden leave provision;
- confidentiality clauses;
- special bonus provisions;
- wide-ranging mobility provisions;
- a requirement not to carry on any other employment or professional activities outside this employment;
- a requirement to relinquish all directorships on leaving;
- special compensation arrangements on losing office.

Although these provisions are more commonly found in directors' service agreements some could also appear in ordinary employment contracts.

Bear in mind that where the contract contains generous bonus provisions these should be subject to stringent conditions, so that you do not end up rewarding failure. This problem has been highlighted in recent years when a number of senior executives have been given generous settlements on leaving companies despite those companies suffering a serious decline in profitability and share values. The financial services sector provides some prime examples!

An example of a director's service contract is set out at the end of this chapter.

Casual employees

Casual employees are those who are employed only for a certain number of hours and who receive payment only for those hours and who do not otherwise benefit from the terms and conditions of employment applying to permanent staff (although you should assume that statutory employment rights will apply). When you employ casual staff the basis of the employment, including its duration and the terms and conditions applying, should be made clear in the offer letter.

An example of wording in a contract for a casual worker is as follows:

You will provide services to the company on a casual basis and as required by the company. However, we cannot guarantee to provide you with work and there is no obligation on your part to accept any work offered.

You will be paid at the rate of £ [insert amount] for all hours actually worked. You will not be entitled to any other company benefits.

You are not an employee of the company and consequently you will be responsible for accounting to HMRC for all taxes payable and any National Insurance or other statutory reductions [alternatively, the company may be obliged to deduct tax and National Insurance, but it should be made clear that, if so, this is 'for administrative convenience only'].

Employee shareholders

The Growth and Infrastructure Act 2013 introduced a new employee shareholder employment status from 1 September 2013. An employee shareholder is defined as someone who is an employee, has between £2,000 and £50,000 of shares in the company, and foregoes the following employment rights:

- certain statutory rights in relation to requesting time off for training;
- the right to request flexible working;
- the right not to be unfairly dismissed (unless the dismissal is automatically unfair or due to discrimination);
- the right to statutory redundancy pay.

Employee shareholders will need to give their employers 16 (rather than 8) weeks' notice if they wish to return from maternity, additional paternity or adoption leave.

Zero hours contracts

Zero hours contracts are those which do not specify any particular number of hours that the employee is expected to work. A person working under this type of contract is not guaranteed work and will be paid only for the hours actually worked. The contract would normally require the employee to be ready to work whenever required by the company.

There has been an increase in recent years in these types of contract because of the flexibility they can give employers. As an employer it means that you can have a pool of employees who can be used as and when the need arises. Generally you are not obliged to offer work to workers on this type of contract, but equally they are not obliged to accept the work offered. In practice such workers are likely to be wary of turning down such work in case it affects their prospects of being offered work in the future.

Whether or not any worker engaged on this type of contract is a self-employed contractor or an employee will depend on the wording of any contract and the reality of the employment relationship. It turns on what has been described as 'mutuality of obligation', such as the extent to which you are obliged to offer work and the worker is obliged to accept it. Any contract therefore has to be very carefully worded if you want to avoid creating an employment relationship. It would depend on the interpretation placed on the relationship by a tribunal or court that would determine whether or not a worker was an employee or contractor.

Regardless of whether the person concerned is an employee or not she would still be a 'worker' for many employment rights such as those within the National Minimum Wage Regulations and the Working Time Regulations. You should also be aware that pensions auto-enrolment applies to 'workers' not just employees, but it remains to be seen how the law will be interpreted by courts and tribunals.

Interns

The ostensible purpose of internships is to provide training to students and graduates to enable them to gain experience in their chosen career. As these are often in highly competitive sectors employers can frequently offer these as unpaid positions. This can be controversial and is viewed by many as a means of employers getting free labour.

A key consideration when offering an internship is the actual nature of the role. If the intern is undertaking the role as part of a course of study, is a school student of age 16 or under gaining work experience, or is only shadowing work carried out by others, then offering no pay may be legitimate. If, however, the intern is undertaking work for the employer then that person is likely to be classified as a 'worker' and therefore is entitled to be paid the National Minimum Wage. It all depends on the nature of the contract with the employer.

Amending contracts

A contract of employment is an agreement between you and the employee and can only be changed by agreement. Although certain common changes such as an increase in pay will be mutually agreed between both parties, any unilateral change by you is likely to be a breach of contract. You should always therefore try to obtain the employee's agreement to any contract changes.

Problems most commonly arise when an employer, for business reasons, tries to make changes to the existing contract that are not accepted by the employee. If the employee cannot be persuaded to accept the new terms the only options are either not to change the contract, or to terminate the existing contract and offer to re-employ on a new one. The danger is that any such action could amount to an unfair dismissal, unless justified by strong business reasons. Imposing the changes without consultation could give rise to claims for breach of contract, and constructive dismissal if the employee resigns.

Further information

Employment Rights Act 1996
Working Time Regulations 1998
www.bis.gov.uk/.../a/11-949-agency-workers-regulations-guidance.pdf

Appendix: Specimen service agreement

The following service agreement is an example of what such a contract will typically look like. It comprises various sections from a number of such contracts with further amendments by the author. You should not use it as it stands because the precise wording to go into any service agreement will depend on what is agreed between the parties and you will need to seek advice to ensure that the agreement covers all salient points and that it is legally sound.

Service Agreement

This agreement is made on the [date] between

(1)   [company name and address] ('the Company') and
(2)   [employee name and address] ('the director')

1 Definitions and interpretations

1.1   In this agreement:
       'Company' includes any successors to the ownership of the Company;
       'Associated Company' means any company or other organization over which the Company (either alone or with any connected person) has direct or indirect control;
       'Board' means the board of directors of the Company from time to time;
       'Chairman' means the Chairman of the Board from time to time;
       'Effective Date' means the date that the agreement is signed by the parties.

1.2   Any reference to a statute or statutory provision includes a reference to any amendment or re-enactment of it.

1.3   Any reference to one gender includes a reference to all other genders.

1.4   Any reference to the singular includes a reference to the plural and vice versa.

1.5   References to any clause, sub-clause, paragraph or schedule is to a clause, sub-clause, paragraph or schedule of or to this agreement.

2 Job title and duties

2.1   You are employed as [job title].
       Further information about your duties and responsibilities are set out in your job description, as amended from time to time.

2.2   You are to exercise the powers and functions and carry out the actions required of your position, and to undertake such other duties consistent with your position which may be reasonably assigned to you from time to time by or with the authority of the Board, and as directed by the Board.

2.3   You shall report to [job title of line manager] or to such other person as the Board may direct.

2.4 The Company reserves the right to transfer you to any subsidiary or associated company on the same terms and conditions set out in this agreement. In any such circumstance your employment will be treated as continuous.

2.5 You agree to serve the Company and any associated company faithfully and well and to use your best endeavours to promote and protect the interests of the Company and any associated company.

2.6 You agree to give the Board any information or assistance it may require relating to the business of the Company, and any associated company about which you have knowledge, and to keep the Board regularly and promptly informed of the development and progress of the Company's and any associated company's business.

3 Date of commencement

3.1 Your period of employment with the Company commenced on [date].
Your period of continuous employment commenced on [date].
OR
You have no period of previous service that would count as continuous employment for the purposes of the Employment Rights Act 1996.

4 Hours of work

4.1 You shall devote the whole of your time, attention and abilities to the performance of your duties during the Company's normal business hours of 9.00 am to 5.30 pm Monday to Friday inclusive [amend as appropriate], and at such other times as may reasonably be necessary for the effective discharge of your duties (unless prevented by illness or other incapacity and except as may from time to time be permitted or required by the Board) and you accept that by signing this agreement you have agreed that regulation 4 (1) of the Working Time Regulations 1998 shall not apply.

5 Place of work

5.1 Your normal place of work will be at the Company's offices at [location]. However, you agree to work at such other places within the United Kingdom as the Company may reasonably require. If you are required to relocate the Company will give you as much notice as possible and will reimburse such removal and other incidental expenses as the Company considers fair and reasonable in the circumstances.

5.2 You may be required from time to time to work abroad. If the Company requires you to work outside the United Kingdom for a period of more than one month it will provide you with written details of any terms and conditions which may apply to that work and to your return to the United Kingdom.

6   Remuneration and benefits

6.1   Your basic salary is £ [salary] per annum, or such other sum as the Company may subsequently determine, and will accrue from day to day. The salary is payable by equal monthly instalments in arrears on the last working day of each month and includes any sums receivable as director's fees.

6.2   The salary will be reviewed annually by the Company with any change taking effect from [date] of that year. Annual salary increases are awarded on merit and depending on your performance.

6.3   You may at the discretion of the Company be entitled to receive a bonus from time to time. Any such bonus will be related to performance, based on targets to be agreed between the parties to this agreement. Details of any agreed bonus or incentive scheme and the terms and conditions applying to it will be set out in a separate document. You shall have no right to receive any bonus if you are no longer employed by the Company or are working out a period of notice.

6.4   You shall in addition receive the following benefits:

–   Membership of the Company's medical insurance scheme for you and your family, including dependent children, provided that you and your family, including dependent children, meet the normal underwriting requirements of that scheme and are accepted at normal rates of premium.

–   Membership of the Company's Life Assurance Scheme for a sum insured equal to four times your annual remuneration (ie basic salary plus bonuses averaged over the previous three years) provided you meet the normal underwriting requirements of the scheme and are accepted at normal rates of premium.

–   Membership of the Company's permanent health insurance scheme provided you meet the normal underwriting requirements of the scheme and are accepted at normal rates of premium.

–   Further information about these schemes is set out in the staff handbook.

7   Expenses

7.1   The Company will reimburse all reasonable hotel, travelling, entertainment and other expenses necessarily and properly incurred by you in the course of carrying out your duties and responsibilities for the Company, subject to the Company's approval of completed expenses claim forms, production of valid receipts or other documentary evidence and compliance with the Company's regulations relating to expenses. Further information about the Company's expenses policy is set out in the staff handbook.

7.2   Any credit card issued to you by the Company must be used only for expenses necessarily and properly incurred by you in the course of your employment and in accordance with the Company's regulations.

8 Car or car allowance

8.1 The Company will provide you with a fully expensed Company car, equivalent in value to a [car make and model] and including a car telephone for business and personal use during your employment. The Company will pay all costs relating to the car as set out in the Company car policy, a copy of which is contained in the staff handbook. You undertake to take good care of the car and to ensure that it is maintained in a legal and roadworthy condition.

8.2 Alternatively you may receive a car allowance of £ [amount] per month. This is on condition that any car you drive shall be a private car and the Company shall have no responsibility for any aspect of owning or running the car except that the Company shall reimburse you the cost of insuring the car and the cost of all petrol (whether for personal or business use).

8.3 It is a condition of your employment that you maintain a valid UK driving licence at all times.

9 Pension

9.1 The Company shall pay a contribution of [x per cent] of your basic salary into the Company's pension scheme subject to any HMRC requirements and overriding legislation.

9.2 A contracting-out certificate is [is not] in force in respect of your employment.

10 Holidays

10.1 You shall be entitled to [insert number] days' holiday each calendar year in addition to all public holidays normally applying in England and Wales. The holiday year runs from [date] to [date]. Holidays may not be carried forward from one year to the next without the express permission of the Board. No payment shall be made during your employment in lieu of holidays not taken.

10.2 On commencement of employment you shall accrue holiday on a pro rata basis for each complete month of service in that holiday year. On termination of your employment you shall be entitled to receive a payment representing holiday accrued, but as yet untaken, on a pro rata basis for the number of completed calendar months you have worked during the current holiday year. Any such payment will be calculated at a rate of [accrual rate, for example 1/260th] of your annual basic salary per day of holiday. [Alternatively, the Company may, at its discretion, require you to take any unused holiday entitlement during your notice period.]

10.3 If at the date of the termination of your employment you have taken holidays in excess of your accrued entitlement this excess will be deducted from any sums due to you from the Company. This will be calculated at a rate of [accrual rate, for example 1/260th] of your annual basic salary per day of holiday.

10.4 The Company will try to accommodate all reasonable requests relating to the time and duration of holidays but reserves the right to arrange holidays in its interest. Your entitlement to holidays and to holiday pay is subject to the rules of the Company from time to time in force relating to holiday entitlement and holiday pay.

11   Sickness or injury

11.1 If, in the opinion of the Board, you are unable to perform your duties properly for a period, or periods, not exceeding a total of 13 weeks (including both normal working days and non-working days) in any period of 12 months because of illness (including mental illness), accident or any other cause beyond your control, you shall be entitled to receive your full basic salary (inclusive of any Statutory Sick Pay to which you may be entitled) for the duration of that period. Thereafter any payment shall be subject to, and in accordance with, the terms of the Company's permanent health insurance scheme.

11.2 If you are unable to work because of illness or an accident you must notify your line manager as early as possible by telephone on the first morning of absence or as soon as reasonably practical thereafter, indicating the reason for your absence and its likely duration. If you are absent for more than three consecutive working days you must complete a self-certification sickness form on your return and give it to your line manager. If you are absent for more than five working days you must provide an appropriate medical certificate from your doctor in the manner required by the rules of the Company. Thereafter you should send in further medical certificates at weekly intervals during the whole period of absence.

11.3 Failure to comply with the Company's rules relating to the reporting of sickness or injury, as amended from time to time, could result in you losing the right to be paid during any such absence.

11.4 Statutory Sick Pay ('SSP') shall be paid by the Company in accordance with the legislation in force at the time of absence. Any payment of remuneration under sub-clause 11.1 for a day of absence will discharge the Company's obligation to pay SSP for that day.

11.5 The Company reserves the right to require you to be medically examined at its expense by a medical practitioner nominated by it and for a report of that examination to be made available to the Board.

11.6 If, in the opinion of the Board, you are or have been unable to perform your duties properly for a period or periods exceeding 13 weeks in total, or if the Board has good reason to believe that you are unlikely to be able to perform your duties properly for a continuous period of 13 weeks or more, the Company shall be entitled at any time to give you at least six months' notice of the termination of your employment less the total of any periods for which you have been paid salary under sub-clause 11.1 during the 12 months prior to the giving of such notice. However, the Company may not terminate your employment if you are receiving, or are entitled to receive, benefits under the terms of the Company's permanent health insurance scheme unless the Company first provides you with benefits no less favourable than the net benefits payable to you by the insurer under that scheme.

12 Outside interests

12.1 During your employment you must not, without the prior written consent of the Board:

(a) be directly or indirectly engaged or concerned in any capacity with any business, trade or occupation where this may conflict with the interests of the Company or adversely affect the effective discharge of your duties. However, this does not prevent you holding, for investment purposes only, not more than five per cent of the issued shares or securities of any companies which are listed or dealt in on any recognized stock exchange. For this purpose 'occupation' shall include any public, private or charitable work which the Board considers may hinder or interfere with the performance of your duties; or

(b) introduce to any other person, company or undertaking, except an associated company, or carry out on your own behalf, any business that the Company is able to carry out.

13 Confidential information and trade secrets

13.1 You shall keep secret and shall not at any time either during your employment, or after its termination, for whatever reason, use, communicate or reveal to any person for your own purposes or those of any other person, company or undertaking, any secret or confidential information about the business, finances or organization of the Company or any associated company, or its or their suppliers or customers obtained in the course of your employment.

13.2 You shall also use your best endeavours to prevent the publication, disclosure or use of any such information.

13.3 Examples of the types of information that will be regarded as secret and confidential will include, but not be limited to, the following examples, whether relating to the Company, an associated company or to any client, customer or supplier of the Company or any associated company:

- relevant hardware, software or source codes;
- details of research and development activities;

- marketing and sales policies and information, price lists, pricing structures, credit management policies and procedures, payment policies and procedures;
- business plans;
- suppliers and their production and delivery capabilities;
- customers and details of their particular requirements;
- financial information and plans;
- product lines and the development of new products;
- production or design secrets;
- technical design, specifications or formulae of products;
- information about officers and employees;
- any information marked 'confidential' or which you have been told is confidential or which you might reasonably expect to be regarded as confidential; or
- any information given in confidence by clients, customers, suppliers or any other person.

13.4 The restrictions in this clause do not apply to:
  (a) any disclosure authorized by the Board or required by any court or tribunal or other authorized regulatory authority; or
  (b) any information that has come into the public domain, except a breach of this clause or of any equivalent provision.

14 Intellectual property

14.1 You agree that any invention made by you in the course of your employment or originated by you using equipment or facilities owned by the Company shall belong to the Company.

14.2 You agree to assign to the Company with full title guarantee all present and future intellectual property rights in any invention made by you during the course of your employment with the Company and agree to disclose promptly to the Company all documents and other materials relevant to any such intellectual property.

14.3 You agree to waive any moral rights that you have or may have against the Company or any of its employees, officers or agents in any intellectual property originated by you in the course of your employment by the Company.

14.4 You agree to take such actions and execute such deeds and other documents that the Company consider may be necessary to substantiate, protect and maintain the intellectual property rights of the Company, without compensation additional to that provided for in your contract of employment. This clause will continue to apply following the termination of your employment for whatever reason.

14.5 You agree that decisions relating to the substantiation, protection and maintenance of any intellectual property originated by you shall be at the sole discretion of the Company and you shall have no claim against the Company in the event of any decision not to proceed with any such substantiation, protection or maintenance.

14.6 You appoint the Company to be your attorney and to take such actions and execute such deeds and other documents as may be necessary in your name and on your behalf and to give the Company or its nominees the full benefits of rights conferred under this agreement.

15 Grievance procedure

15.1 If you have a grievance relating to any aspect of your employment you should raise the matter in the first instance with the Chief Executive [or other appropriate person]. If the matter remains unresolved, it may be raised in writing with the Chairman of the Board. The grievance will then be considered at the next appropriate meeting of the Board, which will give you a written response as soon as practicable following the meeting. The decision of the Board shall be final.

16 Disciplinary procedure

16.1 Except in the case of gross misconduct and subject to the provisions of sub-clause 17.4, the policy of the Company is not to dismiss an employee for a first breach of the contract of employment that is capable of being remedied until that employee has been warned that dismissal could result from that breach. However, you accept that for an appointment at your level it may not always be appropriate to give any such warning prior to dismissal.

16.2 A copy of the disciplinary rules and procedures of the Company are set out in the staff handbook. These do not form part of your contract of employment.

17 Termination of employment

17.1 Your employment may be terminated by either you or the Company giving to the other six months' [or other agreed period] notice in writing.

17.2 If written notice of termination of employment is given either by you or by the Company, the Company may in its sole and absolute discretion terminate your employment immediately by paying you salary in lieu of any required period of notice together with any accrued holiday pay up to the date notice is given. You will not be entitled to any additional compensation in respect of any holiday that would otherwise have accrued during the notice period.

17.3 The Company reserves the right to terminate your employment summarily by oral or written notice and without any payment in lieu of notice if it has reasonable grounds for believing that you are guilty of gross misconduct, gross negligence or any other serious breaches of Company rules or your contract of employment, including any of the following events:

(a) Commission of any criminal offence, dishonesty or serious misconduct, whether during the performance of your duties or otherwise, and which in the opinion of the Board renders you unfit to continue as a director of the Company or which would be likely to prejudice adversely the reputation or interests of the Company or any associated company;

(b) In the event of any bankruptcy order being made against you or by you becoming prohibited by law from being a director or taking part in the management of the Company whether under the Company Directors Disqualification Act 1986 or otherwise;

(c) If any information relating to your suitability for employment by the Company and provided in the course of applying for employment is subsequently found to be false or misleading; or

(d) If you fail or cease to meet the requirements of any regulatory body whose consent is required to enable you to carry out effectively your duties and responsibilities under your contract of employment.

17.4 If written notice of termination of employment is given either by you or by the Company, the Company reserves the right either to require you during the notice period to perform such duties as the Board may determine, or to require you not to undertake any duties and to exclude you from any premises of the Company or any associated company. In either case the Company will continue to pay your normal salary and provide all other benefits during the notice period.

17.5 On the termination of your employment, for whatever reason, you shall immediately:

(a) return to the Company all documents, books, materials, records, correspondence, notes, reports, papers, data, software, manuals and information, in whatever form held (including summaries and extracts of these), relating to the Company or any associated company, and any other property of the Company or any associated company including, but not limited to, any car, computers, software, keys, credit cards which are in your possession, custody, care or control. You will be required to confirm in writing that you have complied fully with the terms of this sub-clause;

(b) delete any information or records, however stored, relating to the business of the Company or any associated company, which you possess or control outside the Company premises. You will be required to confirm in writing that you have complied fully with the terms of this sub-clause;

(c) resign any office or appointment you hold in the Company or in any associated company without any claim for compensation or damages for loss of office and you hereby appoint the Company as your agent to execute any necessary letters of resignation on your behalf; and

(d) transfer to the Company all shares and share certificates you hold in any company as nominee or trustee for the Company, and appoint the Company to execute any such transfers on your behalf.

18 Suspension

18.1 If the Board has reasonable grounds to suspect that any one of the events specified in clause 17.3 has occurred the Board may suspend you on full salary together with associated benefits while the matter is investigated. You have the right during any such suspension to terminate your employment immediately by notice in writing to the Company, but without any claim for compensation.

19 Restrictions

19.1 You agree to be bound by the following restrictions:

(a) You shall not for a period of six months after the termination of your employment, either personally or through an agent, either on your own account or for any other person, directly or indirectly canvass or solicit orders from any customer to supply goods, services and supplies that are provided by the Company or an associated company or which are substantially similar to those provided by the Company or an associated company.

(b) You shall not for a period of six months after the termination of your employment, either personally or through an agent, and either on your own account or for any other person, directly or indirectly canvass or solicit orders from any person, firm or company who within the period of 12 months prior to the termination of your employment was a client or customer of the Company or an associated company and with whom you have had dealings.

(c) You shall not during your employment or for a period of 12 months after the termination of your employment, either personally or through an agent, and either on your own account or for any other person, directly or indirectly solicit or endeavour to entice away from the Company any director, employee or consultant of the Company.

20 Data protection

20.1 You agree that personal data relating to you and to your employment with the Company required for the effective administration of the Company may be collected, held (in hard copy and computer readable form) and processed by the Company.

20.2 You agree that the Company may process sensitive personal data relating to you, including medical details and details of gender, race and ethnic origin. Personal data relating to gender, race and ethnic origin will be processed by the Company only for the purpose of monitoring the Company's equal opportunity policy and for ensuring that equal opportunities in employment are promoted and maintained. You agree that the Company may disclose or transfer such sensitive personal data to other persons if it is required or permitted by law to do so or, in the case of personal data relating to gender, race, ethnic origin, religious belief, age, sexual orientation or disability, for the purpose of monitoring the Company's equal opportunity policy. Where the disclosure or transfer is to a person resident outside the European Economic Area, the Company shall take reasonable steps to ensure that your rights and freedoms in relation to the processing of the relevant personal data are adequately protected.

21 Notices

21.1 Any notice under this agreement shall be in writing and may be delivered personally or sent by first class post (airmail if overseas) or by facsimile machine.

The address of the Company for service of notices shall be its registered office and any such notice should be marked for the attention of the Chairman of the Board. Any notice to you from the Company will be to the address stated in this agreement or to any other permanent address that you notify to the Company. You are required to notify the Company of any changes to your address and telephone number.

22 Collective agreements

22.1 This agreement sets out the entire agreement and understanding between the parties in connection with your employment save only for any terms implied by law. There are no collective agreements that directly affect the terms and conditions of your employment.

23 Variation

23.1 Any term or provision of this agreement may only be amended by written agreement between you and the Company.

24 Miscellaneous

24.1 You consent to the deduction from any sum otherwise payable to you during or on the termination of your employment the value of any claim the Company has against you, including but not limited to, the following:

(a) overpayment of wages or salary;

(b) overpayment of any expenses incurred by you in the course of your employment;

(c) any loans made to you by the Company;

(d) any advances on wages or salary that the Company may have made to you.

25 Severability

25.1 The various terms and provisions of this agreement are severable and if any term or provision in this agreement is held to be illegal, invalid or unenforceable, in whole or in part, under any rule of law or enactment, such term or provision or part shall to that extent be deemed not to form part of this agreement, but the enforceability of the remainder of this agreement shall not be affected.

26 Previous agreements

26.1 The agreement cancels and is in substitution for all previous letters of engagement, agreements and arrangements (whether verbal or in writing) between you and the Company, all of which shall be deemed to have been terminated by mutual consent.

27 Law and jurisdiction

27.1 This agreement shall be governed by and construed in accordance with English law and each party to this agreement submits to the non-exclusive jurisdiction of the English courts.

EXECUTED by:

_____ Director

SIGNED by: _____

in the presence of: _____

Name: _____

Address: _____

_____

Occupation: _____

DATE: _____

Paying Staff

03

Deciding how much to pay

You are free to decide how much to pay for a particular job provided this is above the National Minimum Wage and does not infringe equal pay legislation (see below). In deciding the appropriate pay level you should take into account:

- what the company can afford;
- the market rate for jobs of this type in this sector and location;
- the size of the job in comparison with other jobs in the company;
- what you are paying your other employees;
- the overall value of the remuneration package including benefits.

Finding out the market rate

As you will normally have to compete with other employers for staff it is clearly important to ensure that you are paying at a comparable level for jobs of similar size.

There are a number of sources of information about the going rate for particular types of job. These are:

- job advertisements in local newspapers and professional journals;
- pay surveys and publications;
- employment agencies;
- consultants;
- market research;
- professional bodies and employer organizations.

Job advertisements are a readily available source of information about pay levels. The main danger with this type of information is that the jobs in question may not be directly comparable to those in your own company and they also tend to state the maximum rather than the typical earnings for that type of job. This is particularly the case when terms such as 'total package' or 'OTE' (on-target earnings) are used.

There is also a substantial variation in pay levels depending on the size of the organization, the industry sector and its location. Wherever possible, you should try to compare like with like. There are numerous pay surveys on the market and these can provide a reliable source of data, provided they cover the jobs you are seeking to fill. The main points to bear in mind when using surveys are:

- they can be expensive to buy and are not usually available from local libraries;
- the size of the survey sample is critical – generally the larger the sample the more reliable the data;
- survey data is often collected on the basis of job title, which gives very little information about the real size and range of accountabilities of any particular job, making comparisons difficult;
- survey data quickly becomes out of date and will need to be adjusted to take account of inflation;
- the composition of the survey can vary from year to year, which can lead to some inconsistencies in the data.

Other sources of pay information include a range of personnel and pay publications that are available in some libraries including, for example, the Industrial Relations Services Pay Bulletin, Incomes Data Services Reports, the Office for National Statistics Annual Survey of Hours and Earnings (ASHE) and so forth, and professional bodies such as the Chartered Institute of Personnel and Development (CIPD) and the Institute of Directors (IoD). The surveys by Croner Reward in association with the IoD are particularly useful for determining pay for senior staff. Companies' annual reports are another useful source of information about board-level pay.

It is possible to conduct your own market research by contacting similar companies, or companies with similar jobs. The main problem is that this can be time-consuming and there may be reluctance on the part of many companies to give what they might regard as commercially sensitive information to a potential competitor.

If you are using recruitment consultants to fill a vacancy they will generally have a good idea of the pay level that will be sufficient to attract a good candidate. However, it should be borne in mind that it is in their interests for the recommended pay level to be higher rather than lower, as this will make it easier for them to find a suitable candidate and will increase their fee, which is normally based on a percentage of the salary offered.

Finally, there are a number of reward consultants who will advise on pay levels. However, in view of the fees involved this is usually only a sensible option for senior jobs or where there is a need to review the pay of several jobs.

Internal relativities

In deciding the pay level for a particular job it is not only the external market that has to be taken into account but also the relative pay levels in the company. It is important for motivation and morale to ensure that individuals feel they are being paid fairly in relation to their colleagues. In a small company all that needs to be taken into account is the relative size of jobs based on their content, and the experience and performance of the people doing the jobs.

In a large company it may be necessary to have a job evaluation scheme; see the next section. Such a scheme might be essential to ensure that jobs of equal value receive equal pay, which is a legal requirement. This is, arguably, more important since the introduction of the Equality Act 2010, which allows employees to make enquiries about the pay of colleagues to ascertain whether there is any pay discrimination taking place.

Job evaluation

What is job evaluation?

Job evaluation is the process of systematically assessing the relative importance of jobs in a company so that they can be placed in a rank order. Usually each job is compared with all other jobs in the same company using an analytical framework that enables the user to make logical judgements about job size. It is important to remember that job evaluation is a tool to assist in the decision-making process but the decision itself is based on the judgement of those carrying out the evaluation.

Job evaluation does not determine pay rates; it only helps the company decide how jobs should be grouped. The determination of the appropriate pay and benefits packages for different jobs comes at the end of the job evaluation exercise.

Benefits of job evaluation

There are a number of benefits of job evaluation; the most important are:

- Most people want to feel that they are being rewarded fairly in relation to others in the company and job evaluation can help to ensure that rewards are allocated fairly between jobs.
- Job evaluation provides an analytical way of assessing job size.
- Judgements are made by managers about how much jobs should be paid anyway, so it is better to do this systematically rather than on 'gut-feel'.
- Depending on the method used, it can enable comparisons to be made between completely different types of jobs.
- Without a systematic method of job evaluation it might be difficult to provide a strong defence to any equal value claims (see below).
- Job evaluation can assist in salary planning and pay negotiations.
- Job evaluation can be a valuable tool in the analysis of a company and can help to identify any gaps or overlaps in responsibility.

A systematic method of job evaluation may not be necessary for all companies. If your company is comprised of only a few employees the rank order of jobs will generally be obvious. Similarly in some environments the pay rates are determined solely by the market and trying to assess job size would be superfluous.

Disadvantages of job evaluation

There are of course some disadvantages to job evaluation, including the following:

- Job evaluation is essentially a judgemental process and there will always be some who feel that the approach adopted does not adequately reflect their own jobs.
- Some systems can be time-consuming and costly to install and maintain.
- External consultancy will usually be required to introduce job evaluation.
- Many managers and employees prefer the vagueness surrounding non-analytical ways of determining job size as this gives more scope for negotiation and manipulation.
- Some systems may be difficult for employees to understand, thereby leading to suspicion and mistrust.
- The process of introducing job evaluation can bring to light organizational anomalies that many may have wished to keep hidden.

Equal pay and job evaluation

It has been a requirement of UK law since the Equal Pay Act 1970, and now contained within the Equality Act 2010, that men and women are paid on the same terms where:

a the woman is employed on like work with a man in the same employment; or

b the woman is employed on work rated as equivalent with that of a man in the same employment; or

c the work is of equal value.

In addition, the Equal Pay Directive states that where a job classification system is used for determining pay, it must be based on the same criteria for both men and women and so drawn up as to exclude any discrimination on grounds of sex.

You should note that while it has been generally assumed in this section that an equal pay claim will be brought by a woman, such a claim can also be brought by a man.

The three grounds on which a woman may make a claim for equal pay are where:

1 she is doing work that is the same or broadly similar to that of a man, ie 'like work';

2 the job has been rated the same under a proper job evaluation study; or

3 the work is of equal value to a man's in terms of effort, skill, decision making and the other demands it makes that have not been assessed under a job evaluation study.

Under point 1 above, a tribunal will decide whether the work is broadly similar or whether there are any material differences that would justify different rates of pay. Under point 2, where a woman's job has been rated as equal to a man's under a job evaluation scheme, a tribunal will award equal pay. If it has been rated as lower the woman would not normally be able to bring a claim under this heading unless she could prove that the job evaluation scheme itself was discriminatory.

A woman can make a claim for equal pay for work of equal value where she can prove that her work is equal to that of a man in terms of the demands it makes of her in effort, skill, decision making or other significant factors. Where no job evaluation scheme exists or any such scheme is biased, and the tribunal considers that the comparison made is reasonable, it can appoint an expert to undertake a job evaluation exercise.

For job evaluation schemes to be seen as valid and non-discriminatory they should conform to the following criteria:

- they must be analytical;
- the comparison should be of the whole job;
- factors and weightings must be objective and non-discriminatory;
- the evaluation scheme and the basis for allocating pay rates to jobs should be capable of being explained by the employer;
- the scheme must be based on the same criteria for men and women;
- one overall scheme for all jobs is the safest option;
- a job evaluation scheme may not be discriminatory just because one of its criteria is more common to men, but it should take into account other criteria that may be more common to women;
- the time at which the work is done will not, per se, normally be viewed as justifying a difference in evaluation;
- the job evaluation process must be free of bias, with women being involved in the evaluation of jobs;
- job information must be obtained in a way that is non-discriminatory;
- market issues can sometimes justify a material difference in pay between certain jobs, but care should be taken to ensure that the comparisons are not themselves biased.

Equal pay audits

For equal pay claims presented after 1 October 2014 employment tribunals can order Equal Pay Audits where an employer is found guilty of gender discrimination relating to pay.

Types of job evaluation scheme

Job evaluation schemes divide broadly into analytical and non-analytical schemes. Non-analytical schemes are ranking, paired comparison and classification. These are considered further below.

Ranking

Ranking compares each job with every other job and places them in order of importance to the organization. Evaluators compare whole jobs rather than the separate components of jobs, but may make these comparisons on the basis of one or more key factors, such as the decisions made or the accountabilities of each post.

The advantages of ranking are simplicity and speed and it may be perfectly adequate for a small organization. However, it has a number of disadvantages:

- Its lack of sophistication means that it may be difficult to defend the results as there will be no way of demonstrating any analysis.
- There can be no guarantee that bias has not been built into the system.
- The lack of objective criteria is likely to mean that judgements made about jobs are inconsistent.
- It is difficult to compare very different jobs for which different aptitudes might be required.
- While a rank order can be obtained, the magnitude of the difference between jobs cannot be measured.
- It does not easily enable jobs to be grouped for grading or pay purposes.
- The rationale behind the decisions cannot easily be communicated and the approach is therefore likely to lack credibility with staff.

Paired comparisons

The paired comparisons method of job evaluation is similar to ranking in that complete jobs are compared with all other jobs. However, in this case scores are allocated in terms of whether a particular job is as important, more important or less important than another. In this way, by giving points to each job in turn on the basis of these comparisons, a rank order may be produced.

This approach again has the advantages of simplicity and speed and it may be perfectly adequate for a small organization. Although it is a slightly more sophisticated way of comparing jobs, it suffers from all of the disadvantages of ranking, plus the fact that as the number of jobs increases so do the number of comparisons that have to be made, and the calculations involved.

Job classification

Job classification involves the identification of a number of classes or grades of employee, each of which will have certain characteristics and into which all jobs with these characteristics can be placed. Frequently organizations have a grading structure into which jobs are placed on a felt-fair basis but without any detailed analysis of the size of those jobs. Such systems are very common in the public sector and in large highly structured organizations.

Job classification again has the advantages of speed and simplicity, but with the added advantage that there are clear grade or job family definitions that enable jobs to be more accurately allocated to the appropriate grade or class. The main disadvantages of classification are that:

- It compares job descriptions with grade criteria, rather than jobs with jobs, which is a less reliable way of getting a rank order.
- It can be difficult to grade more complex jobs.
- The grade definitions may be difficult to formulate and may not always be helpful when allocating jobs to grades.

- There is no easy way of justifying why a job has been allocated a particular grade.
- It is not usually accepted as being a valid approach in equal value cases.
- There is no guarantee that bias has not been built into the process.
- This approach can be subject to grade drift whereby, over time, the grades of various jobs will tend to creep up, usually depending on the advocacy skills of the manager seeking any increase.
- It can result in the introduction of too many grades and job categories, which in turn can have implications for the organization structure and will complicate pay policy.

Points rating

Points rating or points factor rating consists of the identification of a number of factors considered to be relevant to all the jobs under consideration, with points allocated to the different levels of these factors. Jobs are then compared against each of these factors, points allocated accordingly, and then the separate factors are totalled to give an overall score.

Once all the jobs have been evaluated the organization will have a rank order of scores that can then be further divided into grades against which pay levels can be set. There are numerous examples of such schemes and a number of factors that commonly occur, such as knowledge and experience, decisions made, complexity, etc. Such schemes may be bought 'off-the-shelf' or can be designed specifically for the organization in question. The main advantages of using an off-the-shelf scheme are that it saves a lot of the time required to design a bespoke scheme and it will have been tried and tested in other organizations. The main drawbacks are that the factors may not be entirely appropriate to the jobs in the organization or may not reflect its culture, and such schemes often need to be maintained by external consultants. Tailor-made schemes are considered further below.

Points schemes have the following advantages:

- As evaluators have to consider each job in terms of a number of factors they are able to be more objective in their judgements.
- Because all jobs are being considered against the same criteria there is likely to be greater consistency in the judgements made.
- Evaluators are able to demonstrate analytical reasons for making particular judgements about jobs.
- The allocation of points makes the process of developing a grade structure or pay bands easier.
- The size of the difference between jobs can be measured.
- The system is more likely to be perceived as fair than one in which the criteria are not known.
- The approach is more likely to be accepted in equal value cases.
- Such schemes are relatively easy to computerize.

The main disadvantages are:

- Their analytical nature can give a spurious impression of scientific accuracy when in fact they are still dependent on evaluators' judgements.
- They can be expensive and time-consuming to install and maintain.
- They are based on an assumption that all the factors used are equally relevant to all jobs, which may not be the case.

Factor comparison

Factor comparison differs from points rating in that jobs are compared with each other on a number of different factors rather than as whole jobs. This produces a number of different hierarchies of jobs as some will be high on some factors but low on others. Comparisons are made of the lists of factor rankings, with judgements about how much of each job is attributable to the various factors, eg what percentage of the job's total size might relate to a factor covering responsibility.

While this approach is analytical and objective, it is relatively little used nowadays because it is time-consuming, complex and costly to install.

Other methods

Over the years a variety of approaches to job evaluation have been developed. A number of these have concentrated on a single factor rather than a range of factors and would therefore be less likely to be accepted from an equal value viewpoint.

Tailored schemes

Tailored schemes are those designed specifically for a particular organization. They have the advantages that they can be designed to reflect precisely the needs of the organization in question, that they will use the terminology recognized within it, and that by involving staff in their design they will give the scheme greater credibility and a sense of ownership on the part of employees. While there is likely to be more development time involved, this can be kept to a minimum if support is provided by an experienced job evaluation specialist who will know from past experience what factors and weightings are likely to best reflect job size in a particular environment.

The job evaluation process

A very important aspect of introducing job evaluation is the process that supports it. Even where a very robust, well-established scheme is introduced it can still fail, not because of any inherent faults in the scheme, but because the process has not been properly managed. While the detail of any process will vary depending on the type of job evaluation method used, there are a number of issues you need to consider when introducing any approach.

Scheme objectives

It is important first of all to be clear about the objectives of any job evaluation scheme and to take account of the organization's business goals, its culture and previous history. You need to be clear about what you expect the scheme to deliver and about those matters you consider central to business success. The organization's culture will affect the way in which the process is carried out.

The range of jobs

The numbers and types of jobs within the organization will affect both the kind of evaluation methodology required and the process. Manual and craft jobs will have different outputs and skills from managerial and professional jobs and both groups may need to be evaluated using different factors. Where only a few jobs are involved, one of the simpler and less analytical methods might be appropriate.

Selecting the method

Once you are clear about the objectives of the job evaluation exercise and you know what types and numbers of jobs are involved, the next stage is to decide the job evaluation method to be used. While the cost of the method and its necessary consultancy support will be a factor in the decision, it is as well to bear in mind that the real costs are likely to be in implementation, and that the consultancy fees are relatively insignificant as a proportion of the total.

There are a number of proprietary schemes on the market, of which the Hay Guide Chart and Profile Method is the most widely used. There are many other schemes including those operated by a range of consultancies and major public sector schemes such as the NJC scheme in local government and the Agenda for Change scheme in the National Health Service. While it is beyond the scope of this book to cover these in any detail, it is as well to note that all these off-the-shelf schemes have the advantage of being tried and tested and so the various factors and scores can be applied with a degree of confidence. Their main drawback is that they often try to cover a very wide range of jobs and organizations with the same selection of factors. Clearly, however, there are differences between the components of jobs on the shop floor and those in the boardroom. For this reason some companies have different schemes for manual and non-manual jobs, and sometimes for different industry sectors.

Some other schemes are tailor-made, with factors and weightings that are specific to a particular organization. This kind of approach can ensure that the factors chosen are those that are the most relevant to that organization, and the fact that it has been involved in the selection and design of them should help to ensure greater credibility. The main difficulty is in getting factor definitions agreed and correctly weighted, although there are statistical techniques for achieving the latter. One other drawback is that the use of different factors, levels and scores in different organizations makes comparison between them more difficult and complicates the pay comparison process.

An extract from the BCHR job evaluation scheme is shown in Figure 3.1.

FIGURE 3.1   Knowledge and skills (extract from BCHR job evaluation scheme)

Interpersonal skills Knowledge and experience	1 Basic – Basic social skills only	2 Limited – Requires an ability to present the right image to external clients and to interface well with other departments	3 Advisory – Requires some influencing skills and an ability to communicate clearly and provide advice	4 Persuasive – Requires some significant motivational, persuasive or influencing skills	5 Critical – Role requires expert counselling skills and an ability to reconcile differences and shape attitudes in conditions of emotional stress
A Basic – Secondary education only required	35	45	55	70	95
B Clerical – Knowledge of elementary systems and procedures and relevant skills	45	55	70	95	120
C Administrative/ technical – Knowledge of more advanced systems and procedures plus relevant skills	55	70	95	120	160
D Advanced technical/basic professional – Requires a body of specialist technical knowledge and an understanding of principles related to that knowledge	70	95	120	160	210
E Professional – Requires a high level of specialist expertise involving professional judgement and the breadth of knowledge necessary to manage others	95	120	160	210	270

FIGURE 3.1   *continued*

Interpersonal skills	1 Basic – Basic social skills only	2 Limited – Requires an ability to present the right image to external clients and to interface well with other departments	3 Advisory – Requires some influencing skills and an ability to communicate clearly and provide advice	4 Persuasive – Requires some significant motivational, persuasive or influencing skills	5 Critical – Role requires expert counsel-ling skills and an ability to reconcile differ-ences and shape attitudes in conditions of emotional stress
Knowledge and experience					
F Senior professional/ managerial – Requires substantial managerial and/or professional knowledge gained through broad and deep experience	120	160	210	270	350
G Directing – Requires sufficient knowledge and experience to be able to direct and control a major function or to contribute substantially to the formulation of strategic objectives	160	210	270	350	455
H Strategic – Requires the knowledge and experience necessary to direct the organization	210	270	350	455	590

Costs

There is usually a cost involved in introducing job evaluation. This stems not just from the cost of buying or designing a suitable scheme, with any necessary consultancy support and the staff time involved in evaluating jobs and maintaining the system, but also from the implementation of any salary increases.

Typically, when you introduce job evaluation you will find that some jobs are underpaid and some are overpaid in relation to others. Since it is very difficult to reduce pay, and it would be demotivating and probably a breach of the employment contract to do so, those who are overpaid will continue to receive their existing level of pay on a personally protected basis, usually for a specified period – a process sometimes described as 'red-circling'. On the other hand, those who are underpaid will usually expect to have their salaries brought up to the appropriate level. It is incumbent on you to do this, as the whole point of the exercise is normally to ensure that pay relativities are right, and any failure to make these adjustments is again likely to be demotivating.

Communication

It is very important to ensure that the job evaluation exercise is effectively communicated to the employees. Precisely what is communicated and in how much detail is something that has to be carefully considered. As a minimum, the employees should be:

- told that a job evaluation exercise is to take place;
- informed of the aims and objectives of the exercise;
- notified of the process and the timescale involved;
- informed of the scheme principles;
- notified about the results of the exercise, although the amount of detail they are given will vary from organization to organization.

Wherever possible you should get the cooperation of any trade unions and they should be involved in the process. In this way they are more likely to buy into the process. If they remain outside it, they can oppose the results at a later date.

Job evaluation panels

Although jobs can be evaluated by an individual, it is more common in organizations of any size to have a job evaluation panel. This reduces the danger of individual bias, as everyone has prejudices about the worth of particular jobs and these will be diluted by a group process; it gives access to a wider range of knowledge about the organization and its jobs; and it is generally perceived to be fairer.

Panel or committee members should be people who have sound judgement and credibility within the organization. You should also try to ensure that as wide a range of job types as possible can be covered by the group's combined knowledge. Similarly, the panel should be representative of the organization's employees. For example, if there are no women evaluators the process may be discriminatory, even if the scheme itself is free of any such bias. However, you should keep the panel as small as possible, otherwise it becomes unwieldy and might involve too much time and resources.

Decisions should be by consensus. If there is no agreement this is likely to mean that the evaluators do not understand the job and require more information or clarification.

Computer Assisted Job Evaluation (CAJE)

Technology can be used in the job evaluation process in a number of ways. At the most basic level spreadsheets can be used to record and calculate points scores and to analyse pay data. At the other extreme there are computer programs that will help a company design its own job evaluation scheme, for example by providing a menu of factors, definitions and levels from which the most appropriate for the company can be selected.

The most common approach, however, is one in which the computer program provides for computer-entry of data, which is then analysed using a standard scheme. It is claimed that the main advantage of this approach is speed. This is because all evaluation schemes rely on the collection of data through job descriptions and questionnaires and these are then usually evaluated by a panel of evaluators. As collection of job information in this way can be very time-consuming, the attraction of direct keyboard entry by a jobholder or the line manager is obvious. Similarly, if the job can then be evaluated by the computer this should reduce the need for time- and resource-consuming job evaluation panels.

In practice these projected time savings are rarely achieved. The main reason for this is that job evaluation is essentially a judgemental process, and while computers are very good at analysing data they are not good at making judgements such as whether one job requires more experience or a higher level of interpersonal skills than another. This means that whoever enters the data, the results still have to be checked or 'moderated'. The moderation process involves reviewing the results to see if they make sense and those carrying out this role are really going through the same process as an evaluation panel. There is, furthermore, considerable complexity in designing a questionnaire that will capture all required job data in the correct form for analysis and it cannot be expected that the results will be 100 per cent accurate.

There is also the key issue of who enters the data. If done by the jobholder, who is generally the person who should know the job best, there is the danger that the information may not be correctly entered. This could also be the case if entered by the manager, who should in any case have a role in validating any employee data input. Many CAJE applications get round this problem by having specialist data inputters whose objectivity and knowledge of the job evaluation program should enable them to assess more accurately the appropriate factor level. This adds a stage to the process. With the non-computerized approach, job descriptions or job description questionnaires are written and then evaluated. With this approach, job questionnaires are completed, the data is entered by someone else, the results are calculated and then these are moderated, often by a panel.

How pay is made up

There are a number of different elements that can make up an employee's total pay. Some of the more common ones are:

- Base pay – which is the contractually agreed rate of pay set out in the contract of employment, before any additions, and usually expressed as an annual, monthly, weekly or hourly rate.

- Overtime – which is the rate of pay for any work over and above the basic hours; the conditions for payment should be clearly described in the contract of employment.
- Bonus – this is any amount additional to the base pay that is paid subject to certain conditions, such as the achievement of performance targets.
- Shift pay – an amount paid to compensate staff for regularly working hours outside the normal working day.
- Regional allowances – to compensate for the higher cost of living in certain locations.
- Other allowances.
- Standby and call-out payments.

Pay structures

In small companies the simplest way to pay people is to pay an individual a weekly or monthly wage or annual salary, which is reviewed annually, generally known as a 'spot rate'. In larger organizations with several jobs of similar size, it is more common to pay jobs within a pay range or grade with the position within that range being generally dependent on the individual's performance and experience. There are many variations on this theme.

The most appropriate approach for you will depend on the number and types of jobs within your company. As companies increase in size, spot rates become more difficult to manage. Pay ranges, on the other hand, give the flexibility to reflect differences in performance. The various types of pay structure with their advantages and disadvantages are described below.

Pay ranges

The most common approach to pay, at least in the private sector, is to apply pay ranges. These may either be applied to individuals or to groups of jobs and typically comprise maximum and minimum salary points, constructed about a midpoint, based on the job size and/or market rate for a particular category of jobs, but usually without incremental steps.

There are no hard-and-fast rules about how wide such ranges should be, but 80 to 120 per cent or 90 to 110 per cent of the midpoint are very common. Similarly, the basis for determining the midpoint, or the maximum and minimum, will vary from company to company. Typically pay ranges overlap, but this is not obligatory. Managers may be given the discretion to appoint anywhere within the range for a particular type of job or certain points may be identified, for example at 90, 95, 100, 105 per cent of the range and so forth. Application of these percentages may be related to performance, and where this approach is used a performance matrix such as that set out in Figure 3.2 can be used to assess the size of any bonus. Where ranges are applied there may often also be one-off cash bonuses for the attainment of agreed targets. The matrix shows the percentage of base salary payable as bonus, related to the position in the salary range, for different levels of performance.

FIGURE 3.2   Performance matrix

Performance rating	Position in range		
	Below 90%	90%–110%	Above 110%
Well above target	15%	12.5%	10%
Above target	12.5%	10%	7.5%
On target	10%	7.5%	5%

The advantages of pay ranges are that:

- They are more flexible than incrementally based grades.
- Managers are usually given relatively wide discretion in deciding salaries and are under no obligation to give an increase if this is not justified by market data or performance, and provided there is no contractual obligation to do so.
- They give the company wide scope to reward individual development and academic attainments or qualifications.
- They can give the company more control over its reward policy.
- They can be based on either job size or market rates, or a combination of the two, and may be applied differently for different job categories.
- They tend to break down the historical attitudes that can arise with grades.

The disadvantages of pay ranges are that:

- Although they are generally less structured than grades with fixed increments, they can be applied just as rigidly, thus generating none of the advantages described.
- Because of their flexibility they require more managing.
- They are likely to result in greater variations in individual pay for similar jobs and could therefore lead to dissatisfaction in some staff.

Competency bands

Pay ranges can be adapted to suit the particular needs of the company. For example, they can be related to competencies by the use of competency bands. Staff would move to different levels within the pay scales on the attainment of certain levels of competence, although the ranges would need to be sufficiently wide to accommodate these.

Job families

Pay ranges can also be applied to job families. In this approach the various job families are identified – for example, administrative and clerical, finance, information technology and so forth – and pay ranges relevant to those groups are applied. This enables the company to reflect the differing pay markets in which these job categories operate and can provide clear career paths. It does, however, make the establishment of one overall reward policy more difficult.

Spot salaries

Spot or spot rate salaries are those where specific individual salaries, rather than a salary range or grade, are paid to staff. In this case the rate paid usually depends on what the individual employee can negotiate with the employer. Obviously this kind of arrangement gives the employer a substantial degree of freedom in agreeing the reward package. Spot rates are most appropriate in small companies with a variety of jobs, for jobs at the most senior level or where the job is such that only a few people with rare capabilities are able to fill it. Where substantial numbers of staff are employed, spot rates can become difficult to apply and manage and could raise equal value issues.

Broad banding

Broad banding entails the introduction of fewer but much broader pay ranges. The typical features of a broad-banded structure are:

- four to six pay ranges covering all employees;
- each pay range containing jobs of perceptibly different size;
- a very wide salary range with significant overlap between ranges;
- the position in the range is determined by a variety of factors, including job size, market pay, performance and the acquisition of new skills and competencies.

The main implications of a broad-banded pay structure are as follows:

- There is less movement between pay bands but more movement within them; moving from one pay band to another would be a significant promotion.
- Staff would have to be prepared to move between jobs without necessarily moving to a higher pay range.
- The actual pay of any employee would be determined by a number of factors including job size, market rate, performance and the acquisition of knowledge, skills or competencies.

A job evaluation process may be necessary to determine the appropriate pay band for jobs and to establish boundaries. This could be installed relatively quickly, but would be likely to be less participative than is usually the case and would be likely to be less effective for defending equal value claims.

Pay discussion will centre more on the individual's pay than the rates for a particular pay band. Team leaders could be placed in the same band as their team members.

Bonuses

The design of bonus schemes can be complex, as any such scheme has to be carefully tailored to the needs of the company and to the type of job involved. For example, the type of scheme that might be appropriate for a salesperson would be completely different from one for a plumber or a secretary. When you are thinking of introducing a bonus scheme, therefore, you need to consider the following issues:

- The reason for the scheme – is it because you want the employees to share in the company's success or is it to reward the achievement of specific targets?
- If it is an incentive scheme, is there clarity about which behaviours you are trying to encourage and does the scheme achieve this?
- If the scheme is to reward performance, do you have a process for setting targets and for assessing whether those targets have been met?
- How is the amount of bonus to be calculated?
- How much is any bonus going to be?
- Are you going to have different schemes for different jobs?
- Are bonuses going to be paid on an individual or a group basis?
- How will you reward office and managerial staff who may not be able to earn bonuses through meeting productivity targets?
- How will any bonus relate to the rest of the remuneration package?
- How often will any bonus be paid?

The National Minimum Wage

The law relating to the National Minimum Wage (NMW) is laid down in the National Minimum Wage Act 1998, the National Minimum Wage Regulations 1999 and in the National Minimum Wage Act (Amendment) Regulations 1999.

The NMW applies to any worker who is not genuinely self-employed. From October 2014 the rate is £6.50 per hour for all workers aged 21 or over. There are lower rates for workers below this age and for certain trainees who may be aged 21 or more.

The hourly rate is calculated by working out a worker's total pay over the relevant pay reference period and dividing by the number of hours worked. The pay reference period is normally a month for monthly paid staff, but for any workers paid over a shorter period, such as a week, it will be that shorter period. The calculation should be based on gross pay (before deduction of Income Tax and National Insurance) and after deduction of certain payments above the base pay, such as overtime, shift payments, expenses, statutory sick pay and maternity pay.

Piece workers, or output workers, including homeworkers, must be paid a 'fair' piece rate linked to the NMW. For this purpose, output work means work that is paid on the basis of the number of pieces made or processed by the worker, or according to some other measure such as the number of tasks or transactions carried out by the worker.

These workers must either be paid at least the minimum wage for all hours worked or, alternatively, be paid the fair piece rate for each piece produced or task performed, determined by reference to the rate of performance of an average worker (called the 'rated output system'). To apply this you must have conducted a test to determine the average speed at which the job can be completed. This test has to be carried out using all workers, or a representative sample, and in similar conditions to those of the piece rate workers. You must then issue the piece rate worker, in advance, with a notice which:

- states that such a test has been conducted (or that the speed has been estimated);
- states what the average hourly output is;
- states that the worker will be treated as having worked for the time that it would have taken him (or her) to complete the job at the average speed;
- states the rate to be paid for the work in question; and
- gives one of the National Minimum Wage helpline numbers.

You are required to pay 120 per cent of the minimum wage for the time established by the testing procedure to ensure that workers who may be below the average speed also receive the NMW. It is essential that you keep adequate records if you use the rated output system.

Further information about the National Minimum Wage can be obtained from the BIS website: **www.bis.gov.uk**.

Guarantee payments

Guarantee payments were introduced to safeguard employees in the event of short-time working. They must be made to any employee who might normally expect to work, for any day when no work is provided because of a lessening of demand for your product or service. These payments are made for a maximum of five working days in any three months and are subject to a limit specified by the government (£25.00 per day from 1 February 2014).

Director's Remuneration Report Regulations 2002

These Regulations give shareholders more opportunity to express concerns over directors' remuneration. They provide that:

- Quoted companies must publish a detailed report on directors' pay as part of their annual reporting cycle. Disclosure requirements both about facts and policies have increased. The report must be approved by the Board of Directors.
- A graph of the company's total shareholder return over five years, against a comparator group, must be published in the remuneration committee report.
- The names of any consultants to the remuneration committee must be disclosed, as must whether they were appointed independently, along with the cost of any other services provided to the company.

- Companies must hold a shareholder vote on the directors' remuneration report at each annual general meeting.

Deductions from pay

Restrictions on deductions

You are not allowed to make deductions from pay unless:

- there is a statutory authority to do so, as with Income Tax and National Insurance;
- there is a clause in the employee's contract agreeing to a specific deduction; or
- the employee has agreed in writing to the deduction.

Overpayments

Where overpayments of wages or expenses have been made these can generally be deducted from earnings. However, there are situations in which any such deduction could be unlawful, such as where the individual has spent the overpayment in good faith. It is therefore always advisable to get the employee's prior agreement before making any such deduction.

Attachments of earnings orders

Where an employee defaults on debt repayments the courts have the power to require the employer to make deductions from that employee's pay.

Check-off agreements

A check-off agreement is an arrangement whereby trade union subscriptions are automatically deducted from pay. It is a legal requirement that you ensure that such deductions are lawful, which can only be done by ensuring that the employee gives his consent in writing to the deduction.

Generally, check-off arrangements can be viewed as a convenient way of ensuring that trade union subscriptions are paid, for maintaining good industrial relations and as a means of enabling the company to monitor the level of union membership. You can, if desired, charge the union an administrative fee for carrying out this arrangement.

Tax and National Insurance

PAYE

Any employee has to pay tax (PAYE – Pay As You Earn) to HM Revenue & Customs (HMRC) under Schedule E and it is your responsibility to deduct the tax and account for it to HMRC. Each employee is given a tax code by HMRC and it is the responsibility of the employee to ensure that the code given is the correct one and the responsibility of the employer to ensure that the correct amount is deducted.

You have to deduct the correct amount, keep records of the pay and deductions and pay the correct amount to HMRC each month. At the end of the tax year a return has to be sent to HMRC showing all the payments and deductions made throughout the year.

The tax code is notified to the employer by a P45 certificate issued by the previous employer or by direct notification from the tax office. In the absence of any such notification an emergency code has to be applied.

National Insurance Contributions

As an employer it is your responsibility to pay National Insurance Contributions (NICs) to HMRC for all employees whose earnings are above the Lower Earnings Limit. These are described as Class 1 NICs and comprise a contribution from the employee and one from you as the employer. It is normal to collect the employee's contribution by making a regular deduction from salary.

All NI payments must be made by the 19th day of the month following the month of deduction and can be incorporated into the monthly PAYE return.

Contributions should be calculated by reference to the employer's pack, which is sent automatically to you before the start of each tax year.

NICs are payable on all earnings and on a range of benefits, but not on expenses. It is not usually payable on redundancy payments.

Contributions do not have to be paid for employees aged under 16 years, and for those over retirement age only the employer's contribution is payable.

What does or does not count for National Insurance purposes is a relatively complex area, although the payment process itself should be fairly routine once it has been set up. To help employers there is a range of information contained in publications available from the National Insurance Contributions Office. This can be accessed online through its website at **http://www.hmrc.gov.uk/ni/index.htm** or by phoning 0300 200 3500.

Itemized pay statement

You must issue any employee with an itemized pay statement at the time of payment with details of:

- gross earnings;
- the amount of any fixed deduction and the reason for the deduction;
- the amount of any variable deduction and the reason;
- the net pay.

Further information

Annual Survey of Hours and Earnings, Office of Manpower Economics, www.ons.gov.uk/ons/rel/ashe/annual-survey-of-hours-and-earnings

Armstrong, M (1996) *Employee Reward*, Chartered Institute of Personnel and Development, London

Armstrong, M and Baron, A (1995) *The Job Evaluation Handbook*, Chartered Institute of Personnel and Development, London

Armstrong, M and Murlis, H (2007) *Reward Management*, 5th edn, Kogan Page, London

HM Revenue & Customs, www.hmrc.gov.uk

Incomes Data Services Ltd, 77 Bastwick Street, London EC1V 3TT

IRS Employment Review, Industrial Relations Services, London, published fortnightly

The Director's Remuneration Report Regulations 2002, www.legislation.gov.uk/uksi/2002/1986/mode

Employee Benefits

04

There is no legal requirement for you to give benefits above the minimum statutory entitlements, but most employers do so because of the need to be competitive in the jobs market and also to encourage a high level of staff satisfaction. Benefits can include:

- pension;
- car;
- share options;
- medical insurance;
- death-in-service benefits;
- holidays (above the statutory minimum);
- sick pay (above the statutory minimum);
- relocation expenses;
- enhanced maternity leave;
- sabbatical leave;
- payment of professional subscriptions;
- season ticket loans;
- subsidized meals or luncheon vouchers;
- sports and social facilities;
- childcare facilities.

The main issues that you have to consider as an employer are the common practice in your market sector, and especially in those companies you might compete against for staff, and whether benefits are applied equally and fairly to all staff. You will also need to consider the tax implications of various benefits packages.

You might also wish to consider whether you want to offer a flexible benefits package, whereby employees can pick and mix from a range of options. More information on flexible benefits is set out later in this chapter.

See research by **www.employeebenefits.co.uk** on 199 companies giving voluntary benefits, defined as products and services made available through an employer but paid for by staff out of their own income. The most common benefits are shown in Table 4.1.

TABLE 4.1 The most common voluntary benefits as reported by 199 surveyed companies

Voluntary benefit	%
Additional voluntary contributions to a defined benefit or money purchase pension scheme	66
Group personal pension	63
Healthcare/hospital cash plan	59
Private medical insurance	58
Gym membership	57
Childcare vouchers	54
Stakeholder pension	52
Life assurance	49
Season ticket loan	49
Leisure/entertainment services	47
Employer's own products or services	46
Legal advice/helpline	40
Retail products, eg electrical goods	40
Travel insurance	39
Optical care vouchers	39
Debt counselling/helpline	37
Health screening	36
Dental insurance	36
HMRC-approved save as you earn (SAYE) sharesave plan	35
Personal accident insurance	35
Financial advice/education	35
Income protection/permanent health insurance	34
Critical illness insurance	30
Retail/leisure vouchers	30

TABLE 4.1 *continued*

Voluntary benefit	%
Non-vocational training	27
Mobile phones	27
Motor insurance	26
House insurance	25
HMRC-approved share incentive plan	21
Pet insurance	19
Fuel for private use	14
Discounted cars through an all-employee ownership plan	11
Mortgage subsidy	4
Luncheon vouchers	3

SOURCE: www.employeebenefits.co.uk

Pensions auto-enrolment

Background

The government has introduced legislation to make it easier for workers to save for their retirement pensions. This requires all employers to enrol workers into a qualifying workplace pension scheme if they are not already in one. If, as an employer, you already have a workplace pension scheme this will need to be reviewed to ensure that it complies with the new rules and regulations. If you do not have a scheme and employ just one worker you will need to provide a suitable scheme. Bear in mind that the scheme applies to 'workers' which is a wider definition than 'employees'.

Definition of worker

The first step in introducing pension auto-enrolment is to decide whether you employ anyone who falls within the definition of 'worker'. This would include anyone who has a contract of employment with the company but could, in certain circumstances, also include agency workers. This might arise, for example, where the person has no employment contract with an agency and works only for your company. Further information on deciding whether a person is an employee or a contractor providing services, and therefore not falling within the definition for the purpose of auto-enrolment, may be found in Chapter 2.

Also excluded from the definition of 'worker' in this context would be a sole director of a company with no other employees, office holders such as trustees and Non-Executive Directors, volunteers and members of the Armed Forces.

Categories of worker

You will then need to decide which of three categories these workers fall into. These categories are:

- Eligible jobholders.
- Non-eligible jobholders.
- Entitled workers.

Eligible jobholders ie those who are eligible for automatic enrolment are workers who:

- are aged between 22 and state pension age;
- are working or usually work in the UK;
- have earnings paid by the employer above the 'earnings trigger' for automatic enrolment (£10,000 p.a. in 2014/15).

Non-eligible jobholders do not have a right to automatic enrolment but can opt-in to a pension scheme. They are workers who:

- are aged between 16 and 21 or between state pension age and 74;
- are working or usually work in the UK;
- have earnings paid by the employer below the earnings trigger for automatic enrolment.

Entitled workers have the right to join a pension scheme and they are workers who:

- are aged between 16 and 74;
- are working or usually work in the UK;
- do not have earnings paid by the employer.

Eligible jobholders must be automatically enrolled into a pension scheme. Non-eligible jobholders do not have to be automatically enrolled but have the right to opt-in to automatic enrolment. Entitled workers do not have the right to be automatically enrolled but they do have the right to join a pension scheme, which may not be the same scheme used for automatic enrolment. A key difference between entitled workers and both eligible and non-eligible jobholders is that the employer does not have to contribute to the pension scheme for entitled workers, unless required to do so by the scheme rules.

Eligible workers have the right to opt-out of a pension scheme and arrangements must be introduced to facilitate this.

Staging dates

The scheme is being phased in from October 2012 to April 2017, starting with the largest employers. The staging dates for companies with fewer than 30 staff will be from 1 June 2015 to 1 April 2017 depending on the company's PAYE reference number. See **www.autoenrolment.info/auto-enrolment-staging-dates**.

Contributions

The rates of employer and employee pension contribution are as set out in the table below:

Pension auto-enrolment Contribution Phasing Summary

	Employee Pays **	Employer Pays
From staging date to 1 October 2017	1%	1%
From 1 October 2017	3%	2%
From 1 October 2018	5%	3%

** less tax relief

Actions required by the employer

If you employ at least one person you will need to;

1 Check your staging date.
2 Assess your workforce to determine which categories your workers fall into.
3 Register with the Pensions Regulator.
4 Review your pension arrangements.
5 Communicate the changes to your staff, including opt-out arrangements.
6 Automatically enrol eligible jobholders.
7 Set up an opt-out process for those who do not wish to join a scheme.
8 Arrange membership of a pension scheme for workers who choose to opt in.
9 Contribute to workers pensions.
10 Maintain records to keep track of the pension scheme and the ages and earnings of all workers.

Shares and share options

You can use employee share schemes to attract and retain staff who are considered critical to the future success of the company, and also as a useful means of linking rewards to company performance. However, they should always be viewed as part of the company's overall reward strategy.

Share schemes can be 'approved' or 'non-approved'. Approved schemes are those that are approved by HM Revenue & Customs. The main advantage of approved schemes is that employees who receive shares or share options under them are not liable to Income Tax under schedule E. The main advantage of non-approved schemes is that they are not subject to the same restrictions as approved schemes, such as the value of shares that may be issued and the terms on which they are offered.

Cars

Cars are usually allocated to employees either because they are needed for the effective performance of the job, or because the status of the job in the company is such that a car is an expected part of the package. It is now common for a car allowance to be paid instead of a car being provided. If a car is provided, probably the most straightforward option is to use a contract hire company.

Whether or not the car fleet is owned by the company, you still have to decide about:

- the choice of makes and models;
- any restrictions on these;
- the replacement policy, ie whether the vehicle will be replaced after a stated number of years or a specific mileage, or whichever of the two is reached first;
- the extent to which you will allow those entitled to a company car to trade up or down (within the approved list) and the related salary adjustment;
- offering a cash alternative to all drivers.

Where an employee is entitled to a company car, you should state in the employment contract:

- the make and model of vehicle the employee is entitled to;
- whether it is available for private use and whether there are restrictions on its use;
- who is allowed to drive the car;
- when it will be replaced;
- who is responsible for the cost of fuel, maintenance, tax, insurance and repairs;
- whether the car user is required to make a contribution in return for private use of the car;
- whether there are circumstances (such as extended leave or during a driving ban) when the vehicle may be withdrawn;
- health and safety rules to be followed;
- the car user's responsibilities in respect of the vehicle.

Information about the taxation of company cars is available from **www.hmrc.gov.uk**.

Flexible benefits

Flexible benefits schemes, also described as 'cafeteria benefits', are formal schemes that allow employees to change their individual pay and benefits package to suit their specific requirements. These can involve a choice within benefits, eg a choice of car models with employees being given the option of upgrading by paying an additional cash contribution, or downgrading with a cash refund, or a choice between benefits. Generally, references to flexible benefits schemes relate to those that provide a menu of benefits options.

Schemes generally allow employees either to retain their existing salary and choose from a range of benefits or to have a salary reduction in exchange for certain benefits.

The CIPD identifies advantages and disadvantages of flexible benefits schemes, which are listed below.

Advantages

Employees choose benefits to meet their needs and value these benefits more highly.

- Employers and employees share the responsibility for providing benefits.
- During periods of change, flexible benefits help to harmonize rewards.
- Employers provide benefits at a known cost that is fixed regardless of the choices that employees make, so allowing them to cap future benefit costs.
- Employees have a true idea of the full worth of the benefits package they receive and employers do not provide benefits that are not valued.
- Employees are given a sense of control and involvement by having a choice.
- Dual career couples avoid having benefits duplicated by their respective employers.
- Employers are seen to be more responsive to the needs of an increasingly diverse, demanding and ageing workforce.
- A competitive benefits package is valuable in attracting and retaining key personnel.
- The awarding of benefits such as a company car becomes less divisive.
- Employers' demands for flexible working practices are more justifiable if employees enjoy flexible benefits.
- They may help to align the total reward strategy to the HR and business strategies.

Disadvantages

- Employers find them complex and expensive to set up and maintain (although new technology is reducing both the cost and administrative burden).
- The choices made may cause problems both to employers and employees.
- The design of any scheme will vary between organizations but most schemes will typically include certain core benefits such as:
  - holidays;
  - life assurance;

- private medical insurance;
- critical illness insurance;
- personal accident insurance.

If you are considering a flexible benefits scheme it is best to get professional advice before doing so because of the complexities involved.

Taxation of benefits

Most benefits are subject to tax, but the following are generally tax-free (though NICs may be payable in some cases):

- contributions paid into an approved occupational or personal pension scheme for the employee;
- cheap or free canteen meals, if these are provided for all employees, even if separate facilities are provided for different groups of employees;
- in-house sporting or recreational facilities;
- redundancy and outplacement counselling;
- a workplace nursery financed and managed by the employer;
- childcare vouchers;
- living accommodation related to the job;
- Christmas party or other annual social event up to £150 per person per annum;
- works buses, or subsidies to public bus services, to get employees to and from work;
- bicycles and cycling safety equipment provided for employees to get to and from work and workplace parking for bicycles and motorcycles;
- removal and relocation expenses up to £8,000;
- genuine personal gifts given for reasons unconnected with the job, for example, retirement gifts other than cash, or wedding gifts;
- long service awards for those with over 20 years' service provided the award does not exceed £50 per year of service;
- awards given under company suggestion schemes;
- provision of a parking space at or near the place of work;
- mobile phones where the contract is between the employer and the supplier;
- equipment and facilities provided for the disabled to carry out their jobs;
- low interest or interest-free loans below £10,000.

Further information

www.adviceguide.org.uk
www.autoenrolment.info/auto-enrolment-staging-dates.html
www.cipd.co.uk
www.hmrc.gov.uk
www.peoplemanagement.co.uk
www.pensionsadvisoryservice.org.uk
www.restpensions.org.uk
www.thepensionsregulator.gov.uk

Performance Management

05

The importance of managing performance

It is vital to the long-term success of your business that your employees carry out their jobs well. This is particularly important if you are in a competitive field where the only differentiator may be the respective performances of individuals and teams within the competing companies.

The effective management of your employees' performance should:

- contribute to business success by ensuring that individual efforts are linked to business objectives;
- improve the motivation and performance of staff by giving them positive feedback and by providing them with opportunities for training and development;
- provide a basis for linking rewards to performance;
- give the company more information about individuals and their needs.

The performance management process

The main steps in the performance management process are:

- setting objectives;
- managing performance;
- appraising (or reviewing) performance;
- rewarding performance.

The omission of any of these stages will result in a process that is incomplete and ineffective. Figure 5.1 shows how performance management fits into the company as a whole.

FIGURE 5.1   The performance management process

How to set objectives

The starting point for objective setting should be your mission and goals. This might sound over-elaborate or too much like management jargon, but it is important for a company of any size to have some view about its reason for existence, as this will help to focus on business priorities. It is also very helpful to your customers for them to know your business philosophy, which in turn will assist you in your marketing. For example, do you 'pile 'em high and sell 'em cheap' or do you provide quality at a price?

Your mission and goals will help you define your corporate or strategic objectives. Once you have established these you should incorporate them into a business plan and cascade them down the company so that there are objectives for each function and then for individual jobs. Overall objectives may then be broken down into more detailed targets.

There can sometimes be confusion over the differences between goals, objectives and targets. Generally goals tend to be broader in scope than objectives, which in turn are broader than targets. However, the particular terminology used is not important as long as everyone is clear about what is meant within the company.

When setting objectives for a particular job you should first consider the main purpose of that job, which should ideally be set out in the job description. From this, and the job's main accountabilities, you should be able to identify the outputs required, or key result areas (KRAs).

From these KRAs you should then be able to identify a number of objectives to be achieved for each KRA. These should be as specific as possible and linked to direct quantifiable outputs. Many objectives will be difficult to quantify, for example improving staff motivation, or giving high-quality advice, and in these cases a competency approach may be required (see below).

As far as possible the objectives you set should conform to what are generally described as SMART criteria (although there are different views about what the acronym actually stands for). This means they should be:

specific;

measurable;

action-based (and achievable);

realistic (relevant and results-oriented);

time-related.

An objective 'to improve sales performance' would not satisfy these criteria, but an objective 'to increase sales of widgets by 20 per cent by the end of the next financial year' would, provided the target was a realistic one.

As an example, suppose you want to increase your sales by 50 per cent during the coming year. Your KRA would be 'sales' and your objective would be 'to increase sales by 50 per cent by the end of the year'. You would then have to consider how you would achieve this, which could involve recruiting additional sales staff, training existing staff or a combination of the two. To ensure that you achieve your aims, you would need to set specific targets and dates for reaching them. An example of a performance plan using this approach is set out in Table 5.1.

You should also make objectives stretching but achievable. If they are unrealistic they are more likely to discourage than motivate the employee. It is also important that they are objectives that the employee can influence by her actions and behaviour.

TABLE 5.1 Performance plan

Key result area	Objectives	The means	Targets
Sales	Increase by 50% in the next financial year.	1 Recruit additional sales staff. 2 Train existing staff in sales techniques. 3 Review sales incentives.	1 Recruit one additional salesperson by end of March. 2 Send three existing sales staff on training courses by the end of the financial year. 3 Develop new bonus scheme for sales staff by the end of the financial year.

The balanced scorecard

One of the complexities of setting objectives is deciding their number and scope. The balanced scorecard, designed by Kaplan and Norton, helps to overcome this problem by identifying four major areas in which objectives should be set. These can be applied, suitably modified, to virtually any type of organization. These areas and the type of questions they address are set out below.

1. Financial

How are we managing the budget?

What financial management processes need to be reviewed?

How is our future income to be generated?

2. Customers

How do our customers see us?

Are we providing the services they require?

Are we providing the best value?

3. Internal processes

What improvements do we need to make to internal processes?

What staff training and development is required?

Do we have the right resources to provide the services required?

4. Innovation

What future research is required?

What services should we develop in the future?

How do we continue to improve?

Analysing competencies

Particular problems arise when you try to set objectives and targets for jobs that do not have clearly identifiable outputs – a secretary, a researcher, jobs providing counselling and advice, and so forth. For such jobs the best approach may be to try to identify those behaviours and skills that have been found to be the key to effective job performance in the past. These are generally described as 'competencies' or 'competences'. Once these have been defined, they can be used as a framework for setting targets and measuring performance.

Some of the more common competencies that have been identified by various organizations are:

- communication skills;
- commercial or business awareness;
- leadership;
- problem solving;
- people management;
- planning and organization;
- initiative;
- self-confidence;
- flexibility and adaptability;
- teamworking.

Each competency has to be precisely defined and then different levels identified, as in the example below.

Example of teamworking as a competency

Teamworking – building and maintaining positive and open working relationships, cooperating and liaising with others to achieve goals. Understanding how teams work best and evaluating the motivation and needs of others.

1	2	3	4	5
Displays little ability in teamworking. Tends to work in isolation and/or does not understand impact of own actions/role on others.	At times displays an awareness of the needs of others. Tends to be overly task-oriented at the expense of achieving team goals or targets.	Shows an ability to take account of the needs of others. Keeps colleagues up to date with relevant information.	Demonstrates a very good insight into the motivation of others. Works positively with others to complete tasks, encouraging participation and adapting own style to suit different situations.	Displays an outstanding ability in all areas of teamworking. Promotes an environment of cooperation and trust within and between teams, effectively overcoming resistance.

This approach is very useful both for managing performance and for recruitment because it provides a framework for deciding the core competencies required for a particular job – the minimum acceptable level for effective job performance, and the differentiating competencies (those that distinguish the superior performers from the acceptable ones).

There is a range of techniques for identifying competencies, the most common of which are:

- expert panels or focus groups that describe the competencies they think are required for average and for superior performance;
- surveys and 360-degree ratings (involving jobholders, superiors, peers, clients) in which observers who know the job are asked to identify the specific behaviours defining competencies;
- an expert system database containing data from numerous competency models, which provides computer-generated competency definitions;
- behavioural event interviews (BEIs), which give detailed narrative accounts of how both superior and average performers thought and acted during critical incidents in their jobs, including successes and failures;
- observation, in which both superior and average performers are studied in actual or simulated work situations.

To try to determine the competencies required for a particular job you need to ask yourself the kind of questions about the job that are set out in the checklist below.

Competency analysis – interview checklist

What is the main purpose of the job?

What are the specific objectives the jobholder has to achieve?

What are the positive aspects of behaviour that support the attainment of these objectives and what are the negative aspects of behaviour that hinder their attainment, considered under the following headings:

- personal drive;
- impact;
- ability to communicate;
- team management;
- interpersonal skills;
- analytical power;
- ability to innovate (creative thinking);
- strategic thinking;
- commercial judgement;
- ability to adapt and cope with change and pressure.

What are the examples of effective and less effective behaviour?

What type of experience and how much of it is required to achieve a reasonable level of competence?

What type of education and training and level of qualifications are required to meet job objectives?

(Adapted from Armstrong, M, 1993, *A Handbook of Personnel Management Practice*, Kogan Page, London)

An example of an objective-setting and staff development guide is set out at the end of this chapter and is reproduced with the kind permission of the Chartered Institute of Public Finance and Accountancy (CIPFA); further examples of competencies are also set at the end of this chapter.

How to manage performance

Managing performance means giving employees effective day-to-day support to enable them to carry out their roles effectively. You should:

- ensure that all necessary equipment and resources are provided;
- ensure that everyone is clear about the results required;
- provide any advice and guidance that may be required;
- give staff the training and development necessary for them to be able to do their jobs effectively and to equip them for larger roles;
- adjust targets, priorities and performance targets according to changes in markets, business aims, economic developments and so forth;
- provide regular and positive feedback on performance.

As an overall aim you should encourage staff to take responsibility for their own performance.

How to appraise performance

Performance appraisal is something that happens throughout the year. Inevitably you will make judgements about how your staff are performing even if this process is not formalized. However, whatever process is used there will be a point or points in the year when you should sit down with each employee concerned and discuss that person's performance. Although there is no hard-and-fast rule, it probably makes sense to do this twice a year. To do it more often is likely to be too administratively time-consuming, and less often may result in issues not being addressed quickly enough.

If you conduct an interim or progress review during the year there is probably no need to complete an appraisal form, although if the employee concerned is failing to achieve her objectives there may be a need to agree an improvement plan. You should keep a file note of any such agreement.

You should remember that the appraisal meeting is really only formalizing what should have been happening anyway, so there should be no real surprises, either for you or the employee. Remember also that the meeting is a two-way discussion.

Main objectives of performance appraisal

The main objectives of any performance review or appraisal process are to:

- review past performance;
- help improve current and future performance;
- identify training and development needs;
- assess potential and produce development plans;
- improve communication;
- improve motivation;
- give the employee the opportunity to raise issues or concerns.

Carrying out an appraisal discussion

Preparation

For appraisal to work effectively you have to prepare thoroughly. This means that you should:

- ask the employee to prepare for the discussion well before the meeting date, ideally using a form such as that set out below;
- ensure that enough time is set aside for the meeting and that it is held somewhere private and where you will not be interrupted;
- confirm the date, time and venue of the meeting;
- consult other managers who may have worked with the employee during the period under review;
- ensure that you have all the information you require readily available;
- consider whether there are external factors that might have influenced the employee's performance;
- plan the discussion.

Performance review scheme – employee preparation form

The purpose of the company's performance review scheme is to ensure that you are able to carry out your job as effectively as possible and to identify your training and development needs. Completion of this form before the appraisal discussion with your line manager will assist in this.

Name:

Review period:

1   Refer to your objectives for this period. How well do you think you have performed against these objectives?

2   What problems have you encountered in achieving these objectives? Are there any actions the company should take to minimize these problems in the future?

3   What do you consider to be your main strengths and weaknesses?

4   What training and/or development do you feel you need?

5   What overall performance rating best describes your performance over the period under review?

A	Exceptional	☐
B	Excellent	☐
C	Good	☐
D	Satisfactory	☐
E	Below standard	☐

6   Please insert any other comments below.

Conducting the discussion

There are rules and behaviours that will help to increase the chances of having a successful appraisal discussion. During the meeting you should:

- put the jobholder at ease with a few informal, friendly comments;
- state the purpose of the meeting;
- generally adopt a positive tone and encourage a supportive atmosphere;
- give praise where it is due;
- focus on facts and results, supported by examples where appropriate;
- encourage the employee to express her views, particularly about her performance;
- listen carefully, summarizing at frequent intervals;
- avoid surprises;
- in discussing less effective areas of performance stress the opportunities for improvement;

- obtain agreement over targets and try to ensure that these are as quantifiable as possible to reduce ambiguity about whether they have been achieved;
- consider and discuss development opportunities.

After the discussion

Following the appraisal discussion you should:

- note the points raised at the meeting;
- complete an appraisal form (see below);
- keep track of performance and ensure that agreed actions are taken.

Performance review form

Name:
Job title:
Period covered by this review:
Name of manager:
Agreed objectives:

Results:
Rating:
(Comment on results achieved, taking into account business conditions, changes to objectives and any other relevant circumstances.)

To be completed by the line manager
For the review period:
    What were the employee's main achievements or strengths?
    What areas of performance need improvement or development?
    What training and development does the employee need?
    What is the overall performance rating?
     A = performance that is exceptional and rarely attained
     B = performance that is well above target in nearly all respects
     C = performance that achieved all major objectives to the standard required
     D = performance that fell just short of requirements in some key areas
     E = performance that was not up to the standard required in most respects

Appraisee's comments:

Appraiser's comments:

Signature of appraisee:
Signature of appraiser:
Date:

To be completed by the reviewing manager

Comments on above review

I confirm the performance rating above/I consider that, following discussion with the line manager, the performance rating should be changed to (delete as appropriate):

Signed:

Name:

Date:

Rating performance

A critical part of reviewing performance is rating the performance of the employee against identified objectives and targets. This rating will normally form the basis for decisions about promotion and bonuses. When rating performance you should:

- take into account overall objectives and individual targets;
- take account of both hard quantifiable measures such as sales targets, and softer, more nebulous measures such as customer relations;
- take into account factors that might have affected performance during the year;
- try to be objective and focus on outputs, setting aside personal feelings about the jobholder;
- weight objectives in favour of those that are more critical to the success of the business;
- use a rating scale as a basis for comparison, and possibly for deciding bonus levels and suitability for promotion (see below);
- consider using a forced distribution in which the percentage of staff receiving particular ratings is restricted (see Figure 5.2).

As part of the performance rating process you will need to develop some kind of measurement scale. It is difficult to be prescriptive about the form this should take, but generally you should avoid negative descriptions such as 'weak' as these could reinforce negative performance and attitudes. You should also be aware that with a five-point scale there is a tendency for most people to tick the middle box, and that with a four-point scale the tendency is to place most people in the upper two boxes. An example of a five-point scale is set out below.

Example performance ratings

Exceptional – superior all-round performance achieving significant objectives that are critical to the success of the business.

Excellent – performance which generally exceeds job requirements with some notable achievements.

Good – performance that generally satisfies all job requirements.

Satisfactory – performance that is to the standard required in most aspects of the job but that requires improvement in some.

Below standard – performance where a significant improvement is required to satisfy job requirements.

Perhaps one of the more effective types of scale is one that describes performance as:

above target;

on target;

below target.

FIGURE 5.2 Typical performance distribution

Showing approximate percentages of staff receiving a particular performance rating in a typical company

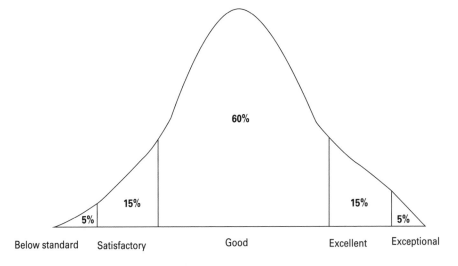

This type of description is more factual and does not imply that someone is a weak performer just by being below target for the period under review. There may have been good business reasons for this.

Finally, where possible, it is advisable to have a two-tier approach in which someone more senior in the company reviews performance ratings by the employee's line manager, generally the manager's immediate manager. This helps to minimize the problems of personal attitudes affecting judgements and is essential in larger companies to ensure consistency between different functions.

Rewarding performance

The fact that you are bothering to assess performance implies that there will be some kind of a reward for good performance. Such rewards typically take the form of pay and/or promotion. As employees will see these rewards as a measure of their worth to the company it is important to ensure that they are allocated fairly, objectively and in direct relation to the contribution made.

There is no one universal formula that can be applied to all organizations. When devising a scheme for paying for performance or contribution it is probably best to get external professional advice. The issues that need to be taken into account in such a scheme include:

- types of jobs involved – some jobs, such as those in sales, have outputs that are easier to measure and that are more directly related to performance than others;
- market practice – taking into account what your competitors are doing for similar jobs;
- the relative importance of different targets;
- the proportion of pay that is to be variable or 'at risk';
- the complexities of measuring performance;
- the extent to which performance should be recognized by permanent increases in pay or by one-off bonuses;
- the frequency of any bonus payments;
- the extent to which rewards are based on long-term or short-term objectives;
- the appropriateness of non-financial incentives;
- the extent to which rewards should be individual- or team-based;
- what the company can afford.

Training and development

A central reason for reviewing performance is to identify staff training and development needs. Specifically you will want to:

- help individuals develop their skills and abilities to improve job performance;
- help familiarize employees with any new systems, procedures and working methods;
- help employees and new starters become familiar with the requirements of a particular job and with the company (induction);
- build up a pool of expertise and skills in the company so that you will not be too adversely affected if you lose staff or if you need workers to cover for absent colleagues.

Effective training will help the company to be successful and avoid problems (such as health and safety problems) and it is therefore important that you develop a training policy. Any training policy will need to include the following stages:

1 analysis of training needs;

2 planned programme of training to meet those needs;

3 implementation of the training programme;

4 evaluation of the effectiveness of training provided.

Right to request time off for training

Under the Apprentices, Skills, Children and Learning Act 2009, with effect from 6 April 2010 employees with a minimum of six months' service in an organization with 250 or more staff have the right to request time off for training if they believe this may make them more productive and effective at work. This operates in the same way as existing arrangements covering flexible working, so you have a duty to consider seriously any such request.

Analysing training needs

When you are trying to assess the training required in the company you should do this for:

the company as a whole;

groups of staff or types of job within the company; and

individual employees.

The need for training will arise when:

● you appoint new staff who will require induction training and training in job skills;

● you introduce new systems and processes;

● you reorganize or redesign jobs;

● there are changes in legislation;

● you require productivity improvements;

● you introduce flexible working arrangements;

● there are significant differences in productivity and performance between individuals and/or groups within the company;

● there are changes in your market;

● you need to ensure equality of opportunity.

Any organizational change will give rise to a training need. To identify other needs, such as those arising from productivity differences between different functions, you will need to maintain and review performance indicators such as sales levels, administration costs and lost productivity. The training needs of individuals should be identifiable through the performance management process.

Planning training programmes

When you are considering what training to provide you need to take into account:

- why you are carrying out the training;
- who is to receive it;
- what should be included in the content;
- the likely costs;
- the likely benefits;
- how the success of the training can be evaluated;
- the most appropriate training method;
- who will provide the training;
- whether it will be carried out in the company or at an external location.

When you are considering the costs of training, you should also consider the costs of not training. Failing to provide training when it is required is a false economy and could result in lowered productivity, more accidents and downtime, an inability to react to changing circumstances, infringement of legal requirements and lowered morale.

Implementing a training programme

When you draw up a training programme you should consider whether the training required is better provided internally through your own resources, or by an external provider. Generally, the training is better provided internally where:

- you are seeking to improve performance in some detailed aspects of an individual's job; and
- you have internal staff who can provide the required expertise and time; or
- the trainee requires practical hands-on experience; or
- you need to train staff in a new internal process or system.

External training may be more appropriate where:

- staff are required to learn about new ideas and approaches;
- you do not have sufficient internal resources and expertise to provide the training yourself;
- the training is of a highly specialized or complex nature that can only be provided by external experts;
- it is for staff development or the acquisition of a broad range of skills.

Training methods

Some of the more common methods of training are:

- On-the-job training – Training provided within the workplace. It is important to ensure that those providing the training are competent, otherwise the trainee may learn bad habits.

- Coaching – Guidance provided by the line manager, supported by the performance appraisal process.

- Self-development – Using appropriate training resources such as CD-ROMs, DVDs, workbooks, etc, to acquire knowledge and skills.

- Project work – Assigning the trainee to a practical problem or task designed to help the company.

- Job rotation – Moving staff into different roles to enable them to acquire a wide range of experience within the company.

- Secondment – Placing a jobholder in another function or department to enable that person to gain insight into its operations.

- Shadowing – Placing a jobholder alongside someone doing a different job so that she is able to learn from that person.

- Mentoring – Providing the employee with a mentor to provide advice on work issues.

- Training courses – Training courses can be internal or external and will typically be provided by specialist external trainers using a range of different training techniques.

Induction training

Every company should carry out some form of induction for new employees. The purpose of this is to:

- Provide a smooth entry into the company and to promote a positive attitude about it.

- Check that there are no matters outstanding following the recruitment process.

- Confirm that the employee has all relevant information, including a statement of employment particulars.

- Collect any information still required, such as the P45 or bank details.

- Draw the employee's attention to the performance standards required and any other important points about working for the company, including health and safety and disciplinary rules.

- Ensure that the employee knows how to operate any essential company procedures and equipment.

- Ensure that the employee knows where all the basic amenities are located.

- Identify any individual training and development needs.

- Agree any more detailed induction, including meetings covering the company's various activities.

An example of an induction training programme is set out below.

Induction programme

Day one

1 Introduction to immediate supervisor and colleagues.

2 Administration – completion of outstanding employment details.

3 Company information.

4 Tour of office.

5 Introduction to facilities (WC, coffee machine and so forth).

6 Products and services.

7 Employment terms – arrangements for payment of salary, pension and so forth, office hours, health and safety rules, first-aid arrangements, fire procedure, security arrangements, car parking, smoking policy, identity cards, disciplinary rules, sports and social activities.

8 Job duties – discuss main tasks and responsibilities.

During first week

1 Introduction to other internal contacts and main external contacts.

2 Company information – more detailed product and service information, business plan and strategy, organization structure, information about regular meetings, competitor information.

3 Employment terms – sickness absence reporting, time off arrangements, annual holiday arrangements, payment of expenses, confidentiality, use of telephone and e-mail, performance appraisal arrangements, explanation of other employment terms.

Evaluating training

Although it can sometimes be difficult to do, you should try to evaluate the results of any training provided. Ways of doing this include:

- using questionnaires before and after the training, to test improvements in skills and knowledge;

- observing trainees while on the training programme and after their return from it;
- using tests of various kinds;
- interviewing trainees to assess what they have learnt from the training;
- measuring changes in a range of performance indicators such as productivity, quality of delivery and achievement of targets.

For certain types of training, such as management development, it may be particularly difficult to measure effectiveness directly. However, if the training has been successful you should notice longer-term improvements across a range of indicators such as lower absenteeism, fewer grievances, lowered staff turnover, improved motivation and higher productivity.

Further information

Apprentices, Skills, Children and Learning Act 2009

Cushway, B (reprinted 1999) *Human Resource Management*, Kogan Page, London

Kaplan, R S and Norton, D P (1992) The balanced scorecard – measures that drive performance, *Harvard Business Review*, January–February, pp 71–9

Megginson, D, Joy-Matthews, J and Banfield, P (2004) *Human Resource Development*, 3rd edn, Kogan Page, London

Spencer, L M, McClelland, D C and Spencer, S M (1992) *Competency Assessment Methods – History and State of the Art*, Hay/McBer, Boston, MA

Appendix 1: CIPFA – Objective Setting and Development Scheme. A guide for staff

Guidance notes

The Objective Setting and Development Scheme aims to encourage communication and generate open discussion between you, your manager (or reviewer) and your team. In addition to clarifying areas of responsibility, a key aim of the Scheme is to provide a systematic way of identifying training and development needs for all staff.
The Scheme will help you to:

Become clear about your individual contribution to the products and services CIPFA offers and to the meeting of your department's business plan and objectives.

Carry out your role competently and confidently.

Understand what you are expected to achieve.

Have your contribution recognized and valued.

Review your work and plan ahead.

Discuss workload, timescales and approach to work with your manager.

Prioritize work and set targets.

Receive accurate and effective feedback on your performance at work.

Think about how you like to learn and what resources are available to you to enable you to learn and develop.

Identify training and development activities you need to become involved in to meet your objectives, improve the way you do things, expand your skills and knowledge or equip you to meet future requirements.

The Scheme will help CIPFA develop a staff able and willing to respond to change, and capable of adapting and learning, rather than being limited by the boundaries of existing skills.

Development is a two-way contract, based on business needs and individual motivation, ie a shared responsibility. It is not ideal for you to think that your development is the responsibility of CIPFA. Likewise, it is not ideal for CIPFA to believe development is entirely the responsibility of each individual.

Your *Mid Year Objectives and Development Review* should normally be six months from the date on which the objectives were initially agreed. Your *Full Year Objectives and Development Review* should normally be one year from the date on which the objectives were initially agreed. If you wish to have a review in a shorter time span, this should take place. Ask your manager for more frequent reviews.

New members of staff should agree their objectives with their manager within three months of joining CIPFA. For the interim period until these are set, appropriate work objectives for the former postholder will apply.

New members of staff can enter the Scheme at the most suitable time during the year. There is no need to wait until November/December to complete Part 1. Let's say you are a new member of staff and you join CIPFA in March. You would probably complete your Objective Setting and Development Plan (Part 1) in June, and have an Objectives and Development Review (Part 2) in December. This would enable you to fit into the Scheme with the rest of your colleagues at the end of the year.

There are three important stages/parts to the Objective Setting and Development Scheme.

Part 1, 2 and 3 – Before the Meeting

Part 1, 2 and 3 are discussions/meetings between you and your manager, not interviews. It is not something that happens to you; it is a process you need to participate fully in.

So how can you prepare?

Use the Scheme's Preparation Checklist

The Preparation Checklist has been developed to help you clarify your thoughts before each stage of the Scheme. You should receive a copy of this at least one month before the meeting.

Be as honest as possible when filling in the Preparation Checklist. One of the main aims of the Scheme is to help you to develop so the more fully you and your manager prepare for the meeting the more successful it will be.

Make sure you have read and understood your department's business plan.

Once it has been finalized, your manager will distribute a copy of your department's business plan to all staff in the department. If this does not happen, please ask your manager for a copy. If you are unclear what any of it means or how it might relate to your work, then ask your colleagues or manager.

Attend the 'Preparing for Your Objectives and Development Review' course

This is a three-hour event to help you get to grips with participating in Objectives and Development Reviews. The course will enable you to identify the skills of a good reviewee and you will get a chance to discuss what is expected of you before, during and after the review. There are a few courses throughout the year. After a year or so, it may be a good idea to attend again as a 'refresher'. Please contact Human Resources (HR) if you are interested in attending.

Part 1, 2 and 3 – At the Meeting

Practical arrangements

It is your manager's responsibility to ensure your Objective Setting and Development Plan meeting and your Objectives and Development Reviews take place where you can feel as relaxed as possible and where you will not be interrupted. It is important that you arrive on time and keep to the time you have set for the meeting. Two hours should normally be enough time.

Remember to take your Preparation Checklist, forms from your previous review(s), and a pen and paper in case you need to make notes during the meeting.

Who does what?

It is important to check and agree with your manager who will complete the appropriate form at the beginning of the meeting. You will also need to agree when it will be written up by, and when you will both be able to check and sign it. Make sure it is an accurate record of your meeting before signing it. If you disagree about any points it is important to try to sort things out at this stage. In the unlikely event that you or your manager just cannot agree or one of you feels unable to sign the form, then your manager's manager or, if necessary, HR will become involved.

Both you and your manager will be contributing to the meeting but it is important that you are prepared to do most of the talking. It is your manager's job to make sure that all the areas are covered and that you are as involved as possible in the setting of work objectives and personal development objectives, and the identification of your own development needs. It is important that you 'own' the agreed objectives, and should be willing to talk to your manager if you think certain objectives are unrealistic.

Once initially completed (and after each review) your manager will copy the Objective Setting and Development Scheme forms (Part 1, 2 and 3) to the appropriate director and also send to HR. HR will feed specific training needs into the training plan for the year. Your forms will be held confidentially in HR. You and/or your manager should also keep a copy of each form for reference.

Setting objectives

It is important to note that setting objectives is not the same as writing a job description. Your job description is a list of your tasks and responsibilities. In objective setting, your work objectives will encompass parts of your job description but will be measurable in some way and time bound.

The key point when setting work objectives is to identify areas of your work where achievement, improvement or performance will have the most impact. It is the main tasks or key result areas you should be concentrating on. We all carry out many tasks and have various responsibilities at work, but you don't need to translate everything you do into an objective.

Don't set too many or too few objectives. Aim for somewhere between 5 and 10, with a mix of work objectives and personal development objectives.

When you set objectives for the coming year, make sure they are SMART: Specific, Measurable, Achievable, Relevant, Time Bound (see Appendix A, below, for examples).

Don't agree to vague or 'woolly' objectives. 'Improve team meetings' is unhelpful. How could you possibly know if you have achieved this or not? A much better objective would be 'ensure all team members have an agenda of the team meeting one week before the meeting and minutes are circulated a maximum of one week after the meeting'. This way you would know exactly what is expected and whether you have achieved the objective or not.

Objectives need to be challenging to enable you to get some satisfaction from achieving them. Don't set objectives that are too easy to achieve, that involve no effort or creativity on your part. If they are too easy then you will have no sense of achievement when you have succeeded.

Be realistic about the time your objectives will take to complete. Are you being realistic if all your objectives are set for the same month?

It may be that you take on extra or different responsibilities in your job and as a result you may need to update your objectives. You and your manager should complete a fresh Objective Setting and Development Plan (Part 1), describing only the updated or new objectives and any development needs, and send to HR. There is no need to duplicate all the information from your original Objective Setting and Development Plan as we will already have this on file.

Try to revisit your job description before each of your Objectives and Development Reviews. It is important your job description is updated, if necessary, to reflect your current responsibilities.

Identifying your development needs

This is not just about courses or workshops you need to attend, but activities or experiences you need in order to meet your objectives, to improve the way you do things, and to expand your skills and knowledge.

Some development activities include projects, observation, discussion with your manager or colleagues, visits to other parts of CIPFA, asking questions, coaching and being coached, attending training courses, seminars, conferences, vocational qualifications, shadowing a colleague, books, journals, newspapers, DVDs, activities outside work.

Make sure your development needs are as specific as possible. If a training course is the most appropriate development activity, then we need to be sure that we are designing and organizing training that actually meets those needs.

For example, 'communication' can mean different things to different people, so if this is an area you need to develop further, you will need to specify what aspect of communication you are meaning. Likewise, 'Microsoft Excel' doesn't give enough information. You may need to learn about absolute references, pie charts and macros. Please refer to the 'example' forms for more information.

Once the appropriate form has been completed, you and your manager will be able to start working on those development needs that require an activity/response other than training courses. Information about any training courses planned in response to your needs will be made available as soon as possible to enable you and your manager to plan your workload, arrange cover, etc. You should plan training courses into your diary like any other project, task or meeting.

Continuing Professional Development (CPD)

You may be a member of a professional body, society or institute (eg CIPFA, Institute of Personnel and Development, Chartered Institute of Marketing, Law Society) and are involved in their CPD scheme. To reduce duplication and save you time we may be able to accept their CPD scheme's documentation. However, we will need to check the suitability of the scheme and supporting documentation. Please contact HR for more information.

Appendix A – SMART Objectives

S SPECIFIC

'To practise and receive monthly feedback on skills in setting work, reviewing performance and coaching.' Not 'improve management skills'.

M MEASURABLE

'Learn how to politely interrupt speakers when I am chairing a meeting with the intention of reducing meeting times by 15 minutes.' Not 'to be more effective in meetings'.

A ACHIEVABLE

'Increase membership of the Institute by 1% over x months.' Not 'increase membership of the Institute by 100% in 6 months'.

R RELEVANT

Relevant to your job, eg if you are a service purchaser: 'Reduce supplier costs by 10% per annum by negotiating discounts.' Not 'paint the outside of the building at weekends'.

T TIME BOUND

'Produce the annual report on training costs by 18 December.' Not 'produce a report on training costs soon'.

1. Communication

Being able to express themselves clearly, effectively and persuasively, verbally and in writing and to understand clearly given communications. Demonstrating an ability to tailor the communication style and content to different situations, objectives and audiences. Being able to win the commitment of others to a decision, view or course of action.

1   Does not communicate effectively with others. Is unable to establish rapport. Fails to give required information at appropriate time. Information given lacks clarity. Fails to listen attentively or understand communications received.

2   Generally communicates clearly but sometimes lacks clarity in presenting views. May sometimes not fully understand clearly given advice and/or instructions.

3   Communicates information clearly, accurately and concisely and at the right time. Information is presented in a confident and structured manner. Listens well and seeks clarification where necessary.

4   Is able to communicate complex information clearly and concisely taking into account the type of recipient and using appropriate verbal and visual aids to reinforce the message. Is aware of, and takes into account non-verbal signals. Listens attentively and is able to recognize implicit as well as explicit messages.

5   An exceptional and highly persuasive communicator. Is quickly able to draw the right conclusions from hints and non-verbal signals and adapt behaviour appropriately.

2. Analytical thinking/problem solving

Being able to resolve complex problems and devise original solutions.

1   Shows little ability to process information and to arrive at logical conclusions through analysis.

2   Is generally able to resolve routine problems and knows where to find any required information. More complex problems would be referred to others.

3   Is able to deal with problems in an organized and systematic way and can analyse both written and numerical data. Seeks advice on complex problems and applies that advice.

4   Is able to deal with complex problems in a structured and organized way and identify the key issues in most situations, using information from a variety of sources.

5   Is able to resolve highly complex problems requiring original thinking, research and analysis. Identifies key issues and analyses the implications of various courses of action.

3. Planning and organizing

Being able to devise and apply systems to take account of relative priorities. Planning and organizing a variety of resources to meet objectives in a changing environment.

1   No evidence of an ability to plan ahead or to understand priorities. Tends to miss deadlines. Needs to be closely managed.

2   Is generally able to plan and organize work to meet routine targets and deadlines but may need guidance in responding to changes in priorities or routine.

3   Identifies priorities and plans and organizes work to meet these. Monitors progress and takes appropriate action to achieve targets. Can be trusted to seek support when required.

4   Successfully plans and coordinates major and complex projects. Focuses attention on key objectives and makes optimal use of resources, redirecting effort as required. Consistently meets deadlines and targets.

5   Displays outstanding planning and organizing skills. Creates, monitors and reviews policies and plans to meet overall business priorities. Anticipates and plans for changes to priorities. Always meets deadlines and targets.

4. Adaptability

The ability to meet, anticipate and deal with new challenges.

1 Generally unaware of and not interested in new developments. Fears change.

2 Aware of new developments and is prepared to change working methods to accommodate these, following guidance or direction.

3 Shows an enthusiasm for new developments and takes steps to keep up to date on these. Happy to try new ideas and approaches and to adapt working arrangements as necessary.

4 Maintains a keen awareness of new developments in the sector and the company and takes all steps necessary to ensure that he or she keeps fully aware of these. Embraces change and acts as a champion for new ideas and approaches.

5 Actively seeks new challenges and opportunities, constantly striving to develop approaches that will give the company a competitive edge. Fully aware of new developments in the sector. Drives change but also takes steps to ensure that implementation is effective.

5. Teamworking and relationships

The ability to work well with others and to deal effectively with both colleagues and customers.

1 Tends to work in isolation and shows little appreciation of impact of own actions on others. Tends to be formal and cool with team members and external customers and contacts.

2 Is generally cheerful and courteous to other team members and external contacts. Tends to put individual aims above team goals. May be overly task-oriented at the expense of team motivation and morale.

3 Shows a clear appreciation of the needs and objectives of others and adapts behaviour accordingly. Enjoys working as part of a team and contributes to the attainment of common goals. Keeps colleagues informed of developments and offers assistance and guidance to others.

4 Shows good insight into the needs of others, exercising tact and diplomacy where necessary. Works positively with others to encourage the attainment of common goals, adapting own personal style to suit different situations. Viewed as a key team member.

5 Shows outstanding ability as an effective and essential team member. Promotes an environment of cooperation and trust within and between teams and team members, setting and achieving stretching goals and effectively overcoming

obstacles while maintaining motivation and morale. Actively develops team members. Able in all situations to tailor words and actions to promote a positive effect on others.

6. Commitment

The desire to achieve the best possible outcome for all parties and being prepared to take all required actions to ensure that targets are achieved on time, within budget and to a high standard.

1   Shows little commitment to the work of the company or interest in customers. Does what is required, but no more. Prefers to play safe by not taking action where this is an option.

2   Shows some interest in the work of the company and the problems of customers but prefers to refer problems to others, rather than attempt to resolve them. Generally works effectively showing concern for quality of own work.

3   Shows a keen interest in the work of the company and the problems of customers. Takes all necessary action to resolve a problem within the scope of his/her own responsibilities. Sometimes suggests improvements to systems and processes.

4   Shows enthusiasm for and a commitment to the work of the company. Takes a keen interest in problems of customers and other external contacts. Is prepared to go the extra mile in resolving problems and will commit himself/herself to resolving an issue rather than passing the problem on. Prefers to take action with all associated risks rather than do nothing. Regularly shows a concern for improving systems and processes.

5   Demonstrates a consistently positive attitude and the highest level of enthusiasm for the work of the company and colleagues. Keeps fully up to date with developments and seeks to enthuse others about these. Takes a keen interest in problems of customers and other external contacts and is prepared to suffer personal inconvenience to resolve problems. Prefers to take action with all associated risks rather than do nothing. Consistently looks for improvements to working methods, systems and processes.

7. Technical awareness

The requirement to understand and carry out tasks and responsibilities to the required standard and to keep abreast of new developments.

1   Does what is required in terms of the job, but no more, to a reasonable standard. Requires guidance on some aspects of the work. Shows no awareness of or interest in external developments.

2 Carries out job duties effectively requiring little guidance. Is aware of new products and changes to work processes.

3 A very effective performer who is technically proficient in all areas of the job. Knows about and understands the implications of technical developments affecting products and processes.

4 A highly effective performer who demonstrates considerable technical competence in all aspects of the work. Regarded as an expert in his or her field and will be consulted by others on technical issues. Understands the implications of the latest technical developments affecting products and processes and is able to advise others about these.

5 A top performer who is regarded as the top technical expert in his or her field within the company. Promotes understanding throughout the company of the latest technical developments affecting products and processes in the sector. Consulted by others requiring definitive information in the field.

8. Leadership

The ability to achieve aims and objectives through others by providing them with focus and direction and by motivating and inspiring them through the use of interpersonal skills such as persuasion, enthusiasm, diplomacy, etc. This includes individuals and teams.

1 Displays little leadership ability. Is unable to define goals effectively or to motivate others to meet them. Shows little influencing skill. May panic or fail to respond under pressure.

2 Tries to influence others but lacks the self-confidence to be fully effective or does not adapt personal style to suit the situation, such as being overly dogmatic or directive where this is not appropriate. May rely too much on authority rather than influence and fail to take account of the needs of individuals. Tends to be irritable under pressure.

3 Is able to define goals and objectives and influence others to achieve these. Takes into account the aims and aspirations of others and adapts behaviour and style accordingly. Expresses confidence in the ability of others. Remains calm under pressure.

4 Encourages ownership of team goals and consistently achieves results through others. Adapts style and behaviour to meet the aims and aspirations of others. Encourages the development of individual and team potential through effective coaching and makes the best use of individual skills and abilities. Deals calmly with conflicting priorities under pressure.

5   Demonstrates an outstanding level of leadership. Formulates goals into an understandable set of plans and objectives and obtains complete commitment to these. Builds multi-skilled teams to meet business needs, modifying roles and responsibilities as necessary. Adapts style and behaviour to meet the aims and aspirations of others and encourages the development of individual and team potential through effective coaching. Recognized as someone who brings out the best in people and commands total loyalty. Adept at dealing with complex high-pressure situations, giving an air of calm assurance and conveying that to others.

9. Commercial awareness

Being aware of ABC's products and services, taking an interest in commercial developments in the sector, the position of ABC within it and of the financial and profit implications of actions taken.

1   Displays little awareness of or interest in ABC products and services or in the market generally. Does not understand impact of own actions on finances.

2   Aware of ABC products and services but has limited interest in market developments. Only vaguely aware of financial implications of own actions.

3   Fully aware of and shows an interest in ABC products and services. Also aware of developments in the wider market and among competitors. Understands financial implications of own actions.

4   Very interested in, and fully up to date on, all ABC products and services, both existing and planned (as far as such information is available). Shows a keen interest in the external market and is fully aware of developments in it and their potential impact on ABC. Fully aware of the financial implications of own actions and takes into account the impact of these on others and the business.

5   Shows extensive awareness of ABC products and services (existing and planned) and of their impact on finances. Researches the external market to maintain a full awareness of the actions of competitors and their implications for the commercial success of ABC. Possesses considerable commercial insight and applies this for the benefit of the company to exploit business opportunities and reduce internal costs.

10. Customer service

Providing a high level of service to customers to ensure that their experience is a positive one and to encourage them to develop a long-term relationship with the company.

1   Displays little understanding of customer needs. Has difficulty in establishing rapport with others and lacks confidence in dealing with customers.

2 Generally shows an awareness of customer needs and some interest in addressing these. Not always able to translate those needs into solutions acceptable to the customer.

3 Displays a clear understanding of customer needs and expectations and responds effectively to these to fully meet customer expectations in terms of results and timing.

4 Displays an ability to understand and anticipate customer needs and expectations and to respond effectively to these so that these expectations are exceeded and the company's reputation enhanced. Will take action to resolve any issues even where this may go beyond job requirements.

5 Displays an exceptional ability to understand and anticipate the needs and expectations of even the most difficult customer and to respond effectively to these. Takes action to resolve any issues even where this goes beyond job requirements and may involve significant personal inconvenience. Will regularly receive customer accolades. Encourages a customer focus in others.

11. Self-motivation

Seeking to enhance own skills and job effectiveness and achieving personal satisfaction through self-development. Demonstrating a drive to achieve.

1 Does no more than is asked. Shows no interest in learning new skills or in improving existing ones. Not prepared to exercise initiative.

2 Occasionally does more than is required without being asked but generally does only what is required. Prepared to put in extra work when asked. Prepared to learn new skills or receive training if asked to do so. Occasionally exercises initiative in resolving problems.

3 Demonstrates enthusiasm for the work, anticipates what needs to be done and generally takes action without being asked. Does more than the minimum required. Seeks opportunities to learn new skills or improve existing ones.

4 A highly-motivated and enthusiastic worker who can be relied on to do all that is necessary to achieve results and who regularly exceeds basic job requirements. Actively seeks new challenges and opportunities. Enthusiastic about learning new skills and developing existing ones and proactive about putting himself/ herself forward.

5 Demonstrates the highest level of motivation and ambition. Strives for excellence in everything he/she does and is strongly focused on meeting and exceeding all targets, whilst maintaining quality. Actively seeks new challenges and opportunities. Consistently seeks opportunities to learn new skills and develop existing ones and commits time to this.

Form to use?	What happens at this stage?	When does this happen?
Part 1	Objective Setting and Development Plan • You and your manager (or reviewer) will discuss and agree your work and personal development objectives for the coming year (or suitable period). • You and your manager will also identify training and development activities you need to become involved in to meet your objectives, improve the way you do things, and to expand your skills and knowledge.	November – December
Part 2	Objectives and Development Review – Mid Year • A chance to reflect on what has gone well and, perhaps, not so well, hindrances to achieving objectives and how you have handled problems and overcome difficulties, the role of your manager and colleagues in helping you to achieve your objectives, improve performance and develop. • You will also discuss the training you have received and development activities you have participated in during the first half of the year, and how these have helped you meet your objectives and learn new skills and knowledge.	June – July
Part 3	Objectives and Development Review – Full Year • As Part 2, but for the whole year.	December – January

Dealing with Absence

06

The absence of staff from work causes obvious problems of productivity, especially when such absences are unplanned. The smaller the company, the greater the effect. Reducing unplanned absence should therefore be a priority of any company.

Planned absences

Many absences are legitimate contractual and legal entitlements. These include:

- annual holidays;
- public holidays;
- attendance on training courses;
- maternity and paternity leave;
- parental leave;
- adoption leave;
- time off to care for dependants;
- time off for jury service;
- time off for public duties;
- time off for trade union duties and activities;
- reservist training;
- attendance at health and safety committees or works councils;
- bereavement or compassionate leave;
- layoffs or short-time working;
- suspension on medical grounds.

You should have policies covering most absences and including:

- what time off is allowed;
- which absences will be paid and which unpaid;
- the procedure for agreeing time off;
- how much time off will be given for particular events;
- actions that will be taken if the facilities given are abused.

Time off for dependants

You must give any employee reasonable time off to deal with an emergency involving a dependant, such as when a dependant falls ill or has an accident. This is to enable the employee to deal with the emergency and to make longer-term arrangements, but it would also apply to attendance at a funeral and making funeral arrangements. A dependant is the partner, child or parent of the employee or someone who lives with the employee as part of the family, or someone who reasonably relies on the employee for assistance. There is no set amount of time allowed and no limit to the number of occasions this time off is given. If you have reason to believe that this right is being exercised more than is reasonable and/or it is causing problems for the company, you should warn the employee about it.

Public duties

Employees have a legal right under the Employment Rights Act 1996 to a reasonable amount of time off to carry out public duties such as being a magistrate, a local authority councillor, or a member of certain statutory and public bodies. This does not have to be paid but the main problem is deciding how much time off is reasonable.

Jury service

You have little choice but to give someone time off for jury service, unless there are convincing reasons why they may be excused, such as serious damage to the business. This time off does not have to be paid.

Trade union activities

You must allow employees who are officials of an independent trade union reasonable paid time off to carry out duties related to industrial relations in the company or to undergo training.

Since the Employment Act 2002 you must also allow time off to Union Learning Representatives (ULRs), who are union members appointed to advise members about their training and education needs.

Safety representatives

You must allow paid time off to safety representatives to allow them to carry out their functions and to undergo training.

Redundant employees

You must give reasonable paid time off to any employee made redundant, and with two years' continuous service, to allow that person to look for a new job.

Reservists

Reservists are required to undertake annual training and it is up to you to decide whether to grant unpaid leave for this purpose (reservists get allowances and pay) or to insist that it is taken as part of the annual leave entitlement. If the reservist is called out for active service you will have little option but to allow this as you will have been required to sign an agreement to this effect. You must keep the reservist's job open for him.

The Reserve Forces (Payments to Employers and Partners) Regulations 2014 enable small and medium employers to receive up to £500 per month for each full month (or pro rata) when a reservist is absent from work on reserve duty.

Bereavement or compassionate leave

Employees have a legal right to a reasonable amount of unpaid time off following the death of a dependant (see above). You can, however, also develop a policy on this, which will then become a contractual entitlement.

Other time-off rights

There are also rights to time off for maternity and paternity (see Chapter 7) and to parental leave (see Chapter 8).

Reducing unplanned absences

To manage absence effectively and to keep unplanned absences to a minimum you need:

- information about the numbers and frequencies of absences;
- procedures to ensure that all necessary processes are in place to enable you to control absences;
- policies to encourage high levels of attendance.

Information

You should keep the following information:

- number of days of absence of individuals;
- number of spells of absence;
- reasons for absences;
- whether absences are certificated or uncertificated;
- employee details.

You should note that, following the Data Protection Act 1998, you need to make employees aware that you will keep records of sickness absence and get their express permission for you to keep such records.

How to calculate absence frequency

Work out the total number of available working days in a specific period. This is the total number of days multiplied by the total number of employees. For example, if the period under review is a working week (five days) and there are 100 employees, then the total number of days available for work is 500 (100 multiplied by 5).

Work out the number of days missed by individuals. Calculate the percentage absenteeism rate by taking the total number of days of absence, dividing by the total number of days available, multiplying by 100. For example, if there are 50 days' absence during a period in which there are 500 days available for work then the percentage rate for absenteeism is $50/500 \times 100 = 10$ per cent.

Calculating individual absences

The Bradford Factor

Calculating the overall level of absence alone is unlikely to give you all the information you need to decide on future action. Frequent short-term absences are likely to be more disruptive to the business than longer-term absences that can be planned for. However, these may not always show up in the absence figures. One way round this is to use a calculation method generally known as the Bradford Factor (having been devised by Bradford University), which takes into account both the length of absences and the frequency of them.

The formula is $S \times S \times D$ where S = the number of specific spells of absence in the last 52 weeks, and D = the number of days of absence in the last 52 weeks. Under this approach: one absence of 20 days is $1 \times 1 \times 20 = 20$; 10 absences of two days is $10 \times 10 \times 20 = 2,000$.

Having collected information about absences you should look for particular patterns, such as higher sickness levels following bank holidays or weekends, and whether absences are higher for particular groups of staff, for certain types of job or in certain locations.

You should also have trigger points that activate processes once absences have reached a predetermined level. These can be either a number of days, or a number of spells of absence or a combination of the two. The main danger with having a trigger point, such as 10 days' annual absence, for example, is that any such target can soon become known to employees and can come to be regarded as the level of absence that management is happy to tolerate.

Procedures to reduce absence

There are a number of procedures that you should introduce and actions that you should take as a manager to keep unplanned absences under control. You should:

- produce clear written guidelines to employees for reporting absences (see example below);
- train managers and supervisors in handling absences;

- ensure that those managers and supervisors take responsibility for controlling absence;
- set targets for absence levels;
- interview those returning to work after absence;
- try to identify likely poor attendees during the selection process.

Absence reporting procedure

On the first day of absence

If you cannot attend work you must notify your manager as early as possible, and by no later than 10.00 am on the first day of absence. You must speak to your line manager and not to one of your colleagues. You should telephone personally, and only in exceptional circumstances should a friend or relative do this for you. If you do not have a telephone, you should make this known to your line manager so that alternative arrangements can be made. You should explain the reason for your absence and say when you expect to return to work. You should complete a company self-certification form on your return to work.

On the fourth working day

You must let your manager know of your continued absence and say when you expect to return.

By the eighth calendar day

You must get a doctor's certificate and send it to your manager no later than your eighth calendar day of sickness. You need to keep your manager informed during your period of sickness. Continued absence must be supported by medical certificates otherwise you may lose your right to any sick pay.

Fit Notes

Fit Notes were introduced from 6 April 2010 to improve communication between employers and GPs. The idea was that the somewhat negative message that an employee was unfit for work could be replaced by a positive statement indicating what work that person might be able to do. In practice this change seems to have made little difference to employers. A Fit Note, like the Med 3 certificate it replaced, is for social security or SSP purposes and while it should be taken as strong evidence of incapacity an employer can challenge its validity if there is strong evidence for doing so. See **www.gov.uk/government/uploads/system/uploads/attachment_data/file/183291/fitnote-employers-linemanagers-guidance.pdf**

Return to work interviews

One of the most effective ways of controlling absence is the return to work interview. You should:

- make a point of discussing any absence with the employee on his return to work;
- make it clear that he was missed;
- adopt a friendly and interested tone;
- if any problems arise from the meeting try to ensure that these are addressed.

The purpose of the meeting is to:

- find out the reason for the absence;
- find out whether there are any particular problems and, if so, what action is being taken to address them;
- find out whether the employee has consulted a doctor (if the reason is sickness);
- review any other recent absences;
- welcome that person back and inform him about work developments;
- offer support where appropriate;
- agree any necessary actions.

A meeting is also valuable during sickness when an employee has been off sick for some time as it is important to show that the company continues to take an interest and to try to find out when a return to work can be expected. Generally your tone at any such meeting should be supportive, unless clear problems or a particular pattern have emerged, in which case you may need to be more formal.

The whole emphasis is on getting the employee to reduce the level of absence, or to return to work at the earliest opportunity, but you should not allow someone to return before being fit to do so, as all employers have a duty of care to their employees.

Policies to encourage good attendance

There are a number of policies that should be introduced, and actions taken by you to try to ensure that attendance levels are kept high. You should:

- provide good physical working conditions;
- carry out risk assessments and ensure that health and safety rules and procedures are followed;
- ensure that all staff receive the appropriate training, especially when working with machinery or in a hazardous environment or when undertaking physical activities;
- review working arrangements where there are high levels of absence;
- ensure that there is adequate training of supervisors and line managers, particularly in relation to maintaining motivation and morale;
- ensure that, where possible, there are opportunities for promotion and/or development;

- where possible encourage teamworking, as peer group pressure can help to encourage good attendance;
- operate flexible employment policies such as flexible working hours and job-sharing;
- focus on outputs and performance targets, rather than just attendance hours;
- where possible provide crèche or childcare facilities;
- agree reasonable absences for emergencies and medical appointments, bearing in mind that some of these rights are enshrined in statute;
- consider the introduction of programmes to promote good health;
- consider redesigning jobs to relieve people of high levels of monotonous routine or stress.

Incentives to encourage good attendance

You could consider financial incentives to encourage good attendance. However, there is little firm evidence that these have a long-term effect and they can result in staff complaining that they are penalized for being ill. Probably the best type of incentive is something along the lines of a full attendance draw, in which employees with full attendance over a certain period may be entered into a draw for a prize, such as a holiday or cash. This has the merit that it stresses the importance the company places on good attendance and it cannot really be said to penalize those who are sick.

Developing a sickness policy

You should produce a written policy for managing sickness. Without this there will be confusion about the rules applying to sickness, leading to inconsistent and possibly unfair treatment of employees. The policy should cover:

- what an employee should do if unable to come to work, including who should be contacted to report the absence and how that contact should be made;
- whether a self-certificate is required (see example on page 143);
- at what stage a medical certificate or Fit Note will be required;
- the intervals at which certificates should be provided;
- the action to be taken on returning to work;
- to whom the policy applies;
- entitlement to sick pay and any conditions attaching to it, such as length of service;
- any rules relating to sickness such as the requirement to have a medical examination;
- action that may be taken if the rules are not followed;
- the actions that will be taken by the company to keep in touch with the employee;

- the right to statutory sick pay (SSP);
- what will happen when the sick pay entitlement expires.

An example of a sickness policy is set out below.

Sickness absence policy

Introduction

It is recognized that from time to time staff may be unable to attend work because of ill health. This document sets out the procedure to be followed by all staff and the entitlement to sick pay in the event of such absences.

Notification of absence

If you are unable to attend work because of sickness or injury you must notify your line manager by telephone of the reason as soon as possible on the first day of absence and, ideally, within one hour of your normal start time.

Notification can be by you or by someone on your behalf.

You must maintain regular contact with your line manager on any subsequent days of absence.

If you are absent for more than seven days you must get a doctor's certificate for the entire period of absence and send this to your line manager.

The company may, at its discretion, request a doctor's certificate for periods of absence of less than seven days. The company will reimburse any cost of obtaining a certificate in these circumstances.

For long or frequent periods of absence the company may require you to be examined by the company's medical adviser.

Returning to work

On your return to work you must report to your line manager, who will interview you.

If you return to work within seven calendar days you must complete a self-certification form, which is available from your line manager, on your first day back.

Sick pay

The company will pay you sick pay, provided you comply with the notification arrangements, on the following scale:

Years of employment	Full pay	Half pay
Less than 1 year	SSP only	SSP only
One to two years	one month	one month
Two to five years	two months	two months
Over five years	three months	three months

Payment is in relation to any period of 12 months, starting with the first day of sickness. Anyone starting part-way through the calendar year will be paid in proportion to his or her length of service. Similarly, part-time staff will be paid on a pro rata basis.

When you have exhausted your entitlement to sick pay the company will continue to pay you statutory sick pay (SSP), provided you have an entitlement to it. The company will offset any other payments received for the sickness or injury against company sick pay.

Withholding sick pay

The company may withhold sick pay if:

> you do not comply with the company's requirements for the notification of sickness absence;

> you refuse to undertake a medical examination at the company's request;

> you work for another employer during your period of sickness absence, in which case the company will also take disciplinary action.

Accidents at work

Any accident at work must be reported to your line manager as soon as possible, and an accident report completed.

Sickness absence and annual leave

If you fall sick while on annual leave and you produce a doctor's certificate relating to the period of sickness, the company will treat this as sick leave and not annual leave.

Long-term sick leave

If you are on long-term sick leave, which is a period of 13 weeks or more, you must keep your manager informed of your progress on a weekly basis. You must produce medical certificates to cover the absence.

Benefits

All the benefits to which you are entitled will continue to be paid during your period of sickness absence and your annual leave entitlement will continue to accrue during this period.

Frequent or prolonged absence

The company reserves the right to terminate your employment because of frequent or prolonged absences.

Pay during absence

You do not have to pay for any unauthorized absence. For sickness absence there is a statutory entitlement to statutory sick pay (SSP). It is for you to decide whether you wish to pay anything above this legal minimum with a company sick pay scheme. If you do so, you should ensure that the scheme is not so generous that it encourages staff sickness and you should make it clear that abuse of the system is a disciplinary offence.

Many company sick pay schemes apply a sliding scale of entitlement (see example sickness absence policy on page 140). The most generous schemes, particularly those in the public sector, may give up to six months' full pay followed by six months' half pay, the entitlement typically increasing with length of service. In contrast small employers often just give SSP (see below).

Statutory sick pay (SSP)

Employees are entitled to SSP once they have been sick for four days in a row (including Sundays, holidays and rest days). No payment is due for the first three days, which are known as 'waiting days'. Any sickness absence is described as a 'period of interruption of work', abbreviated to 'PIW'. Any day of absence has to be a 'qualifying' day for payment of SSP – a day on which the employee would normally have been expected to work if he had not been sick.

Periods of absence that are less than eight weeks apart are linked to count as one period of sickness, or PIW, for payment of SSP. This means that if someone is sick for a second time during this eight-week period, and the total absence is four days or more, SSP would have to be paid from the first day of that second absence. The maximum entitlement is to 28 weeks of SSP in any PIW.

Statutory sick pay is treated as part of normal earnings and is subject to Income Tax and National Insurance Contributions.

Reclaiming SSP

Up to the end of the 2013/14 tax year under the Percentage Threshold Scheme some employers were able to reclaim SSP payments to sick employees if they were more than 13 per cent of their NIC liabilities for that month. This scheme has now been abolished and employers will not be able to claim back any SSP payments with effect from the 2014/15 tax year.

Employees not entitled to SSP

There are some employees who are not entitled to SSP including those:

- whose earnings are below the Lower Earnings Limit for National Insurance Contributions;
- who are pensioners;
- who have received certain state benefits within the preceding 57 days;
- who have not worked under the contract of employment;
- who fall sick during a stoppage arising from an industrial dispute, unless they did not take part and had no interest in it;
- who are in legal custody or in prison;
- who are sick during the maternity pay period (see Chapter 7).

Notification of absence

There are rules about how absence should be notified and you can withhold payment of SSP if notification is late without a good reason. However, you must:

- make the rules about notification clear to employees;
- indicate how notification must be made;
- accept notification by someone else on behalf of the employee;
- not require notification earlier than the first day of sickness or by a specific time on that day, or more than once a week;
- accept any written notification that the employee is sick, even if this is not on a form provided by you.

Although you can accept any reasonable written notification, you can use a self-certification form such as that set out below, or use one that is available from the local social security office.

Self-certification form

This form must be completed after any absence from work because of sickness or injury. It must be completed on the first day back.

If you have been away for more than seven consecutive days you will need a medical certificate or Fit Note. Failure to produce one could result in loss of sick pay.

Name:
Job title:

Date of first day of absence:
Date of last day of absence:
Reason for absence (please state as precisely as possible the nature of the illness or injury):

Did you visit your doctor or a hospital during your absence? Yes/No

I confirm that the above details are correct and that I have not worked during my period of absence.

Signed:
Date:

Manager's statement – to be completed by your line manager

I confirm that the above information is correct.
Signed:
Date:
Position:

Records

You are required to maintain records of SSP payments for at least three years after the end of the tax year they relate to.

Withholding SSP

You are entitled to withhold SSP from the employee if you feel that:

- the employee's incapacity is not genuine; or
- you have not been correctly notified; or
- evidence of incapacity has not been provided.

If you do withhold SSP the employee has the right to ask you for a written statement of the reason for refusal, which you must provide.

Dealing with persistent absence

Short-term sickness absences

When dealing with short-term absences you should:

- obtain an explanation from the employee about the reasons for these absences;
- where there are frequent short-term absences not supported by medical evidence, ask the employee to consult a doctor, as there could be a serious underlying medical condition;
- if there are no good reasons for the absence, deal with the matter under the company's disciplinary or capability procedure (see Chapter 12);
- consider whether the absences are likely to be temporary and whether the company can help in any way;
- tell the employee what improvement in attendance is required and what is likely to happen if no such improvement is forthcoming.

If the absences continue and you decide to take disciplinary action you should take full account of the employee's past performance, age, length of service and the likelihood of improved attendance in the future.

Poor attendance is a legitimate reason for dismissing someone, but only after you have investigated the matter thoroughly, and the employee's circumstances, as well as the effect on the business and your other employees, have been taken into account.

Long-term absence through ill health

Where an employee has been absent with a long-term illness, before taking any decision to dismiss you should:

- maintain regular contact with the employee;
- obtain the employee's written agreement if you intend to seek medical advice;

- notify the employee of any action you propose to take, particularly if his employment is at risk;
- consider whether suitable alternative work might be available;
- consider how much disruption is being caused by the employee's absence;
- consider whether the work can be covered in some other way;
- consider whether there is an alternative to dismissal, such as redeployment;
- consider whether the employee has a disability, in which case you may need to make reasonable adjustments, as required by the Equality Act 2010;
- take into account the employee's age, length of service and so forth;
- discuss the position and possibilities with the employee.

You have to get the employee's permission to obtain any medical records and the employee has the right of access to any reports about him (see example consent form, below). The employee can refuse to allow any reports to be provided. However, where the employee refuses to cooperate by providing medical evidence, a decision can still be made on the basis of the information available and the employee should be notified of this.

If the illness persists and there is no likely prospect of an early return to work, you may have no option but to dismiss the employee.

Consent to medical report

This form is a request for your consent to a medical report. Under the Access to Medical Reports Act 1988 you have the right to:

withhold your consent for an application to be made to a doctor;

ask your doctor to let you see the report and to amend any part of the report you consider to be inaccurate or misleading;

attach your written objections to the report if the doctor refuses to amend it;

withhold your consent to the report being supplied to the company.

Employee declaration

Having been made aware of my statutory rights I give my consent to a medical report being obtained from my doctor or medical specialist by the company.
I understand that the clinical details in the report will be treated as confidential, but that the content will be used by the company management as part of the information required for deciding on future action.

I understand that if I wish to see the report before it is sent to the company I must arrange to do so with my doctor or medical specialist within 21 days of making the application.

I do not wish to see the report before it is sent to the company.*/I wish to see the report before it is sent to the company.*

Signature:
Date:
Doctor/specialist's name and address:

*Delete as appropriate

Frequent lateness and unauthorized absences

In considering what action should be taken about persistent lateness and unauthorized absences, account should also be taken of the circumstances surrounding these, such as current travelling difficulties. However, actions that can be taken to reduce these problems include:

- monitoring attendance records for individuals and groups;
- asking employees to telephone by a particular time on every occasion they are absent;
- having return-to-work interviews;
- restricting overtime.

Finally, there may be a need to take disciplinary action.

Company health check

You might want to check how healthy your company is in its approach to managing absence levels. The checklist below may help in this.

- Do you have sickness records that show:
  - the number of days off for each employee;
  - the reasons for the absence;
  - numbers and duration of each absence for individual employees, different functions and the company as a whole?
- Are these records sufficiently comprehensive to enable you to identify patterns?
- Is the information computerized with built-in trigger mechanisms?
- Do you calculate the costs of absence?
- Are there clear procedures for reporting absences?
- Are any such procedures clearly notified to employees?
- Are targets set for absence levels at company and functional levels?

- Is there top management commitment to the encouragement of good attendance?
- Are line managers and supervisors made responsible for managing absence?
- Are managers and supervisors trained in handling absence?
- Are checks built in to the recruitment process to try to identify probable poor attendees?
- Are employees made fully aware of the importance the company attaches to good attendance?
- Are return-to-work interviews held?
- Are other strategies used for encouraging good attendance, such as health programmes, teamworking, incentives, job redesign or performance management?

Further information

Access to Medical Reports Act 1988
Data Protection Act 1998
Disability Discrimination Act 1995
Employment Relations Act 1999
Employment Rights Act 1996
Equality Act 2010
Getting the Most out of the Fit Note: Guidance for Employers and Live Managers, Department for Work and Pensions, 2013
Huczynski, A A and Fitzpatrick, M J (1989) *Managing Employee Absence for a Competitive Edge*, Pitman, London
Reserve Forces Act 1996
Statutory Sick Pay (General) Regulations 1982

Maternity and Paternity Rights

07

This chapter describes the maternity and paternity rights applying to all employees, which include:

- time off for antenatal care;
- medical suspension during pregnancy;
- maternity leave;
- paternity leave;
- maternity pay;
- paternity pay;
- the right not to suffer a detriment or be dismissed because of pregnancy, maternity or paternity;
- adoption leave;
- adoption pay.

Time off for antenatal care

Any pregnant employee is entitled to paid time off, during working hours, to receive antenatal care. This applies irrespective of the employee's length of service or working hours. After the first appointment you can ask for written proof that she is pregnant and that an appointment has been made. It is also the case that from 1 October 2014 fathers and partners, including agency workers, can take unpaid time off to attend up to two ante-natal appointments of up to 6.5 hours each.

Medical suspension during pregnancy

You must assess the risks to the health and safety of any new or expectant mother and change her working conditions or hours of work if any such risk exists. This includes offering alternative employment. If none of these changes are possible then you must suspend her on full pay for as long as the risk remains.

Maternity leave

All pregnant employees are entitled to 52 weeks' maternity leave regardless of length of service or hours of work.

You can give an employee rights to maternity leave in the contract of employment and then either these contractual rights, or the statutory rights, whichever are more favourable, will apply. The same rule applies to maternity pay.

A pregnant employee must let you know when she intends to begin her maternity leave by the 15th week before the expected week of childbirth (EWC). She is required to confirm:

- that she is pregnant;
- the date her maternity leave is to begin;
- the EWC.

An example form for an employee going on maternity leave is set out below.

Example form for employee going on maternity leave

Please complete this form and return it to your line manager as early as possible and no later than the end of the 15th week before your expected week of childbirth.

If you are unable to give this notice, please notify us at the earliest practicable date.

You must attach your Mat B1 certificate, or other evidence of pregnancy, signed by a midwife or doctor.

Name:

1 Please state your expected week of childbirth.

2 What date will your maternity leave begin?

3 What date do you intend to return to work?

I confirm that I am pregnant and that I will be taking maternity leave as set out above.

Signed:
Date:

You should ask her to produce evidence of the EWC in writing (although you are not required to do so) and this will normally be produced on form Mat B1.

If she is unable to give the required notice, as long as she lets you know as soon as reasonably practicable she will have satisfied the notification requirement. A woman can also change her mind about when she wants her leave to start, provided she gives you 28 days' notice, if reasonably practicable. You must respond to this notification within 28 days. An employee who does not comply with these requirements may have to forfeit her maternity leave and could lose her right to statutory maternity pay (SMP). However, you should be very cautious about taking action in these circumstances. A model letter recommended by the Department for Business, Innovation and Skills (BIS) to acknowledge notification of maternity leave is set out below.

Model letter for employers to acknowledge notification of maternity leave

This letter should be used when only the statutory levels of leave and pay are provided. (Employer must respond within 28 days of receipt of employee's notification.)

Date:

Dear

Congratulations and thank you for telling me about your pregnancy and the date that your baby is due. I am writing to you about your maternity leave and pay.

As we have discussed, you are eligible for 52 weeks' maternity leave.

Given your chosen start date of [insert date], your maternity leave will end on [insert date].

If you want to change the date your leave starts you must, if at all possible, tell me at least 28 days before your proposed new start date or 28 days before [insert date leave starts] (your original start date), whichever is sooner.

If you decide to return to work before [insert date leave ends], you must give me at least eight weeks' notice.

As we discussed, you are eligible for 39 weeks' Statutory Maternity Pay/not eligible for Statutory Maternity Pay [delete as appropriate].

Your maternity pay will be £[insert amount] from [insert date] to [insert date] and £[insert amount] from [insert date] to [insert date].

OR

The form SMP1 (enclosed) explains why you do not qualify for Statutory Maternity Pay. You may, however, be entitled to Maternity Allowance. If you take this form to the Jobcentre Plus or Social Security Office at [insert local details], they will be able to tell you more.

As your employer I want to make sure that your health and safety as a pregnant mother are protected while you are working, and that you are not exposed to risk. I have already carried out an assessment to identify hazards in our workplace that could be a risk to any new, expectant or breastfeeding mothers. Now you have told me you are pregnant I will arrange for a specific risk assessment of your job and we will discuss what actions to take if any problems are identified. If you have any further concerns, following this assessment and specifically in relation to your pregnancy, please let me know immediately.

If you decide not to return to work you must still give me proper notice. Your decision will not affect your entitlement to SMP.

If you have any questions about any aspect of your maternity entitlement please do not hesitate to get in touch with me. I wish you well.

Yours sincerely,

Premature birth

If an employee gives birth before the EWC, the maternity leave period starts on the date of childbirth.

Pregnancy-related illness

If a pregnant employee is absent from work wholly or partly because of pregnancy during the four weeks before her EWC, the maternity leave period will begin from the first day of absence.

Compulsory maternity leave

You must not allow a woman to work during the two-week period immediately following childbirth. This period extends to four weeks if she works in a factory.

Contractual rights during maternity leave

During maternity leave the employee's contract of employment continues to exist. This means that you must apply to her all the terms and conditions of employment that would have applied had she not been absent, with the exception of wages or salary. Remember that when calculating the entitlement to maternity pay during the maternity leave period you must include any pay rises given to your employees during that period, and during the period used to calculate the rate of maternity pay to be applied.

Particular problems can arise where bonus payments are involved. Whether or not the employee is entitled to such payments will depend on the wording of the conditions relating to payment. You will generally need to take advice about whether they should apply.

Returning to work after maternity leave

The employee does not have to notify you about her return but can just turn up for work on the due date. However, if she wishes to return before the end of the maternity leave period she must give you at least eight weeks' notice of her intention to return. If she does not give this notice, you can postpone the date of return until this notice provision has been satisfied.

You should bear in mind that the employee cannot return during the compulsory two-week leave period referred to above.

If she is unable to return at the end of the maternity leave period because of sickness, this should be treated as normal sickness absence.

The employee must be allowed to return to the job she was doing immediately before her period of maternity leave began and on the same terms and conditions of employment.

Refusal to allow the employee to return to work

If you do not allow an employee to return to work after maternity leave, she may make a claim to an employment tribunal that she has been unfairly dismissed for reasons relating to the maternity leave. You would have to be able to satisfy the tribunal that there was a valid reason for dismissal, or redundancy, which was unrelated to the exercise of maternity rights. In practice, this is likely to be difficult to prove.

Dismissal during maternity leave

You must not dismiss any woman for reasons connected with pregnancy or childbirth. Any dismissal will be automatically unfair if it is because of:

- pregnancy;
- the fact that an employee has given birth;
- suspension from work on maternity grounds;
- the fact that the employee took maternity leave;
- the fact that the employee tried to take advantage of the benefits applying during the maternity leave period.

Similarly, if you make an employee on maternity leave redundant without having first offered her suitable alternative employment, in preference to her colleagues if need be, this will also be automatically unfair.

It is possible for you to dismiss an employee who is pregnant or on maternity leave for legitimate reasons, but in practice it is likely to be very difficult to prove that it was not because of the pregnancy or maternity leave. There are also other practical difficulties in that any dismissal would need to be preceded by a meeting with the employee and if she is on maternity leave this might prove difficult to arrange. Dismissal without any such meeting is likely to be procedurally unfair.

Dismissal of replacement

It is fair to terminate the employment of any temporary employee you may have engaged to cover for the period of maternity leave provided you have made it clear on appointment that the employment was only for the duration of the maternity leave and would end on the return of the jobholder. This counts as a dismissal for Some Other Substantial Reason (see Chapter 14). It can sometimes happen that you prefer the replacement worker but you cannot retain this person in preference to your original employee.

Statutory maternity pay

Statutory maternity pay (SMP) applies for up to 39 weeks during the maternity leave period. To qualify for SMP the employee must:

- have been employed continuously for at least 26 weeks by the start of the 15th week before the EWC, known as the 'qualifying week';
- have average earnings of at least the Lower Earnings Limit for payment of National Insurance Contributions;
- still be pregnant at the 11th week before the EWC or have given birth earlier;
- provide you with evidence of the expected date of childbirth;
- have stopped working.

Statutory maternity pay comprises: a higher rate equivalent to 90 per cent of the employee's normal weekly earnings for the first six weeks, and a lower rate for the remainder of the period (£138.18 per week from April 2014).

Recovery of SMP

You can recover 92 per cent of the gross amount of SMP paid by deducting that amount from the total of employees' and employer's National Insurance Contributions payable.

If you qualify for small employers' relief (your gross National Insurance Contributions in the preceding year were less than £45,000) you are able to claim 103 per cent of the SMP paid out.

Keeping in Touch days

An employee on maternity leave is entitled to 10 'Keeping in Touch' (KIT) days, which allow her to do a limited amount of work for her employer during the maternity pay period and still retain her SMP for that week. However, any work done on any day, for example attending a one-hour training session, will count as a whole KIT day. There are no restrictions on when KIT days can be used for SMP, though the maternity leave regulations prohibit a woman from working for two weeks after childbirth. Once those days have been used up, the woman will once again lose a week's SMP for any week in which she does any work for her employer.

A woman is entitled to be paid for any KIT days worked, but the rate will need to be agreed and must be at least equivalent to the SMP rate.

Maternity policy

An example of a company maternity policy is set out below.

Maternity policy

The following document sets out the company's policy on maternity leave, maternity pay and all other issues relating to pregnancy and maternity.

This represents the law at the date of this document and may have to be amended in the light of future changes to the law.

The policy is designed to be as comprehensive as possible. However, if you have any questions about the policy please contact your line manager.

Time off for antenatal care

If you are pregnant you are entitled to take paid time off during your normal working hours to receive antenatal care. This should be at times agreed with your supervisor or line manager and preferably at the start or end of your working day. Antenatal care includes appointments with your GP, hospital clinics and relaxation classes. Fathers and partners also have the right to take time off to attend up to two ante-natal appointments of up to 6.5 hours each.

Procedure for notifying absence for antenatal care

You should advise your line manager that you will be absent as far in advance of your appointment as possible, and you may be asked to produce your appointment card.

Pay

There will be no deduction of salary for attendance at authorized antenatal appointments.

Maternity leave

Entitlement

All pregnant employees are entitled to take 52 weeks' maternity leave, no matter how long they have been employed by us and no matter how many hours they work each week, subject to the rules set out below.

When does your maternity leave start?

You can choose to start your maternity leave at any time after the start of the 11th week before the week in which your child is due except in the following cases:

(a) If you are absent because of an illness related to your pregnancy at any time during the four weeks before your child is due, the company reserves the right to require you to start your maternity leave on the first day of that absence.

(b) If your child is born earlier than your planned date of starting maternity leave, then the maternity leave starts on the day the child is born. You should write as soon as possible to notify the company, enclosing Form Mat B1, unless you have already handed this over by then.

Note: if your child is stillborn after the 24th week of pregnancy you retain your maternity leave rights (and your right to statutory maternity pay subject to the SMP rules stated below).

Notification requirements

At least 28 days before you start your maternity leave you must give notice in writing addressed to your line manager. That notice must state:

that you are pregnant;

the week in which your child is due (note that for these purposes a week begins on a Sunday);

when you want your maternity leave to start.

You should enclose a Form Mat B1 signed by your GP or midwife with your letter, unless this has been given to the company earlier.

If you are unable to give 28 days' notice because you have to start your maternity leave sooner than you anticipated, provided that you give notice as soon as you can, you will not lose your right to take maternity leave.

Keeping in touch

You are allowed to work for up to 10 days during your maternity leave without losing your entitlement to maternity pay. These 'Keeping in Touch' (KIT) days need to be discussed and agreed with your line manager.

Returning from maternity leave

If you return to work at the end of your maternity leave period you need not formally notify us in advance of your return and you will return to work in the same job that you left before you started your maternity leave. If, for health and safety reasons, you were doing a different job from your usual one while you were pregnant, you may be required to return to that different job for a short time if you are still at risk when you return to work.

You may wish to return to work before the end of your maternity leave period, but if you choose to do so you must give us eight weeks' advance warning of the date of your return.

If you cannot return to work because you are ill you should notify your line manager, who will advise you how much, if any, sick leave you are entitled to. Please note that in some circumstances if you cannot return to work at the appointed time you will lose your right to return to work altogether.

If you decide not to return to work at the end of your maternity leave period you must notify your line manager at once in writing of your decision.

Maternity pay

To qualify for statutory maternity pay (SMP) you have to be pregnant (or have given birth) at the start of the 11th week before the baby is due. If you have at least 26 weeks' service by the end of the 15th week before the expected week of childbirth you will be entitled to receive SMP whether or not you intend to return to work. (Note that if your normal weekly earnings are less than the Lower Earnings Limit for National Insurance Contributions for the previous eight weeks then you will not qualify for SMP.) If you do not qualify for SMP you may be entitled to claim maternity allowance. Your local Benefits Agency office will be able to advise you how to claim this.

Statutory maternity pay is payable for a maximum of 39 weeks, for the first six weeks at the higher statutory rate of nine-tenths of your salary followed by the lower statutory rate for the remaining period. You will be given a statement of your exact entitlement when you start your maternity leave.

To claim SMP you must give 28 days' notice in writing of your absence on maternity grounds and you must give the original Mat B1 form, not a photocopy, to your line manager. You can only receive SMP once you have stopped work.

Once you start your maternity leave, your maternity pay will be paid into your bank account on the same date when you would have received your salary, and will be subject to deductions for Income Tax and National Insurance.

Contractual benefits

You will continue to receive your contractual non-remuneration benefits during your maternity leave period.

Holidays

While you are absent on maternity leave you will continue to accrue holiday entitlement in the usual way. You must take this additional holiday within 12 months of your return to work.

Pension contributions

Your maternity leave period will be treated as pensionable service and the company will therefore continue to make contributions on your behalf into the pension scheme based on the maternity pay you receive rather than your usual salary.

Health and safety

If you are employed in a job that has been identified as posing a risk to your health or that of your unborn child you will be notified immediately and arrangements will be made to eliminate that risk.

For this reason you are required to notify your line manager as soon as you are aware that you may be pregnant. Arrangements will then be made to alter your working conditions or, if this is not possible, you will be offered a suitable alternative job for the duration of your pregnancy.

If there is no alternative work, the company reserves the right to suspend you on full pay until you are no longer at risk.

These alternative arrangements may continue after the birth of your child if you are still considered to be at risk.

If you have any concerns about your own health and safety at any time you should let your line manager know immediately.

Paternity leave

See 'Forthcoming changes' below. Any new father is entitled to two weeks' paid paternity leave provided he has at least 26 weeks' continuous service with you by the 15th week before the expected week of childbirth. This leave must be taken within a period of 56 days beginning with the date on which the child is born.

Under the Additional Paternity Leave Regulations 2010 fathers are entitled to up to six months additional paternity leave provided the mother has returned to work, thus giving parents the option of dividing a period of paid leave entitlement between them.

The leave is for a maximum of 26 weeks and a minimum of two weeks, and it must not start until at least 20 weeks after the birth or placement for adoption and must end not later than 12 months after the birth or placement for adoption. The leave may only be taken in multiples of complete weeks.

Where this leave is taken during the mother's 39-week maternity pay period it will be paid at the same rate and on the same basis as statutory maternity pay. Parents are required to self-certify by providing details of their eligibility to their employer.

The employee has rights on returning from paternity leave similar to those applying to women returning from maternity leave. This means that he has the right to return to the same job and must not be subject to any detriment, or be unfairly dismissed for reasons connected with the taking of this paternity leave.

Statutory paternity pay

See 'Forthcoming changes' below. Statutory paternity pay may be paid to any employee who meets the 26-week service qualification and whose average weekly earnings are above the Lower Earnings Limit for National Insurance Contributions. The rate of statutory paternity pay is determined by Regulations, but from April 2014 is the lesser of £138.18 per week or 90 per cent of the employee's average weekly earnings. This should be administered in the same way as statutory maternity pay and amounts paid out reclaimed in the same way.

Forthcoming changes

Additional paternity leave and pay will no longer be available for babies due after 5 April 2015 or for children who are placed for adoption on or after that date as it is to be replaced by shared parental leave. This will allow eligible mothers, fathers, partners and adopters to choose how to share time off work after their child is born or placed. This could mean that the mother or adopter shares some of the leave with her partner, perhaps returning to work for part of the time and then resuming leave at a later date. The regulations introducing this came into force on 1 December 2014.

Adoption leave

Rights to adoption leave are similar to those for maternity leave. Adoptive parents have the right to take adoption leave for a period of up to 52 weeks. This right is in addition to the right to parental leave.

As with statutory paternity leave, the employee has the right to return to the same job following absence on adoption leave, and must not suffer any detriment or be unfairly dismissed for reasons relating to adoption leave.

Statutory adoption pay

Statutory adoption pay is paid to any employee who meets the 26-week service qualification and is earning at least the Lower Earnings Limit for National Insurance Contributions. It is paid for a period of up to 39 weeks and the rate is determined by Regulations, but from April 2014 is the lesser of £138.18 per week or 90 per cent of the employee's average weekly earnings. This should be recovered in the same way as statutory maternity pay and statutory paternity pay.

Forthcoming changes

From 5 April 2015 the Government is changing the rights on adoption leave and pay as follows:

- The main adopter will be able to take paid time off for up to five adoption appointments and the secondary adopter will be entitled to take unpaid time off for up to two appointments.
- Employees will no longer need to have 26 weeks' continuous employment to be eligible for adoption leave.

- Statutory Adoption Pay will change to bring it in line with maternity pay so the first six weeks will be paid at 90 per cent of the employee's normal earnings.
- Some surrogate parents will become eligible for adoption leave.
- Eligible employees will be able to opt into the new Shared Parental Leave scheme.

Further information

Additional Paternity Leave Regulations 2010
Employment Rights Act 1996
Maternity and Parental Leave etc Regulations 1999
Statutory Maternity Pay Manual (CA29)
Trade Union Reform and Employment Rights Act 1992
www.dwp.gov.uk
www.gov.uk

Working Hours and Holidays

08

Working Time Regulations 1998

Working time limits

The Working Time Regulations 1998 limit a worker's average working week, including overtime, to a maximum of 48 hours over seven days. The average figure for working hours is calculated over a reference period of 17 weeks.

In calculating the reference period certain days are 'excluded'. These include days when the worker was on sick leave or maternity leave or any periods for which the worker agreed to work more than 48 hours per week. However, where such excluded days arise, the reference period must be extended by a number of days equal to the number of excluded days to get the total of 17 weeks. These additional days must be from the period immediately following the reference period.

For example, if the worker has one week of sickness during a 17-week reference period the number of hours worked in the one week immediately following the reference period would be added to the calculation to get to the total of 17 weeks (see Figure 8.1).

The formula used to calculate working time is A+B/C, where A = the number of hours worked in the reference period, B = the number of hours excluded from the reference period and C = the number of weeks in the reference period.

Exclusion

The working time limits do not apply to any workers who can decide their own working hours.

Opting out of the Regulations

Workers can agree to work longer than the 48-hour limit by signing an 'opt-out'. This must be in writing and signed by the worker (see example in Chapter 2). You need to keep a record of all employees who have signed such an opt-out.

FIGURE 8.1   Working time calculation

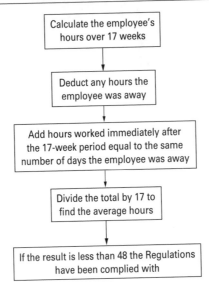

Workers can cancel this agreement at any time but they must give you seven days' notice or any longer period you agree with them, although this cannot be more than three months.

As an employer you are obliged to take all reasonable steps to ensure that workers are not required to work more than an average of 48 hours per week unless they have signed an 'opt out'.

The meaning of working time

Working time includes all those hours that the employee is required to be working for you, including lunch breaks, travelling, undertaking job-related training and working abroad. It does not include routine home-to-work travel, rest breaks or training that is not job-related.

Time off

You must ensure that workers are given the time off that they are entitled to during the working period. Workers are entitled to a rest period of 11 uninterrupted hours between each working day and one day a week off (which can be averaged over a two-week period).

Young workers

A young worker is a worker who is over school leaving age but is not yet 18. Such workers are entitled to 12 uninterrupted hours off in each 24-hour period of work. They are also entitled to two days off each week, but this cannot be averaged over two weeks.

Rest breaks

Any worker required to work for more than six hours without interruption is entitled to a rest break of 20 minutes, which must be taken during the six-hour period.

If a young worker is required to work more than 4.5 hours at a stretch he is entitled to a rest break of 30 minutes.

Annual leave

All workers, including part-time workers, are entitled to 5.6 weeks' annual leave. The number of days' leave is related to the number of days normally worked. For a five-day week, therefore, the entitlement will be $5.6 \times 5 = 28$ days' annual leave, but for a three-day week it will be $5.6 \times 3 = 16.8$ days per annum. All public holidays count towards the annual leave entitlement.

Leave accrues at the rate of one-twelfth of the annual entitlement per month during the first year of service. A full-time worker with three months' service would be entitled to three-twelfths of the annual entitlement of 28 days' leave (ie seven days). A part-time worker working three days a week with one month's service would accrue 1.4 days (28 days × three-fifths = 16.8 days × one-twelfth).

You should agree with the workers concerned how and when notice of their intention to take leave should be given. If there is no such agreement the notice that the worker must give you should be at least twice the period of leave to be taken. You may in turn refuse the worker permission to take the leave but must respond within a period equal to the period of leave requested.

Calculating a week's pay

For workers paid a fixed wage or salary, a week's pay is that which is due for the basic hours worked. It excludes overtime unless this is a guaranteed part of the contract.

If the worker is a piece worker or receives variable bonuses or commission related to output, a week's pay is the average hourly rate multiplied by that worker's normal working hours (see also Chapter 3).

To calculate the hourly rate, the weekly pay over the previous 12 weeks should be divided by the number of hours worked during that period. If no pay was received for any of those weeks, then this should be replaced by a week before the 12-week period to make it up to the total of 12 weeks.

A week's pay is the total eligible pay (excluding voluntary overtime but including relevant bonuses) over the 12-week period divided by 12.

Common issues relating to working time

Signing opt-out agreements

You cannot force a worker to sign an opt-out agreement and any action taken against a person for not doing so is likely to be unfair.

Workers with second jobs

If you know that a worker has a second job you should agree an opt-out with that person if the total time worked is likely to be more than 48 hours a week. It may be a wise precaution to insert a clause in the employment contract requiring employees not to take on other employment without the agreement of the company. However, if a worker does another job without your knowledge it is unlikely that you would have any liability in the event of the Regulations being breached.

Rest breaks

You do not have to pay for rest breaks but this is a matter to be agreed with your employees or their representatives.

Employees voluntarily working longer hours

If employees voluntarily wish to work more than 48 hours a week you would have no liability under the Regulations, provided you made it clear to the employees that they are not required to work longer than 48 hours.

Time off in lieu of overtime

Some organizations have employees who are required to travel or work outside normal working hours. Compensation for these hours, where given, may be payment of overtime or by giving time off in lieu (TOIL). How to implement a TOIL policy is set out below.

Implementing a TOIL policy

1 Review existing contracts to ensure that there are no provisions preventing the introduction of time off in lieu, eg any commitment to give paid overtime.

2 Review past practice in relation to overtime and time off to ensure that there are no precedents that could give rise to any contractual entitlement.

3 Ensure that any members of staff who may be required to regularly work more than 48 hours per week sign an opt-out agreement. This will have normally been carried out under the Working Time Regulations anyway.

4 Consult staff about the proposed agreement, especially in relation to the number of hours to be carried over and the period in which any time off may be taken.

5 Ensure that the policy is coordinated with any other time off provisions, including those required by UK statute, so that the company can meet operational requirements.

6 Arrange for the recording of TOIL on existing timesheets.

Example policy for time off in lieu of overtime

The company recognizes that the nature of its work means that staff may often have to work or travel outside recognized office hours. The company also recognizes its duty to protect the health and safety of its staff by ensuring that they do not work too many hours and that they are recompensed for any extra time that they do have to work.

What is lieu time?

Lieu time is time off which you are allowed to take in lieu of overtime pay, for hours worked beyond the working day (ie evenings and weekends). Overtime is compensated only in time off, not in addition to base pay, and all references to 'overtime' in this document mean unpaid overtime.

Accrual of lieu time

1   If you need to attend an evening or weekend meeting or event in the course of your work, or have to travel outside normal working hours you should ensure that your line manager is aware of this, preferably before the date concerned, and you should record the hours worked on your time sheet.

2   Time off must be equal to time actually worked, ie there is no provision for time-and-a-half, double time, etc – if you work two hours, you can claim two hours' lieu time, regardless of the day or time that the work is actually carried out.

Redemption of overtime

1   Lieu time should be taken in the same month that it is accrued, and not carried forward from month to month. If this is not possible, it must be taken within the following two months. Lieu time accrued and not redeemed as outlined will be lost.

2   No more than 15 hours' lieu time may be accrued in any one month.

3   Use of lieu time must be clearly marked on your time sheet.

4   Reasonable notice should be given to your line manager when lieu time is to be taken, and it is your responsibility to ensure that the proposed time off fits with your work commitments, etc.

5   Line managers have the discretion to vary these arrangements to suit operational requirements.

Annual holidays

Apart from the requirement under the Working Time Regulations to give all employees a minimum of 5.6 weeks' paid holiday a year, it is for you to decide the company's policy on annual holidays. You can also decide the arrangements for booking holidays. If you are likely to require staff to take their holidays at certain times of the year you should take care to ensure that this is specifically referred to in the employment contract.

Any holiday pay should be equivalent to the employee's normal pay including commission and any overtime that cannot be refused (though technically this only applies to the 20 days guaranteed under the European Working Time Directive).

Employees do not have any legal right to carry over unused annual holiday from one holiday year to another, or to receive payment in lieu of holidays, except when leaving the company.

Parental leave

Employees with at least one year's service and who are parents of children under 5 years of age are entitled to 18 weeks' unpaid leave up to the child's fifth birthday for each child. You can agree with the employees the amount of leave to be taken at any one time, but if you do not have any such agreement you will have to apply what is called the 'fall back' scheme. Under this scheme employees can take parental leave in blocks of one week or more, subject to a maximum of four weeks in any one year. Any such request for leave should generally be made 21 days before the date on which it is due to begin. You have the right to postpone the leave for up to six months if the business is likely to be unduly disrupted by the employee's absence.

During the period of the absence the employee maintains full employment rights and is entitled to return to the same job.

You are entitled to ask for reasonable evidence of an employee's responsibility for a child and the date of birth of that child.

Parents of disabled children have the right to 18 weeks' leave up to the child's 18th birthday.

Sunday working

Staff working in shops, including betting shops and racecourses, cannot be forced to work on Sundays. If they have previously agreed to do so they can opt out by giving you three months' notice in writing of their intention not to work on Sundays. Any disciplinary action by you against employees protected in this way, or who have opted out of Sunday working, would be automatically unfair.

Employment of schoolchildren

You may not employ any child:

- under the age of 13;
- during school hours;
- before 7.00 am or after 7.00 pm;
- for more than two hours on a school day;
- for more than two hours on a Sunday.

Flexible working arrangements

Flexible working

From 30 June 2014 the rules relating to flexible working changed. Prior to that date only parents of children under the age of 17 (or 18 if the child is disabled) and certain carers could submit a request to work flexibly. Now every employee has the statutory right to request flexible working after 26 weeks of employment.

The right is not to work flexibly but to request flexible working. Eligible employees can request a change to working hours, working time or working location. This includes a wide range of working patterns, such as job sharing, working from home, part-time working, compressed hours and flexitime. The employee must have 26 weeks' continuous employment and must not have made a flexible working request in the past 12 months.

There is no set procedure for dealing with a request for flexible working but there is a duty on employers to deal with requests in a 'reasonable manner'. The request can only be rejected on one or more of eight business grounds where agreeing to the request might result in:

- additional costs;
- an effect on the ability to meet customer demand;
- inability to reorganise work among existing staff;
- inability to recruit new staff;
- a detrimental impact on quality;
- a detrimental impact on performance;
- insufficiency of work during period of work proposed by the employee; or
- planned structural changes.

All requests, including any appeals, must be considered and decided on within a period of three months from first receipt, unless an extension is agreed. The request can be treated as withdrawn if the employee, without good reason, fails to attend two consecutive meetings to discuss the request or an appeal.

Where multiple requests are received each should be dealt with on its own merits which may require a value judgement to be made. Requests should be treated on a first-come-first-served basis which could mean that some less meritorious claims take priority over later, but more deserving, ones. It will also need to be borne in mind that having agreed to a flexible working request the business context will have changed for any subsequent ones.

Bring Your Own Device (BYOD)

Bring Your Own Device (BYOD) is the practice of employees using their own laptops, phones and tablets to conduct business at work. With the expansion of home and flexible working, security risks have increased with staff using their own devices and the Government has now published a set of guidance notes on managing these risks. These set out best practice in ensuring that personal devices do not access sensitive data and that employees are not able to compromise security by finding ways around the controls. The guidance should be read together with the Information Commissioner's BYOD data security guidance published in March 2013.

Part-time workers

A part-time worker is any worker who does not work as many hours as your full-time workers. The general rule is that you should treat part-timers no less favourably than full-time workers. This means that they should receive exactly the same pay and benefits as full-time employees in comparable jobs, applied on a pro rata basis where appropriate. They should also be given the same opportunities for promotion and training and development.

Job-sharing

Job-sharing arises when two employees voluntarily share the responsibilities of one full-time job.

Contracts

In preparing a contract for job-sharers you will need to incorporate the following additional clauses:

- that an offer to one person is conditional on the other also accepting it;
- the days and hours to which the job-share relates;
- how entitlement to public holidays will be decided;
- that if one job-sharer leaves and a replacement cannot be found the remaining job-sharer will have to convert to full-time working or may instead be dismissed.

Terminating employment

If one job-sharer leaves, any dismissal of the remaining job-sharer will only be fair provided:

- the remaining job-sharer is consulted about the action to be taken;
- that person is offered the additional work;
- an attempt is made to find a replacement job-sharer;
- an assessment is made of whether the business requirements are such that full-time coverage is necessary;
- you consider whether the work undertaken by the person who has left can be carried out in some other way;
- you try to find alternative work for the remaining employee;
- dismissal is the last resort, once all other arrangements have been explored.

Holidays

One of the main complexities with job-sharing is how to deal with public holidays, especially when one job-sharer works all Mondays when most public holidays occur. Probably the simplest option is to allocate each employee an additional amount of annual holiday equivalent to the total number of public holidays, with the job-sharer who would usually be working on the day the bank holiday falls having that day deducted from the annual entitlement.

Homeworkers

Working from home has become more common in recent years and it can offer employees a lot more flexibility, particularly if they have family responsibilities. If you are considering employing homeworkers there are a number of key issues to be addressed:

- How will you ensure that homeworkers are given equal opportunities for promotion, training and bonuses?
- How will you measure and reward performance?
- How will you ensure participation in company and union activities?
- What changes do you need to make to the contract of employment?
- How will you monitor working hours, holidays, sickness and time off?
- Do you need to change any of your employment policies and procedures to ensure equal access to these?
- What are your health and safety responsibilities to homeworkers and what actions do you need to take to cover yourself?
- How do you need to modify your recruitment and selection processes to ensure that you select staff with the appropriate skills and attitudes?

You have to ensure that all your employment policies and procedures are sufficient to provide statutory safeguards and to ensure continued employee motivation and performance. The implications of homeworking for your policies and procedures are summarized in Table 8.1.

TABLE 8.1 Implications of homeworking on employment policies and procedures

Policies and procedures	Implications
Equal opportunities policy	You need to ensure that all staff are given the option of homeworking, not just those with family responsibilities. You need to ensure that all staff have equal access to promotion, training and bonus opportunities, especially if one particular group, for example women, is over-represented. Good opportunity for using staff who may acquire a disability.
Disciplinary rules	Will generally be the same but some may not apply, for example dress code, and others may need to be inserted.
Disciplinary procedure	Generally, no change.
Grievance procedure	Generally, no change.
Maternity leave	This is a statutory right so will apply as normal. You need to ensure that there is a formal process for notifying return to work. You need to ensure that no work is done in the two weeks following childbirth.
Maternity pay	This is a statutory right so will apply as normal.
Holidays	Generally, no change.
Hours of work	You need either to ensure that staff do not work more than 48 hours per week or that they sign an opt-out. They must also be given breaks at least every six hours. Homeworkers may have to provide time sheets.
Paternity leave	This is a statutory right applying equally to homeworkers.
Statutory paternity pay	This is a statutory right applying equally to homeworkers.
Adoption leave	This is a statutory right applying equally to homeworkers.

TABLE 8.1 *continued*

Policies and procedures	Implications
Parental leave	This is a statutory right applying equally to homeworkers. Office-based employees may view this as unduly generous to homeworkers.
Time off for dependants	This is a statutory right applying equally to homeworkers.
Other time off	Generally, no change. Again may be viewed as generous by office-based staff.
Sick pay	Generally, no change.
Job descriptions	May need to be modified as certain duties and responsibilities arise from working in an office environment.
Person specifications	Will need to be modified to reflect characteristics required of someone who may be deemed suitable for homeworking. Different competencies are likely to be required.
Selection process	Selection tests will need to establish suitability for homeworking.
Pay	If office staff receive luncheon vouchers or benefit from a subsidized canteen should homeworkers be given a commensurate allowance? Regional weighting allowances are likely to need adjusting. Where overtime or shift pay is given there will need to be processes for managing these. Bonuses and PRP will need to be applied equally to homeworkers and office staff but with greater emphasis on IPRP with the former. Performance measures may need to vary (for example team-working will not apply to homeworkers but may be part of an incentive scheme for office staff). Job evaluation factors and related grades/pay ranges may be affected. There is a need to ensure that there are no equal value problems.

TABLE 8.1 *continued*

Policies and procedures	Implications
Benefits	Most benefits should be unaffected, although some will not apply to homeworkers, for example season ticket loans.
Union membership	Arrangements must be made to ensure that homeworkers have equal rights in terms of union membership. This is mainly the responsibility of the union but it could become critical in the event of a dispute about union recognition where the 'appropriate bargaining unit' is in dispute.
Employee relations	Similar considerations to above, but where partnership arrangements are in place processes will need to be introduced to ensure active participation of homeworkers.
Health and safety	There will be a need to carry out an initial health and safety audit to ensure that the working conditions and equipment are suitable and there are minimal risks to health. You will need to check that insurance cover is adequate for any equipment used and that there are no mortgage or local authority restrictions. You must keep lists of outworkers and send this information to the local authority twice a year and to the Health and Safety Inspector if requested (Factories Act 1961).

Employer's checklist on homeworking

The following checklist may help ensure that you have taken all appropriate actions when considering the employment of homeworkers.

Checklist on homeworking

Equal opportunities. Do you have systems and procedures that ensure that office and home-based staff have the same conditions of employment and equal access to opportunities for promotion, training and development?

Recruitment. Have you adapted your recruitment and selection processes to ensure that those selected for homeworking have the required skills, attitudes and competencies?

Hours of work. Have you introduced procedures to ensure that the hours of work of homeworkers are monitored?

Reward structure. Have you developed reward systems that reflect the differences between homeworkers and office-based staff, and that provide homeworkers with incentives and participation in company bonus schemes?

Disciplinary rules. Have your disciplinary rules been adapted for homeworkers?

Union recognition. Have you identified the appropriate bargaining unit for homeworkers for the purposes of union recognition? How are homeworkers catered for in your participation arrangements?

Health and safety. Have you undertaken a risk assessment and health and safety audit of your homeworkers' working environment? What guidance have you issued?

Insurance. Is the appropriate home insurance in place?

Notification. Have you notified the local authority?

Further information

ACAS Code of Practice on handling in a reasonable manner requests to work flexibly
BIS website: www.bis.gov.uk
Homeworking – a guide for employers and employees: www.acas.org.uk/flexibleworking
The right to request flexible working: An ACAS guide
Working Time Regulations 1998

Writing a Staff Handbook

09

Most companies will want to produce a staff handbook that gives details of all the terms and conditions and benefits applying to staff. Much of this information is often too detailed and lengthy to be included in any offer letter or written statement of particulars of employment.

This chapter describes some of the main areas that are usually included within any staff handbook and gives extensive examples of what this content would typically look like. This is not intended to be a comprehensive summary of everything that could be included in a staff handbook, as this is primarily a matter of choice for the company in question.

The subjects most frequently covered in staff handbooks are:

- welcome and introduction to the company;
- mission statement and values;
- product or service information;
- terms and conditions of employment;
- the induction process;
- ethical considerations, for example gifts, confidentiality and conflicts of interest;
- limits of authority, particularly in terms of finance;
- holiday and leave provisions;
- termination of employment;
- outside employment;
- disciplinary and grievance procedures;
- pay and benefits, including bonuses, loans, cash awards and so forth;
- car policy;
- share options;
- pension scheme;
- travel and business expenses;

- performance appraisal;
- staff development;
- intellectual property;
- use of computers and e-mail;
- equal opportunities policy;
- harassment policy;
- whistle-blowing policy;
- health and safety, including policies on smoking, fire safety, first aid, AIDS, use of drugs and so forth;
- personnel records;
- employee communications;
- trade union membership;
- dress code;
- charitable giving;
- names of relevant people in the company.

Welcome to the company

The first section of any handbook should comprise some kind of welcoming note, a description of how the handbook should be used and the name of the person in the company whom the employee should contact for further information or assistance. The wording could be along the following lines, although it should obviously be adapted to suit your circumstances:

I am pleased to welcome you to the company and hope that your association with ...
is a long and happy one. This handbook is provided for your guidance and information and describes the terms and conditions applying to your employment with the company. These, together with your letter of appointment and written statement of particulars, form part of your contract of employment. You will be notified in writing of any changes to these terms and conditions.

If you require any further information, or would like anything explained in more detail, you should contact ....

Background information

The next section of the handbook should contain information about the company. In particular, you may wish to include information about:

- the company's history, including how and when it was formed;
- the company's mission statement and values;
- the company's climate and culture (what it is like to work in the company);

- how the company is organized;
- company size, location and associated ventures;
- key personnel in the company;
- future aims.

Terms and conditions of employment

Salaries

In this section you should set out, more or less, the same information set out in the offer letter or written particulars of employment (apart from the precise salary offered to an individual). The wording is likely to be similar to the following:

Salaries are paid monthly in arrears, on the 25th of each month, by direct transfer to your bank/building society account.

Your salary will be reviewed on a regular basis, and at least annually. Any such review is entirely at the company's discretion. In carrying out any review we will take account of your performance and that of the company as a whole, as well as any other relevant factors. However, there is no guarantee that salaries will be increased at any particular time.

Expenses

You should include any rules about expenses. A typical clause is:

The company will reimburse you for reasonable expenses incurred by you arising from your employment. Claims must be authorized by your line manager and supported by the production of valid receipts or such other documentary evidence as the company may require from time to time. You must also comply with the company's procedure for claiming expenses.

Benefits

You need to describe the main benefits provided by the company such as a pension, company car, share options, bonuses, medical insurance and any conditions attached to them. In the case of a pension you may have to refer the employees to the pension provider for more information.

Mobility

You may need to give more information about any mobility requirements contained in the job. An example of the type of wording that might be appropriate is as follows:

Your normal place of work is set out in your contract of employment.

The company has the right, as a term of your employment, to change your normal place of work to any other company premises. If we do so, you may, at our discretion, be entitled to financial or other relocation benefits.

You may from time to time be required to work at other locations throughout the UK and Europe depending on business requirements. Appropriate travel and accommodation arrangements will be made in such circumstances. We may also need you to work outside the UK for periods of more than one month and, if we do so, we will let you know the length of your stay abroad, the currency in which you will be paid, any benefits in kind you will receive while abroad, and the terms and conditions of your relocation package. We will also give you details of the terms and conditions applying to your return to the UK.

Hours of work

You should explain in detail any rules and regulations applying to hours of work. An example of a section of this kind is set out below:

The normal working week is 35 hours and the hours of work are from 9.00 am to 5.00 pm, with a one-hour break for lunch. However, you are expected to work such additional hours as are reasonably necessary to perform your duties, without additional pay.

The Working Time Regulations provide that average working time, including overtime, must not exceed 48 hours for each seven-day period (to be averaged over a period of 17 weeks) unless you agree that this provision should not apply to your employment. You will usually be asked to agree that this provision should not apply to your employment with the company.

At any time during your employment either you or the company may give three months' notice in writing that the opt-out from the 48-hour limit shall cease to apply with effect from the expiry of that notice.

The company will monitor your working time in accordance with the requirements of the Working Time Regulations and to ensure that your health and safety are protected. It will monitor working time primarily by when you enter and leave the company's offices. For the purpose of these Regulations, the meaning of 'working time' is all the time between your entering and leaving the company's offices.

You must let us know if there is any other time that you consider should be treated as 'working time' and you must keep records of it.

You must comply with any requests made, or measures imposed, to enable the company to monitor your 'working time', which will be primarily through our existing time sheet and office systems. Failure to do so will be a disciplinary offence.

If you have any concerns about the number of hours you are working, they may be raised with your manager, on a completely confidential basis, who will take whatever steps are necessary to address the situation.

Holidays

You should describe the holiday entitlement for employees and particularly any rules relating to the taking of holidays, payment in lieu and carrying over of any entitlement from one year to the next. The section should also cover how any entitlement to outstanding holiday not taken will be dealt with on termination of employment. An example is set out below:

Your holiday entitlement is 20 working days in addition to public and bank holidays in any calendar year. You also earn an additional day of holiday for every completed year of service up to a maximum of 25 days. Your holiday accrues at the rate of 1.67 days per month.

If you joined part-way through the year you will only be entitled to holiday that accrues in the remainder of that holiday year.

If you leave part-way through the year, holiday entitlement will be calculated on the basis of the part of the year worked, and you will either receive pay in lieu of those days that are untaken at the date of leaving or, alternatively, if you have exceeded the amount of holiday to which you are entitled, pay in lieu of the excess days will be deducted from your final salary or repaid by you.

Holidays cannot be carried forward from one year to the next, without the company's written consent.

All requests for holidays should be approved in advance by your line manager. All holiday requests should be approved at least one week in advance.

If you are ill while on holiday the days of absence will only be treated as sick leave, rather than holiday, if you produce medical certificates as evidence of your illness.

Time off for dependants

There is a statutory entitlement to time off to care for dependants. You should describe the company's arrangements for administering the rules relating to this time off. An example is set out below:

Although all employees have an entitlement to paid holidays it is recognized that there may be occasions when unpaid leave, with or without notice, may be required to deal with an emergency involving a dependant. We will give you a reasonable amount of time off when such an unexpected or sudden problem arises, for example when a dependant falls ill or if a childminder fails to turn up.

You should notify your supervisor as soon as possible about any such absence, including the reason for it and how long you expect to be away from work.

Parental leave

There is a statutory entitlement to parental leave. You should set out the company's rules relating to the taking of this leave. An example is set out below:

Once you have completed one year's service you are entitled to a maximum of 18 weeks' unpaid parental leave for any child under 5 years of age. This is subject to the production of a birth certificate in the parents' names or other evidence of parental responsibility.

You may take this leave at any time in the year, up to a maximum of four weeks in any one year, and you must give at least 21 days' notice of the required dates. The company reserves the right to postpone the leave for up to six months for operational reasons, although we will try to be as flexible as possible.

For adopted children (subject to the production of documentation) there is an entitlement to 18 weeks' leave to be taken within the first five years after the date of adoption or until the child's 18th birthday.

On recruitment, where it is known that there is a child or children under 5 (or adopted) you must declare how much parental leave has been taken with any previous employer in respect of each child. This will be checked with them.

Any abuse of this benefit is likely to be treated as gross misconduct and could lead to dismissal without notice.

Bereavement leave

Any entitlement to compassionate or bereavement leave should be described. An example is:

> You are allowed a day off with pay to attend the funeral of a close relative (such as a parent, grandparent, husband/wife, brother or sister) plus an additional three days' compassionate leave with pay. Any other compassionate leave must be agreed with your supervisor and will be unpaid.

Absence

You should describe in this section any rules relating to the reporting and control of sickness absence. An example is set out below:

> If you have to be absent from work for any reason, you should contact your supervisor as early as possible, preferably within one hour of your normal start time, and no later than 10.30 am, on the first day of absence, to let him/her know.
>
> If you are absent because of illness, you should give an indication of the nature of your illness and how long you think you are likely to be away from work. You should contact us yourself, but if, exceptionally, you are unable to do so you should get someone to telephone on your behalf as soon as possible. If you are away for more than one day you should contact us on a daily basis.
>
> You are required to provide a certificate for any period of sick leave in excess of four days. Where the illness is no more than seven days in total this may simply be a statement from you that you have been ill. Beyond seven days, you must provide us with a medical certificate from your GP. When deciding what sort of certificate you need to provide us with, you should bear in mind that weekends and bank holidays count as days of absence.
>
> You will receive statutory sick pay, in accordance with the statutory rules during any period of sickness absence. Any additional payment will be at the company's discretion and will depend on your individual circumstances.
>
> The company may require you to be examined by a doctor of our choice and at our expense and you will be required to agree that the company can have access to the medical report produced as a result of that examination.

Maternity and paternity

You should set out details of any maternity, paternity and parental leave policies. There are legal requirements about the amount of maternity, paternity and parental leave and pay to which employees are entitled, but employers often give more than the minimum entitlement. Your company's policy, and any conditions attached to it, should be set out in this section. An example of a maternity policy is set out in Chapter 7.

Disciplinary procedure

The disciplinary procedure will usually be too lengthy to be contained within the written statement of employment particulars and should therefore be described in detail in the handbook. An example of a disciplinary procedure is set out in Chapter 12.

Grievance procedure

Any grievance procedure should be set out in the staff handbook if it is not already fully contained within the written statement of particulars. For small companies this procedure can frequently be summarized in one sentence and can therefore easily be contained within the written statement. An example of a grievance procedure is set out in Chapter 13.

Confidential information

Any company will have a certain amount of commercial and other information that it will want to safeguard. The rules relating to the treatment of such information can be set out in the handbook. An example is set out below.

During your employment with the company you will acquire or have access to information in written, verbal or electronic form relating to the company, its customers, suppliers, employees and so forth, and to products and processes. Some of this information will be confidential in nature, and although this will depend on the circumstances, if you are in any doubt you should treat any such information as confidential. Examples of the type of information that the company will generally consider to be confidential are set out below, although this list is not intended to be exhaustive:

Technical information relating to the company's products and processes or arising from the company's research and development activities.

Information relating to the company that will not be generally known to the company's competitors such as any business plans, pricing information, customer data, etc.

Personnel information relating to the company's staff.

Any internal incidents or conversations relating to company staff, customers, directors, suppliers, guests, visitors and so forth that you might hear about or witness during your employment and which could potentially damage the company or anyone associated with the company.

Information described as confidential by the company.

Information about the company's business dealings must be kept confidential unless you have express permission from a company director to disclose the information. You will also be required, if requested by the company, to sign an agreement with a customer or potential customer not to disclose any confidential information relating to that customer if they make such a request.

You must not disclose any confidential information in any form about the company, its directors, employees, contractors, customers or any other persons or organizations connected with the company to any third party either during your employment or afterwards without the written agreement of the company.

Any breach of this policy during employment will be treated as gross misconduct.

Intellectual property

Any invention by an employee belongs to that employee unless it arose directly out of the work that person was required to do. You may therefore wish to make it clear that any inventions arising in the course of employment belong to the company. The following example seeks to do this:

> While you are employed by the company it is a term of your employment that the work you produce belongs to the company. You must disclose and deliver to the company all information developed or discovered by you working alone, or with others, during the course of your employment.
>
> You must also waive any rights to such material and give the company control over how it is used in the future, without any further reference to you. This obligation continues following the termination of your employment for whatever reason.

Restrictions during and after employment

Exclusive employment

You may wish to discourage your employees from taking second or other jobs while they are in your full-time employment, not least because they might then end up working more than the 48-hour limit set out in the Working Time Regulations. An example of a clause aiming to do this is set out below:

> You are a full-time employee of the company and must therefore devote the whole of your working time and energies to the company's business. You should not take on any employment outside the company without the express permission of one of the directors.

Restrictive covenant

Most companies will wish to protect their commercial interests following the departure of an employee. This most commonly means trying to prevent that person from setting up in competition or using company products and information for the benefit of a competitor. The main problem with any such restriction is that you cannot seek to prevent someone from earning a living and so any restrictions should be no more than is reasonable to protect your interests. These particular restrictive covenants or restraint of trade clauses are often contained in the written statement of employment particulars, particularly for senior jobs. An example of a restrictive covenant is set out below.

The company will require you to agree that you will not:

1 During your employment, and for a period of six months after the date of termination of your employment, for any reason, have any commercial involvement in any capacity in any business that competes with the company without the written consent of a director of the company.

2 For the six months following the date of termination of your employment for any reason, solicit or offer employment to any of the company's employees.

3 For the six months following the date of termination of your employment for any reason, directly or indirectly, try to solicit or entice away anyone who has been a customer of the company and with whom you have had personal dealings during your employment, or to try to persuade them to cease, reduce or adversely affect their business with the company.

You will also be required to agree that you will not: a) during or after your employment with the company make or publish any derogatory or disparaging statement about the company, or any of its officers or employees; b) without the company's prior written consent, at any time during or after your employment with the company, disclose information obtained from a third party and which you know to be confidential, or use any material for which the company or its customers or suppliers owns the copyright.

You must also agree to notify any new employer of the restrictions contained in this agreement and the company reserves the right to do so in any case.

You are required to agree that the restrictions set out above are reasonable and necessary for the protection of the company. If any restriction on its own is considered by a court to go beyond what is reasonable to protect the legitimate business interests of the company, but would be considered reasonable if amended, these clauses will still apply with those amendments.

Company property

You may wish to incorporate a clause relating to the return of company property on leaving the company. The following is an example:

> You are responsible for any company property issued to you and must ensure that you take all necessary precautions to prevent loss or damage. You should immediately report any such loss or damage to the company.
>
> When you leave the company you must return all company property including any confidential information, equipment, lists of customers, internal procedures, correspondence and any other information relevant to the business, in whatever form it is held. You must return any company vehicle together with keys, and any car telephone and any personal or notebook computers that are the property of the company. You must not keep any copies of any company documents or information received or created during and in connection with your employment, in whatever form held, and must not allow them to be used by any other person.

Gifts

A satisfied customer will often want to give some small gift as a token of satisfaction with the service provided and equally, a potential contractor may wish to give a gift as an inducement. It is wise to have a clear policy on this so that staff know how to react in either circumstance. An example is set out below:

> You must not accept any gifts, entertainment or other favours, other than those that it would be discourteous to refuse and which are of nominal value, from any third party with which the company has had business dealings. You should report any such offer to your line manager.

Bribery Act 2010

Following the introduction of The Bribery Act 2010, effective from 1 July 2011, you should have an anti-corruption policy that is made known to all employees and which should be incorporated into any staff handbook, employment contracts and disciplinary rules.

Equal opportunities policy

There are strong legal safeguards against discrimination on a range of grounds including sex, race, religion or belief, age, disability, etc. To ensure that you do not infringe the law and that you treat all staff fairly, you should have an equal opportunities policy. An example is set out in the extract below.

Equal opportunities policy

It is the policy of the company to give equal opportunity in employment regardless of sex, marital status, sexual orientation, race, ethnic origin, religion or belief, age, trade, union membership or non-membership or disability. This applies to recruitment, training, pay, conditions of employment, allocation of work and promotion.

Implementation

As an equal opportunity employer our key criterion for selection, promotion, training and reward is ability to do the job to the required standard. For this reason we will not discriminate on any grounds unrelated to performance, regardless of whether these are prohibited by law. Discrimination includes discrimination by association, for example where a person is discriminated against because of their association with someone who has one of the protected characteristics defined by the Equality Act 2010.

It is your personal responsibility as an employee to ensure that this policy is followed. Any questions or doubts about the application of the policy should be referred to your line manager.

The policy applies not only to our staff but also to our relationships with our customers and suppliers.

If you feel that you have been discriminated against you should raise the matter through the grievance procedure.

Discipline

Your cooperation is essential in ensuring the success of this policy. Discriminatory actions or behaviour by employees will be treated as serious misconduct and could lead to dismissal.

Health and safety policy

The staff handbook is the ideal place to describe your health and safety policy. What you actually put into the policy will depend largely on the nature of your business, with those companies working in a manufacturing or similar environment, or operating potentially dangerous machinery, plant and processes requiring much more detail in their policy than would apply in a typical office environment. Generally, however, it might contain information and procedures relating to first aid, accidents at work, fire safety, risk assessment and so forth.

Smoking at work

Smoking at work is illegal in Scotland, Wales and England. A policy on smoking at work can be contained within that on health and safety, but making it a separate document highlights it. An example is set out below:

> Smoking is not permitted in any of our offices or other premises.
> This applies to staff at all levels in the company and regardless of their office location.
> Visitors to the company, including actual and potential customers, should be asked to observe the company's rules in this respect.
> Any infringement of this policy could lead to disciplinary action.

Harassment policy

(See also Chapter 13.) Harassment of staff, which primarily means sexual or racial harassment, can potentially be very serious for the business, as well as for any employee concerned. One of the main problems is likely to be in deciding when mere banter goes beyond what may be considered to be reasonable bounds. For this reason it is a good idea to have a written policy so that there should be little doubt about what is, or is not, acceptable. An example is set out below.

Example harassment policy

Introduction

Sexual or racial harassment at work is unlawful, and both the company and the harasser may be held liable to pay damages for such unlawful actions.

The following sets out the company's policy on harassment.

Policy

The company deplores all forms of sexual or racial harassment and will seek to ensure that the working environment for staff is free from such actions. The following section gives examples of the type of behaviour that is unacceptable to the company.

You are expected to comply with this policy.

Examples of harassment

Sexual harassment can take many forms, from mild sexual banter to actual physical violence.

It is not always obvious what behaviour might constitute sexual harassment but it is up to you to try to recognize that what is acceptable to one employee may not be acceptable to another.

Sexual harassment is unwanted behaviour of a sexual nature by one employee towards another. Examples include:

insensitive jokes;

provocative comments about appearance;

threat of dismissal, loss of promotion and so forth for refusal of sexual favours.

Racial harassment can also take many forms, from relatively minor abuse to actual physical violence. Examples of racial harassment include:

insensitive jokes related to race;

deliberate exclusion from conversations;

racial abuse.

The examples above are not exhaustive. Depending on the circumstances, some types of harassment may constitute gross misconduct, punishable by summary dismissal under the company's disciplinary procedure.

Informal remedy

If you consider that you are, or have been, a victim of minor sexual or racial harassment or other intimidation you should make it clear to the alleged harasser that the behaviour is unacceptable and must stop. If you or a colleague feel unable to do this by word of mouth, then a written request (explaining the distress that the behaviour is causing) handed to the harasser may be effective. You may also discuss your complaints with your line manager, in total confidence.

Formal procedure

Where informal methods fail, or serious harassment occurs, employees should bring a formal complaint under the company's grievance procedure. The complaint should be made in writing to the Managing Director and state:

the name of the harasser;

the nature of the harassment;

dates and times when harassment occurred;

names of witnesses, if any, to any incidents of harassment;

any action already taken by the complainant to stop the harassment;

any suggested remedy.

The Managing Director will carry out a thorough investigation as quickly as possible, and in any event within two weeks, and if there is a case to answer action will be taken against the harasser under the company's disciplinary procedure.

Harassment outside work

A decision of the Employment Appeal Tribunal upheld a ruling that employers can be held liable for incidents of sexual harassment which take place at work-based social events whether or not they are outside the workplace. Accordingly, the company may take disciplinary action against anyone who subjects a member of staff to harassment outside the workplace.

Other matters

There are a number of other policies and terms of employment that could be included in any staff handbook. For further information on any particular aspect you should consult the appropriate chapter of this book. You may wish to include general information that you do not intend to be part of the employee's contract, and where this is the case it should be made clear. This might apply, for example, to information about sports and social facilities. You should remember that written policies and agreements made collectively are all part of an employee's contract of employment.

When you are preparing a handbook it is probably a good idea to produce a draft that can be discussed with managers and staff. When you are happy that the content is appropriate and readily understood, the handbook can then be suitably bound and circulated. Once it has been produced, you will need to ensure that it is kept up to date, and for this reason it is probably sensible to keep it in a loose-leaf binder.

Further information

Essential Facts – Employment (2013) Croner, Kingston upon Thames, Surrey
The Bribery Act 2010
The Equality Act 2010

Personnel Records and Data Protection

10

Personnel records

Every company needs to keep records of its employees. Not only are these in many cases a legal requirement, but without personal information about employees it would be extremely difficult for you to manage a company. You need to keep such records to:

- provide a store of personal information about individual employees;
- assist in planning the company's future people requirements;
- help in the recruitment and selection process;
- provide training and development information;
- provide information to help in performance appraisal;
- provide information for pay purposes;
- provide general employment information for dealing with such issues as changes to terms and conditions of employment, relocation, redundancy and disciplinary procedures;
- provide information for health, safety and welfare;
- provide information for statutory returns.

The main information you should keep for each employee includes:

- personal details of the employee including address and contact details, next of kin, National Insurance number, etc;
- bank account details for payment of salary;
- the employee's employment history;
- details of the job, including job title, function, location, grade and so forth;
- the terms and conditions attached to the job;

- the employee's absence record;
- the employee's disciplinary record;
- any training given to the employee;
- any performance appraisal information;
- job evaluation data.

You should be able to analyse the information in various ways, for example by age, length of service, pay rate and sex. You should also keep information on the ethnic origin of employees and whether any are registered as disabled. You should also be able to summarize information about labour turnover, retention rates, absence, time-keeping, salary and wage costs, and accidents.

You should, of course, keep personal files confidential and although the Data Protection Act 1998 gives employees the right of access to personal information held about them, this does not necessarily mean that they can have unrestricted access to the whole personal file (see below).

Human Resource Information Systems

The management of employee data can be incorporated within a computerized Human Resource Information System (HRIS). There are many of these systems on the market and the most comprehensive ones will enable you to manage combined functions including those relating to:

- personal information on employees;
- payroll data including pay progression, grades and bonuses, etc;
- staff benefits;
- terms and conditions of employment;
- attendance and sickness records;
- holidays and time off;
- performance, training and development plans;
- disciplinary action and grievances;
- resource planning and employee potential;
- recruitment processes;
- knowledge management.

In selecting such a system the critical issue is to decide what you actually require, and then to assess the capability of the system to deliver this.

Data protection

The Data Protection Act 1998 came into effect on 1 March 2000. The Act regulates the use of personal data and gives individuals the right of access to that data as well as requiring the holders of such data to be open about its use and to follow certain principles in how that information is obtained, used and stored. Whereas the earlier 1984 Act related only to data held on a computer, this later Act applies to manual records as well.

Those about whom information is held are referred to as 'data subjects' and those who hold and control the data are described as 'data controllers'. As an employer you will be a data controller, although it is common for companies to appoint one person who has responsibility for implementing the Act.

Personal data comprises any information held about an individual. This need not be particularly sensitive information and could just be a name and address to fall within the definition.

Personal files

As an employer, the two most important considerations for you to bear in mind are that employees have a right to any information held about them and also that those employees must have given permission for such information to be held. Although it is not entirely clear that an employee has an automatic right of access to his personal file, it is probably wise to assume that he does.

Data protection principles

Any personal data you hold must conform to the following eight principles:

1 The data must have been obtained fairly and lawfully and the employee must have agreed to data being held and processed.

2 The data must be held only for specific and lawful purposes and not processed in any manner incompatible with those purposes.

3 The data should be relevant, adequate and not excessive for the purposes for which it is used.

4 It should be accurate and kept up to date.

5 It should not be kept for any longer than is necessary.

6 It should be processed in accordance with the rights of people under the Act.

7 Measures should be taken to guard against unauthorized or unlawful processing of personal data and against its accidental loss, destruction or damage.

8 Personal data should not be transferred to a country or territory outside the European Economic Area, unless that country or territory provides an adequate level of protection.

Individual right of access

An employee has the right to be given a copy of any personal data held and processed by the employer and can ask for the removal or correction of any inaccurate data. You must respond within 40 days of receiving such a request provided that:

- the request is in writing;
- any fee requested (up to a maximum of £10) has been paid;
- the employee has supplied any information that is required to confirm his identity and the location of the relevant information;
- you have not already complied with an identical or similar request by the same individual, except after a reasonable interval has elapsed.

Exemptions

There are some exemptions from these provisions including:

- references given by you;
- references received if disclosure would give information about another individual, unless that third party had consented to the disclosure;
- where the disclosure of data might be likely to prejudice the conduct of your business, such as if there are proposed redundancies or mergers;
- if disclosure would be likely to give away your negotiating position, for example in relation to salary negotiations;
- personal data disclosed for the purpose of legal proceedings in relation to legal rights;
- data that might compromise national security or hamper detection of crime and tax evasion, etc.

As indicated above, for information about individuals to be legitimately held you need to get the permission of those individuals to the holding of this data. Probably the best way of doing this is to incorporate an appropriate clause in the contract of employment (see the example written statement of particulars in Chapter 2).

Sensitive personal data

Some information is categorized as sensitive personal data. This includes any data relating to:

- ethnic or racial origin;
- political opinions;
- religious beliefs or other beliefs of a similar nature;
- trade union membership;
- physical or mental health;
- sex life;
- the commission or alleged commission by the employee of any criminal offence;
- any proceedings arising from a criminal offence or alleged offence or the result of such proceedings.

Sensitive personal data such as those itemized can only be held with the express consent, ideally in writing, of the employee concerned, unless you need the information to comply with a statutory requirement. If you require this sensitive personal data to be held you must be very clear in explaining the reasons for doing so and ensuring that you get the individual's consent.

Ensuring compliance with data protection principles

To ensure that you comply with the requirements of the Data Protection Act you should:

- decide what information needs to be kept in personnel records;
- notify employees of what information is held and the reasons for holding it;
- appoint someone as data controller;
- clarify the rules about access to data;
- ensure that confidentiality is maintained;
- ensure that information that is kept is accurate and up to date;
- review existing forms such as application forms to ensure that the information requested is justified;
- make unauthorized disclosure of confidential information a disciplinary offence;
- train line managers in the implications of data protection.

Notification

If you keep personal information about living individuals on a computer it is likely that you will need to notify the Information Commissioner. You can check whether you need to do so with the Commissioner either through the internet or by telephone (enquiry line: 0303 123 1113).

Data protection policy

It is a good idea to have a written policy on data protection, which could be included within the staff handbook. An example policy is set out below.

Example data protection policy

It is a legal requirement for the company to comply with the Data Protection Act 1998. It is also company policy to ensure that every employee maintains the confidentiality of any personal data held by the company in whatever form.

Data protection principles

The company needs to keep certain information about its employees, customers and suppliers for financial and commercial reasons and to enable us to monitor performance, to ensure legal compliance and for health and safety purposes. To comply with the law, information must be collected and used fairly, stored safely and not disclosed to any other person unlawfully. This means that we must comply with the Data Protection Principles set out in the Data Protection Act 1998.

These principles require that personal data must be:

obtained fairly and lawfully and shall not be processed unless certain conditions are met;

obtained for specified and lawful purposes and not further processed in a manner incompatible with that purpose;

adequate, relevant and not excessive;

accurate and up to date;

kept for no longer than necessary;

processed in accordance with data subjects' rights;

protected by appropriate security;

not transferred to a country outside the European Economic Area without adequate protection.

In processing or using any personal information you must ensure that you follow these principles at all times.

Data protection coordinator

To ensure the implementation of this policy the company has designated [job title] as the company's data protection coordinator. All enquiries relating to the holding of personal data should be referred to him/her in the first instance.

Notification of data held

You are entitled to know:

what personal information the company holds about you and the purpose for which it is used;

how to gain access to it;

how it is kept up to date;

what the company is doing to comply with its obligations under the 1998 Act.

This information is available from [job title/department].

Individual responsibility

As an employee you are responsible for:

checking that any information that you provide in connection with your employment is accurate and up to date;

notifying the company of any changes to information you have provided, for example changes of address;

ensuring that you are familiar with and follow the data protection policy.

Any breach of the data protection policy, either deliberate or through negligence, may lead to disciplinary action being taken and could in some cases result in a criminal prosecution.

Data security

You are responsible for ensuring that:

any personal data that you hold, whether in electronic or paper format, is kept securely;

personal information is not disclosed either verbally or in writing, accidentally or otherwise, to any unauthorized third party;

items that are marked 'personal' or 'private and confidential', or which appear to be of a personal nature, are opened by the addressee only.

You should not use your office address for matters that are not work-related.

Monitoring of e-mails and telephone calls

You have the right to monitor telephone calls made and e-mails sent by your staff, provided you notify them that you intend to do so. It may be advisable to incorporate a clause in the contract of employment stating this fact.

You can also monitor or record communications without the caller's consent for the purposes of:

- recording evidence of transactions;
- ensuring compliance with regulations or rules;
- gaining routine access to business communications;
- maintaining the effective operation of your systems;
- monitoring standards of service and for training purposes;
- combating crime and the unauthorized use of the system.

Developing an e-mail policy

You may consider it a wise precaution to develop an e-mail policy. If you do so, any such policy should:

- make it clear that the company owns the system;
- notify employees that they do not have an individual right to privacy when using the system;
- notify them that e-mails are likely to be monitored;
- set out permissible uses and those that are prohibited;
- prohibit the use of unauthorized passwords;
- notify employees that they must report any inappropriate use of the system.

All employees should be given a copy of the policy and be asked to sign a declaration that they have read and understood it.

An example of an e-mail and internet policy is set out below.

Example e-mail and internet policy

The use of e-mail and the internet is important for the maintenance of efficient operations and effective communications. However, their inappropriate use could lead to a loss of efficiency, personnel problems and also possible legal claims against the company. This policy sets out how these systems should be used by all employees, describes your individual responsibility and states how the company will respond to inappropriate use.

Appropriate use

When using e-mail or the internet you must comply with the following rules:

the system must only be used on authorized company business;

the style and content of any e-mails must conform to those applying to written correspondence;

e-mail should not be used as a substitute for other forms of communication that may be more effective;

where the content of any e-mail is confidential, the sender must ensure that all steps are taken to protect this confidentiality, by specifying that it is confidential and to be read only by the addressee;

passwords should be memorized and not written down;

only authorized passwords should be used;

all necessary steps must be taken to ensure that no other person has unauthorized access to your computer;

you should ensure that there is backup storage for any critical information, so that data is not lost in the event of a system failure.

Failure to follow these rules will be likely to lead to disciplinary action and could result in dismissal.

Inappropriate use

The system is not to be used for any of the following purposes:

  any messages that could be construed as bullying or harassment or as sexually or racially discriminatory;

  accessing or downloading pornography;

  online gambling;

  excessive personal use;

  downloading or distributing copyright information;

  disclosing confidential information about other employees;

  making derogatory comments about the company or its management, its customers or suppliers;

  accessing information using another person's password.

The system is the property of the company and its use will be monitored. Any misuse of the system will be subject to disciplinary action and could lead to summary dismissal. Hard copies of e-mail messages will be used as evidence.

  Any employee who has a complaint about the use of the system should raise the matter informally through his/her line manager or formally through the company's grievance procedure.

Further information

Data Protection Act 1998
Information Commissioner's Office: www.ico.org.uk

Handling Organizational Change

11

An inevitable consequence of running a business is the need to make changes from time to time. These may be to reflect changes in markets and the demand for products, developments in technology and production methods, the loss or acquisition of employees and so forth. Whatever the reason, you will at some stage find yourself having to make changes to the company's structure, processes, procedures or people, and perhaps all of them simultaneously. Any change can be unsettling for people, creating uncertainty and suspicion, and therefore has to be handled carefully.

Some of the main issues to be taken into account when implementing any organizational change are set out in this chapter.

Changes in responsibilities

You will often wish to change the responsibilities of employees, perhaps to give them additional roles reflecting changes in business requirements and the individual's own development, or possibly to transfer someone to a role to which she may be more suited. Where responsibilities are increased you need to:

- ensure that the person concerned is also given any necessary training;
- ensure that the person concerned is clear about the requirements of the new role;
- provide any necessary support in the early stages of the change, including reviewing the employee's pay package to ensure that the changes to the job are appropriately reflected;
- consider the effect of this change on other jobs.

You need to keep an eye on the situation to ensure that the new responsibilities do not create too much stress for the person concerned, because as an employer you have a duty of care to your staff, and higher levels of stress are likely to lead to higher levels of absence and staff dissatisfaction.

The other side of the coin is that you may wish to reduce someone's responsibilities, possibly because you feel that she is not up to the job or because she is overloaded. The main points to bear in mind when doing this are:

- Significant reductions in responsibility, which lower the status of the individual concerned, might be viewed as a breach of contract serious enough to allow the individual to resign and claim constructive dismissal (see Chapter 14).

- Any changes should be agreed with the employee and an amended employment contract produced.

- You may have to maintain the employee's current level of earnings for a less responsible job unless that person voluntarily agrees to a pay reduction. Imposing the changes might again be seen as a breach of contract by you.

- Where such changes are proposed for performance reasons you should ensure that you have adequate evidence to support your conclusions.

- Finally, you should ensure that any change to responsibilities does not result in an overlap or duplication with other jobs and also that no vital responsibilities are neglected in the transition.

Changes to organizational structure

When you make any changes to the structure and reporting lines in the company you should bear in mind that changing someone's reporting line, for example from reporting directly to the managing director to reporting instead to another director, might diminish the status of the individual concerned and could possibly be a breach of contract. Similarly, flattening the structure by increasing spans of control may be more efficient and lead to improved communication and swifter decision making, but it will inevitably lead to fewer promotion opportunities.

Any restructuring needs to ensure that all main responsibilities are covered but not duplicated. One way of ensuring this is to plot the main areas of responsibility against the jobs you have, perhaps by using a matrix such as the one shown in Figure 11.1. This identifies the jobs that have the main or prime responsibility for delivering key business objectives, and those that have a supporting or shared role.

Changes to processes and procedures

When you make changes to any of your internal procedures, working methods or processes you should bear in mind that:

- Any proposed changes should be first discussed with those who will be most affected by the changes and who have detailed day-to-day knowledge of how they work.

- The changes will need to be effectively communicated to anyone affected by them.

FIGURE 11.1   Accountability matrix

Job	Operations Director	Finance Director	Sales Director
Accountability			
1. Achieve production targets	P	S	S
2. Maximize sales	S	S	P
3. Research new products	S	S	P
4. Develop new markets	S	S	P
5. Maintain customer relations	S	S	P
6. Control company finances	S	P	S
7. Train and develop staff	P	S	S

P = Prime accountability, S = Shared accountability

- The staff and supervisors will need to be given the appropriate training.
- Where the changes affect working methods and the use of plant and equipment the safety implications of the changes need to be fully considered.
- If you have full consultation processes the appropriate staff representatives will need to be consulted about any proposed changes.
- The impact on productivity and earnings will need to be fully taken into account.
- The changes will need to be monitored and modified if necessary.

Obtaining commitment to change

Any change creates uncertainty and may be seen as threatening. To obtain commitment to change you should:

- consult staff as far as possible about the proposed changes;
- explain the reasons for them;
- demonstrate how they will improve matters;
- highlight the advantages to the company and the people affected;
- give safeguards to ensure that no one is adversely affected by the changes, for example by guaranteeing existing status and pay levels where possible;
- involve people as fully as possible in the change process, so that they feel that it is their process.

Introducing participation

You may wish to consider giving your employees more involvement in the running of the company, a process generally described as 'participation'. If you involve them in making decisions about the company you are likely to gain a greater degree of commitment to any changes you might propose.

To introduce participation successfully you should adopt the following approach:

- agree the aims and objectives of participation;
- consider how these affect your policies, procedures, jobs and management generally;
- show your full support for participation by both your words and actions.

Where you are involving unions in the process try to ensure that they are seen to support it. If they do not, you may have to exclude them. If they are supportive you can use any existing consultative machinery as a means of communication.

Be prepared to commit the time and resources necessary for its successful introduction and to provide any necessary training.

Relocation

There is sometimes the need to relocate staff, for example because of plant closure, centralization or decentralization of operations, to reduce costs and so forth.

Where such relocation is within the same local area there may be few problems, although you may need to consider reimbursing staff for any additional travelling costs for a certain period. However, where the relocation is to premises that are some distance away, and there is no hard and fast rule for gauging whether such a relocation is significant, you will have to discuss the change with the staff affected, taking into account their domestic circumstances, and offer them a comprehensive relocation package. Such a package would typically include:

- reimbursement of all costs associated with moving, such as legal and estate agent's fees, survey fees, insurance and removal costs;
- reimbursement of indirect costs such as new carpets and curtains or telephone installations up to a fixed limit;
- assistance with arranging a mortgage;
- payment of any excess housing costs;
- payment of a disturbance allowance;
- reimbursement of any house-hunting costs.

There are a number of relocation agencies that can assist with such a move. Staff who are unwilling or unable to relocate are, in effect, redundant, and should be offered the appropriate redundancy package.

Business transfers

The Transfer of Undertakings (Protection of Employment) Regulations 2006

These Regulations have superseded the Transfer of Undertakings (Protection of Employment) Regulations 1981 (TUPE). They are critical if you are thinking of acquiring the whole or part of another business, or if you are the target of a takeover or merger. They apply to any situation where there is a transfer of business ownership; this can include not just the sale and purchase of businesses, but also contracting out, licensing, franchising and granting of concessions. There have been further changes arising from the Collective Redundancies and Transfer of Undertakings (Protection of Employment) (Amendment) Regulations 2014 and these are set out below.

The two broad categories are business transfers and service provision changes, although some transfers will be both a business transfer and a service provision change. Where a business transfer takes place the key question is whether there is a transfer of a 'stable economic entity' that will retain its economic identity after the transfer.

To decide if there is a stable economic entity that is capable of being transferred you should consider the following factors:

- Is the type of business being conducted by the transferee (incoming business) the same as that of the transferor (outgoing business)?
- Has there been a transfer of tangible assets such as buildings and moveable property? (Not essential.)
- Have the majority of employees been taken over by the new employer?
- Have the customers been transferred?
- Is there a degree of similarity between the activities carried on before and after?

If the answer to all or several of the above questions is 'yes', it is safe to assume that there has been a transfer of a stable economic entity. The absence of a profit motive is not a determining factor.

A service provision change occurs when a client who engages a contractor to do work on its behalf is either: a) reassigning such a contract, or b) bringing the work 'in-house'. It will not be a service provision change if: a) the contract is wholly or mainly for the supply of goods for the client's use, or b) activities are carried out in connection with a single specific event or a task of short-term duration.

The Regulations provide that where a business is transferred:

- the employment contracts of employees of the former employer (the transferor) are automatically transferred to the new employer (the transferee), as are any relevant collective agreements;
- all the transferor's rights, duties, liabilities and powers connected with the employees pass to the transferee;
- dismissal of any employee where the sole or principal reason for the dismissal is the transfer will be automatically unfair, unless it can be shown that it was for an economic, technical or organizational (ETO) reason entailing a change in the workforce;

- elected employee representatives or recognized trade unions have the right to be informed and in most cases consulted, prior to the transfer taking place.

This is a complex area of law that has not been made any easier by contradictory decisions arising from the various courts. The main difficulty concerns the meaning of what constitutes an economic entity and the stage at which an employee's link with the previous company can be said to have been broken, thus enabling the new employer to change terms and conditions. Most interpretations suggest that the Regulations only apply where there has been a significant transfer of assets or a major part of the workforce. The question appears to be whether the identity of the previous company has been taken over. The Regulations would not apply, for example, to a transfer arising from a change of share ownership. If you are contemplating such a takeover the safest course would be to assume that you will not be able to change the terms and conditions of employment, including pay, of the staff transferring.

Transferors are obliged to give the transferee written information about the employees who are to transfer and all the associated rights and obligations relating to them. This information includes the identity and age of the employees who will transfer, information contained in the employees' written particulars of employment and details of any claims that the transferor reasonably believes might be brought.

If the transferor does not provide this information, the transferee may apply to an employment tribunal for such amount as it considers just and equitable. Compensation starts at a minimum of £500 for each employee in respect of whom the information was not provided or was defective.

Further information is available from **www.acas.org.uk** and **www.bis.gov.uk**. In view of the complexity of this area you should ensure that you obtain professional advice before making any final decisions.

Disclosure of information in the transfer of an undertaking

If you are proposing to transfer the ownership of your business to a third party or to take over another business, or to merge companies (and have at least 10 employees), you have a duty to inform and consult 'appropriate representatives' of any of the affected employees. These are employee representatives elected by the employees, or representatives of any recognized trade union.

However, you must consult any recognized trade union. You must let them know, well before any transfer takes place:

- the fact that a transfer is to take place;
- the approximate date of the transfer;
- the reasons for the transfer;
- the 'legal, economic and social implications' of the transfer for the affected employees;
- what actions you intend to take in relation to the employees (if no action is to be taken, they must be told of that fact).

If you are the transferor you must indicate what action the purchaser intends to take in relation to transferred staff. If the purchaser does not intend taking any action, you must notify the employees of that fact. If you are the purchaser you must give the transferor the information needed in sufficient time to be able to comply with this requirement.

You must undertake any consultation with a view to achieving an agreement. This means that you should enter full discussions to try to seek consensus about the way in which the transfer will be carried out and how it will affect employees. You must consider any representations made by appropriate representatives, reply to them and state the reasons for rejecting any of them.

In common with the consultation on redundancy, you can argue that there are special circumstances that make it not reasonably practicable to carry out consultation. However, you must take all reasonable steps to consult and the onus would be on you to prove that special circumstances prevented you from doing so. In practice, such circumstances are likely to have to be exceptional, for example where a transfer has to be kept secret to avoid commercially damaging the company.

Changes to the TUPE Regulations from 31 January 2014

The Collective Redundancies and Transfer of Undertakings (Protection of Employment) (Amendment) Regulations introduced the following changes to the TUPE Regulations effective from 31 January 2014:

- for transfers after 1 May 2014 employee liability information should be provided 28 days before the transfer, rather than 14 days as previously;
- there is scope to negotiate changes to terms and conditions that derive from a collective agreement after 12 months from the transfer date;
- dismissals arising from a change in the location of the place of work are no longer automatically unfair;
- for a service provision change to apply the services provided must be essentially the same as those provided before the change;
- dismissals will only be automatically unfair if the sole or principal reason is the transfer (previously 'a reason connected with the transfer');
- businesses with fewer than 10 employees are not required to invite the election of representatives for consultation purposes if there are no existing arrangements.

Further information will be available from the ACAS website: **www.acas.org.uk**

Further information

Cushway, B and Lodge, D (1999) *Organizational Behaviour and Design*, 2nd edn, Kogan Page, London

Department for Business Innovation and Skills (2009) Employment rights on the transfer of an undertaking: a guide to the 2006 TUPE Regulations for employees, employers and representatives, BIS, London, available at: www.bis.gov.uk

The Transfer of Undertakings (Protection of Employment) Regulations 2006 (2006) SI 2006/246, HMSO, London, available at: http://www.opsi.gov.uk/si/si200602.htm

http://www.acas.org.uk

Handling Disciplinary Issues

12

There will invariably be times when you have to take disciplinary action against staff, either because of their conduct or because of their work performance. This chapter describes what disciplinary rules should be applied, the procedure to be followed and the actions you can take.

As an employer you have an obligation to set the required standards of behaviour and performance, to ensure that these are brought to the attention of employees and to inform them what will happen if these standards are not reached.

It is also a legal obligation under the Employment Rights Act 1996 and the Employment Act 2002 for any employer to include within the written statement of employment particulars (see Chapter 2) details of any disciplinary rules that apply to the individual (or where such rules can be found – for example, in a staff handbook), to whom any appeal against disciplinary action should be made, and the procedure for doing so. Finally, it is important for any employer to follow the ACAS Code of Practice on Disciplinary and Grievance Procedures.

Disciplinary rules

Disciplinary rules govern the behaviour of employees in the workplace and help to make employees aware of the acts and omissions that might lead to disciplinary action. Once rules have been established it is important to ensure that they are applied fairly and consistently.

You should set out disciplinary rules that make it clear what standards of behaviour are required of your employees. You cannot hope to cover everything that might require disciplinary action, but you should have rules relating to:

- absence, including the rules on sickness absence and the arrangements for reporting absences;
- health and safety, including the requirements for the use of safety equipment, protective clothing, smoking, alcohol, health and hygiene, etc;
- gross misconduct, including the types of offence that the employer considers serious enough to warrant summary dismissal, ie instant dismissal without notice;

- use of company facilities and equipment, such as the extent to which employees can use the office telephone and e-mail facilities for personal reasons;
- discrimination, such as any rules describing what constitutes discriminatory behaviour or harassment;
- performance standards, such as any specific targets that might have been made part of the job requirements;
- activities that are prohibited.

You must also ensure that, whatever rules are drawn up, employees are made aware of them and have easy access to them. They should be made particularly aware of the likely consequences of breaking the rules and of actions or omissions that might constitute gross misconduct (see below).

Drawing up disciplinary rules

Disciplinary rules apply in any workplace and often they have grown up through custom and practice and been passed on by word of mouth. However, this can lead to uncertainty and it is therefore preferable that they are written down, making it easier to ensure that employees are notified of them and to prove when any breaches have occurred. The aim of these rules is not to form the basis for disciplinary action but to ensure that such action is avoided in the first place.

When drawing up a set of rules you should follow these principles:

- Ensure that the rules are written down and that employees are made fully aware of them. It is important to be able to demonstrate that a breach of the rules has occurred, especially if the result is disciplinary action.
- Ensure that all rules are non-discriminatory and are applied equally regardless of sex, sexual orientation, marital status, race, religion, disability, age, etc.
- The rules should be readily available to all employees and managers should ensure that they are made aware of and understand them.
- An explanation of the rules should be given to all new employees as part of the induction process.
- Particular care should be taken to ensure that the rules are fully understood by employees with limited knowledge of English or who have little work experience.
- When it is intended to change a rule, to introduce a new one or to remove an old one, employees should be consulted in advance and notified of any agreed changes.

Gross misconduct

You should give examples of what the organization considers to be gross misconduct. This is misconduct that is considered to be so serious that it is likely to lead to summary dismissal, which is dismissal without any prior notice or warning.

Common examples of gross misconduct are:

- theft, fraud and deliberate falsification of records;
- fighting at work;
- serious bullying or harassment;
- wilful damage to the employer's property;
- misuse of an organization's property or name;
- bringing the employer into serious disrepute;
- drunkenness or drug abuse;
- serious breaches of health and safety rules;
- serious insubordination;
- inappropriate use of the internet, e-mail or telephones;
- serious breaches of confidentiality (excluding whistle-blowing under the Public Interest Disclosure Act, 1998).

You should state that the breach of any of these rules could render the employee liable to dismissal. This is preferable to stating that any breach will lead to dismissal as this could imply an element of pre-judgement.

While the above events would be regarded as gross misconduct in most companies, there may be other matters that should also be included for your own company. An increasingly common problem where employees have access to the internet is the downloading of pornography which would be regarded as an inappropriate use of it.

You should make it clear that any list of examples of gross misconduct is for guidance and is not intended to be comprehensive.

Reviewing disciplinary rules

It is important that you review disciplinary rules periodically, especially in the light of changes to employment legislation or work practices, to ensure that they continue to be relevant and effective. Any changes to the rules should only be introduced after giving reasonable notice to employees and, where necessary, consulting employees' representatives.

You should also review disciplinary records to ensure that rules and procedures are being applied fairly and consistently and to identify any problems to be addressed. Managers and supervisors who are required to apply the disciplinary rules should be thoroughly trained in their application, the reasons for them and how to deal with any breaches.

Disciplinary procedure

The ACAS Code of Practice on Disciplinary and Grievance Procedures states that the disciplinary process (and grievance procedure) should contain the following elements:

- employers and employees should raise and deal with issues promptly;
- employers and employees should act consistently;
- employers should carry out any necessary investigations to establish the facts of the case;
- employers should inform employees of the basis of the problem and give them the opportunity to put their case before any decisions are made;
- employers should allow employees to be accompanied at any formal hearing;
- employers should allow employees to appeal against any formal decisions.

The previous Code set out a three-stage procedure, and failure to follow this could result in any tribunal award being increased by 50 per cent. The current Code, introduced in 2009 does not have this requirement but a tribunal can still adjust any awards by up to 25 per cent for unreasonable failure to comply with it. This can mean increasing the compensation payable by an employer or decreasing any award to an employee if either unreasonably fails to comply with the provisions of the Code.

To comply with the requirements of the Code, an employer investigating any disciplinary issue should:

1 establish the facts of each case;
2 inform the employee of the problem (in writing);
3 hold a meeting with the employee;
4 allow the employee to be accompanied at any disciplinary meeting that is likely to result in a warning or some other action;
5 decide on the appropriate action; and
6 provide the employee with an opportunity to appeal.

Items 2, 3 and 6 above equate to the three stages set out in the previous Code.

You should provide a copy of the disciplinary procedure to all employees, perhaps as part of the staff handbook. It is generally not considered a good idea to make the procedure part of the contract of employment because this would mean that any breach of it in dismissing an employee would be a breach of the contract, which might enable that employee to bring a claim of wrongful dismissal. However, the Employment Act 2002 makes the provision of a disciplinary procedure an implied term of the contract, so failure to provide one would be a breach of that implied term.

The general aim in any disciplinary process should be to try to avoid taking formal disciplinary action. This means that, as far as possible, matters of concern should be dealt with informally, with the employee being told what behaviour is unacceptable, or how his performance falls short of the standards required, and what he must do to remedy the position. No formal records should be kept of any informal warnings, although it is clearly sensible for any manager to keep a diary note as a reminder.

Implications for small businesses

It may not be practicable in small organizations to adopt all the good practice guidance set out in the Code and it is stated that employment tribunals will take account of an employer's size and administrative resources when deciding if that employer has acted reasonably.

An example of a disciplinary procedure based on the Code's recommendations is set out below.

Disciplinary procedure

The company recognizes that it is essential to maintain high standards of performance and behaviour. This procedure seeks to ensure fair treatment for anyone whose performance or conduct falls below those standards.

The procedure sets out the process to be followed when disciplinary action is taken. The procedure may be activated at any stage, except that the company will only proceed directly to Stage 3 – Dismissal in cases of gross misconduct.

It is our intention that wherever possible any shortcomings will be dealt with informally by your line manager and we will provide any assistance, advice or training required to achieve the necessary improvement.

General guidelines

1   You have the right to be accompanied by a colleague or a trade union representative at any meeting held under this procedure.

2   Except in more serious cases, the formal procedure will normally only be activated once the informal process has failed to achieve the desired results.

3   Any complaint will be thoroughly investigated under this procedure before any action is taken, and you will be notified in writing of the nature of any such complaint and will be given the opportunity to respond.

4   You will be fully informed of the stages of the procedure and the possible consequences, and of your right of appeal.

5   If dismissal (including dismissal on grounds of capability, conduct, redundancy, or non-renewal of a fixed-term contract) or other disciplinary action short of dismissal (excluding warnings under this procedure) is contemplated, you will be notified in writing of the basis for this.

Stage 1. Written warning

If your conduct or performance does not improve following any informal warnings, or for more serious cases, you will be informed in writing of what you are alleged to have done and why this is not acceptable. You will be invited to a meeting with your line manager to discuss the position. Any allegations will be explained to you and you will have the opportunity to respond, to ask questions, present evidence, call witnesses and raise any points about information provided by witnesses.

Following this disciplinary meeting you will be sent a letter describing the outcome of the meeting. You will be asked to sign a copy of any warning letter to confirm your understanding of the content. The letter will clearly state what has to be done to remedy the position, a deadline date by which any improvements must be made and the likely consequences of failure to achieve the desired results. A copy will be held on your personal file but this will be disregarded for disciplinary purposes after six months.

Stage 2. Final written warning

If your conduct or performance does not improve following the written warning given at Stage 1, or for more serious cases, the company may have to consider issuing a final written warning. You will be invited in writing to a meeting with your line manager to discuss the position. Any allegations will be explained to you and you will have the opportunity to respond, to ask questions, present evidence, call witnesses and raise any points about information provided by witnesses.

Following this disciplinary meeting you will be sent a letter describing the outcome of the meeting. You will be asked to sign a copy of any warning letter to confirm your understanding of the content. The letter will clearly state what has to be done to remedy the position, a deadline date by which any improvements must be made and the likely consequences of failure to achieve the desired results. A copy will be held on your personal file but will be disregarded for disciplinary purposes after 12 months.

Stage 3. Dismissal

If your conduct or performance does not improve following the final written warning given at Stage 2, or for more serious cases, the company may have to consider dismissal. You will be invited in writing to a meeting with your line manager to discuss the position. Any allegations will be explained to you and you will have the opportunity to respond, to ask questions, present evidence, call witnesses and raise any points about information provided by witnesses.

Any decision to dismiss you must have the prior agreement of the Managing Director. The decision will be confirmed to you, together with details of the appeal process and the name of the person to whom any appeal should be made.

Summary dismissal

Where there has been gross misconduct the company may consider that summary dismissal may be the only reasonable option. Gross misconduct includes serious breaches of discipline such as striking another member of staff or a manager, theft or fraud, substance abuse in the workplace, etc. Summary dismissal is dismissal without notice or pay in lieu of notice.

If the company has reasonable grounds for suspecting gross misconduct, you may be suspended on full pay for a period of up to five working days while the circumstances are investigated. This investigation will be conducted by a manager not previously involved and with no direct line management responsibility for you, to ensure impartiality. This investigation will include a meeting with you and any relevant witnesses. Following the initial investigation you will be asked to attend a meeting with the manager concerned, where the findings will be reviewed and a final conclusion reached. If the case of gross misconduct is upheld you will be summarily dismissed. The decision will be confirmed to you in writing and this letter will also give details of the appeal procedure.

Appeals against disciplinary action

1   You have the right to appeal against disciplinary action taken at any stage of this procedure.

2   You have the right to be accompanied by a colleague or trade union representative at any appeal hearing.

3   Any appeal against disciplinary action must be made in writing within two weeks of the disciplinary action.

4   An appeal against any disciplinary action or dismissal should be made to the Managing Director stating the grounds of your appeal. He will carry out a full review of the facts, which may include a further meeting with you and the relevant line manager. Following this review, he will reply in writing within five working days.

Applying disciplinary rules and procedures – general guidelines

There are a number of general guidelines you should follow when applying disciplinary rules and procedures. These are as follows:

- Make sure that any disciplinary rules are set out in writing and that copies are made available to all new employees.
- Ensure that any rules are clear and unambiguous and where there is any danger that they may be misunderstood they should be clearly explained to the employees affected.
- Disciplinary rules must be applied fairly and consistently and without discriminating against any particular employee group.
- Although it is important to be consistent when applying disciplinary rules, they should not be applied too rigidly, especially where observance in the past has been relatively lax.
- Where there is believed to have been a breach of the rules the circumstances in which this has occurred should be thoroughly investigated before any action is taken.

● Any written warning should make it very clear what improvement is required and the likely consequences if this does not occur. The wording should be specific and avoid vague injunctions.

● Employees should be clear about what constitutes gross misconduct.

● Bear in mind that warnings may sometimes be implied, for example by failing to give someone a pay rise, but where it is intended that this is part of the disciplinary procedure this should be made clear in writing and the employer is obliged to follow the full written process.

● No employee should be dismissed without the sanction of a senior manager.

● Ensure that all managers and supervisors responsible for the discipline of staff are trained in applying the disciplinary procedure and in conducting disciplinary investigations and hearings.

● Review procedures regularly to ensure that they still meet the needs of the company and are being applied fairly.

● Ensure that any disciplinary investigations are carried out as quickly as possible. Where it is decided that disciplinary action is justified, you do not have to be clear beyond any doubt about the employee's guilt but must act reasonably in the circumstances.

● Any employee subject to an investigation should be notified in writing of what he is accused of, be made aware of any evidence against him and be given a chance to explain.

● Employees have the right to be accompanied at any disciplinary meeting that might result in a disciplinary sanction.

● Any disciplinary procedure should provide a right of appeal to a more senior manager and set out the process for lodging the appeal.

The right to be accompanied

All employees have the right to be accompanied by a fellow employee or a trade union official at certain disciplinary or grievance hearings they are invited to by the employer. This right applies to any disciplinary meetings held as part of the dismissal and disciplinary procedures or which could result in:

● a formal warning being issued to the employee;

● some other disciplinary action including, for example, suspension without pay, demotion or dismissal;

● the confirmation of a warning or other disciplinary action, such as at an appeal hearing.

This right to be accompanied does not apply to any informal discussions or counselling sessions, or meetings to investigate any incidents that could lead to a disciplinary hearing. If it becomes clear during any investigation or informal meeting that disciplinary action may be required, then the meeting should be discontinued and a hearing arranged at which the employee will have the right to be accompanied.

It is up to the employee to make a request to be accompanied, although the employer has an obligation to make the right known, and any request made must be reasonable. It would not be reasonable, for example, for an employee to ask to be accompanied by someone who might prejudice the discussions, or who might be based at a geographically remote location when there is a suitably qualified person on-site.

Employees cannot generally ask to be accompanied by someone other than a fellow employee or trade union official, such as a legal representative, unless there is provision for this in the company's disciplinary procedure. The trade union official can be from any union, whether or not recognized by the employer, but should be appropriately trained in the role.

Any employee who agrees to accompany a colleague employed by the same employer is entitled to take a reasonable amount of paid time off to do so. The companion is allowed to address the hearing to put the employee's case, sum up the employee's case and to respond on the employee's behalf to views expressed at the hearing. However, the companion has no right to answer questions on the employee's behalf if the employee does not wish this.

Investigating disciplinary complaints

When a disciplinary issue is raised you should thoroughly investigate the matter before taking any action. This includes making full enquiries into the circumstances and giving the employee an opportunity to provide an explanation. Following this investigation you should consider whether there is a case for taking disciplinary action, whether the matter can be dealt with informally or whether there is no reason for any further action. In particular, you should consider:

- what the employee is alleged to have done or not done;
- the circumstances in which this took place;
- the consequences arising from this;
- the employee's job;
- the employee's age and length of service;
- the employee's past performance and disciplinary record;
- the evidence of any witnesses;
- any records or other information that can shed light on the situation;
- any changes that may have recently occurred in the job or working environment;
- whether there have been previous incidents related to this one;
- whether the employee has received the appropriate counselling or training.

While it is accepted that you cannot hope to investigate every single aspect of allegations against an employee, it is critical that any such investigation is reasonable in the circumstances. What is reasonable depends on the facts of the case and clearly, where an employee readily admits an offence, no further investigation may be necessary.

Having taken into account all of the above, you then need to consider whether:

- there is a case to answer;
- there is an alternative to disciplinary action, eg training or redeployment;
- the matter is serious enough to require a disciplinary hearing.

Who should conduct any investigation is clearly a critical consideration and ideally it should be a relatively senior manager who has had no direct involvement relating to the allegations. In a small company it may not always be easy to find such a person but it would still be expected that any investigation should at least be conducted impartially. The role of the manager carrying out the investigation is to assemble the facts and any supporting information, to decide whether there is a case to answer and then to notify the employee of the allegations. Depending on the nature of the alleged misconduct, there may be a need to interview other staff, and sometimes members of the public, to gather evidence. The decision about the next step to take will need to be based on the balance of probabilities.

Holding a preliminary interview

Before taking any disciplinary action you will need to hold a meeting with the employee to discuss the allegations and to give him an opportunity to respond. Generally at such a meeting it is advisable to have more than one member of management present so that there is a witness to anything that may be said, and it is also reasonable to allow the employee to be accompanied, although the statutory right only applies to disciplinary hearings, not to the preliminary investigation. You should make it clear that the meeting is to investigate the facts and that it is not a formal disciplinary hearing.

If new facts emerge during the meeting then it may be necessary to have an adjournment to investigate these. At the end of the meeting you should tell the employee what will happen next, which will usually be:

- no further action; or
- further consideration; or
- a disciplinary hearing.

If you decide to pursue the matter under the disciplinary procedure the employee then has the right to be notified in writing of the allegations against him.

Suspension with pay

For some more serious offences there may be a need to suspend the employee on full pay while the matter is investigated before taking any action. You should generally avoid this as it amounts to the imposition of a penalty before any disciplinary hearing has taken place. However, if you feel that such a sanction might be required then it should be provided for in the contract of employment. The company's disciplinary procedure should make it clear which level of manager has the authority to suspend an employee.

The situations in which you may have to suspend an employee include those where:

- the alleged offences are so serious that to allow the employee to remain at work might weaken your case for summary dismissal because of gross misconduct, if this is subsequently proven;
- the employee's continued presence at the workplace might undermine any effective investigation of the complaints made against him;
- attendance at the workplace by the employee might have a disruptive effect or might enable him to take actions to undermine the case against him, eg by removing records or files;
- the employee might be able to disrupt the business.

Any suspension for the above reasons should be described as 'precautionary' and it should be made clear that it is not a disciplinary sanction.

Conducting a disciplinary hearing

Preparing for a disciplinary hearing

To prepare for a disciplinary hearing you should:

- make sure that the circumstances have been fully investigated and that all the necessary facts and information are available at the hearing;
- arrange a suitable time, date and venue for the hearing;
- notify the employee concerned in writing of the precise nature of the complaint being made and of the arrangements for the hearing;
- notify any manager who may be required to attend of the arrangements for the hearing;
- inform the employee of his right to be accompanied by a fellow employee or a trade union representative;
- review the evidence being put forward and explore whether there are any other circumstances that might affect the position;
- ensure that the employee is notified in time to be able to prepare his case and to consult with any fellow employee or representative;
- where a trade union official is the subject of the disciplinary procedure, ensure that the relevant full-time trade union officer has been notified;
- ensure that all relevant information relating to the employee, including details of any previous disciplinary action, is available at the hearing;
- arrange for someone to take notes;
- if there are likely to be any communication difficulties, try to arrange for someone to be present who may be able to assist with these;
- where witnesses are being asked to attend ensure that they are aware of the arrangements for the hearing, or if they are unable to be present, get witness statements from them;

- ensure that the hearing is free from interruptions;
- ensure that some other manager is available to act as a witness.

An example of a letter asking an employee to attend a disciplinary hearing is set out below.

Example letter asking an employee to attend a disciplinary hearing

Dear

Disciplinary hearing

I have received a complaint from [insert name] that you [insert nature of complaint including dates and times of any alleged incident].

I have also been told that you made the following admissions: [insert admissions].

To investigate this matter, a disciplinary hearing has been arranged in accordance with the company's disciplinary procedure. This will take place on [insert date] at [insert time] at [insert location] and you are required to attend, accompanied if you wish by your trade union representative or a colleague. Please let me know the name of any person who will be attending the hearing with you and the names of any witnesses you would like to be present. I will arrange for them to be released from their duties so that they can attend the hearing.

I have already arranged for the following persons to attend the hearing: [insert names].

Yours sincerely,

When conducting the disciplinary hearing you should adopt the following process:

1 Introduce everyone present and state the reason for their attendance.
2 Ask that all mobile phones and portable devices are switched off and ensure that employees and their representatives remove all personal belongings during any adjournment.
3 Explain that the purpose of the hearing is to consider whether disciplinary action should be taken.
4 Explain how the hearing will be conducted.
5 State precisely the nature of the complaint and why the possibility of disciplinary action is being considered.
6 Give the employee an opportunity to respond to the points made and to present any evidence on his behalf.
7 Ensure that all the facts relating to the complaint emerge and that any special circumstances are noted.

8   At the end of the hearing summarize the main points made by both parties and highlight any that may need to be checked further.

9   If it is felt during the hearing that there is inadequate information to make a decision the hearing should be adjourned so that this can be checked.

10 At the end of the hearing the employer's representatives should adjourn to consider their decision.

11 Summarize the hearing's conclusions and ensure that the employee is clear about what is likely to happen next.

During the hearing

- Both sides should be able to call witnesses.
- The employee and/or his representative must be able to ask questions of the manager presenting the employer's case and of any witnesses called by the manager.
- The manager must be able to ask questions of the employee and of any witnesses called by the employee.
- The employee and/or his representative can argue the employee's case.
- The arguments of both sides, including any pleas of mitigation, must be considered.

If it turns out that the employee has a satisfactory explanation, no further disciplinary action will be necessary. In all cases the burden of proof must be established 'on a balance of probabilities'.

If an employee refuses to attend a disciplinary hearing you can still hold it in his absence, provided he has been appropriately notified of it and has been told that the hearing will go ahead whether he attends or not. If, however, he is unable to attend because of absence through ill health, you should postpone the meeting until he returns to work.

Any disciplinary hearing should comply with the rules of natural justice which, in essence, means that the accused person should know the nature of the accusation, should be given an opportunity to state his case and the tribunal should act in good faith.

After the hearing

Notifying an employee of the result of a disciplinary hearing

Following a disciplinary hearing you should notify the employee in writing of:

- the result of the hearing;
- the reason for the decision taken;
- what specific improvement is required;
- the period over which such improvement must take place and how it will be assessed;
- the likely consequences if the required improvement does not occur;
- his right of appeal and how any such appeal should be made.

Records

You should keep a record of any disciplinary hearings and actions, which should include:

- the nature of the breach of discipline;
- the employee's defence of mitigation;
- the action taken;
- the reasons for the action;
- whether an appeal was made;
- the outcome of any appeal and subsequent developments.

This information is usually kept on the individual's personal file and it is common practice for these to be removed after a certain period, eg 12 months, if the employee commits no further offences. If such a provision is included in the disciplinary procedure it is important for you to remember that you cannot then subsequently refer to any such incidents that are out of time. These records should be treated as confidential and be kept no longer than necessary in accordance with the Data Protection Act 1998.

You should give the employee a copy of any notes held, although it would be legitimate to withhold information in certain cases, eg to protect a witness.

Taking disciplinary action

Generally, following a disciplinary hearing you will have three main options:

1 to drop the matter because there is no case to answer; or
2 to provide counselling or training that might help to resolve the matter; or
3 to take disciplinary action.

Before deciding what disciplinary action to take you should consider whether:

- there has been as much investigation as may be considered reasonable in the circumstances;
- the company has followed the requirements of its disciplinary procedure;
- sufficient account has been taken of any explanations given by the employee;
- you have a genuine belief in the guilt of the employee;
- on the balance of probabilities, it is more likely than not that the employee is guilty of the misconduct complained of;
- the misconduct is serious enough to warrant the disciplinary action being considered;
- any mitigating circumstances have been taken into account;
- the disciplinary sanction being considered is within the band of reasonable responses open to you.

You should also take into account the employee's employment and disciplinary record and the disciplinary action taken in any previous similar cases.

Disciplinary warnings

Once it has been decided that disciplinary action is necessary you will need to decide what type of action is appropriate. Generally, a staged approach should be adopted, as follows:

1 The first step should be an informal warning, or warnings, from the individual's line manager or supervisor. This is not part of the formal procedure and no record should be kept.

2 If the informal warning has no effect, or if the misconduct is more serious, you may need to give a formal warning, which is the first stage of the formal procedure. In this case, instead of just telling the employee about the improvements required you will need to put in writing the nature of the complaint, what needs to be done to remedy the situation, the timescale for improvement and the likely consequences of no such improvement taking place.

3 If the formal written warning has no effect, or you consider the misconduct to be sufficiently serious, you may need to issue a final written warning specifying that any further breaches will result in dismissal. For serious misconduct you may wish to proceed straight to this stage.

4 If none of the previous steps has any effect you may need to proceed to the final stage of dismissal.

Although following the stages recommended above should help to ensure that you have handled the issue fairly, it does not necessarily mean that you have to go through all these stages for every offence. For more serious offences you may leapfrog a number of stages, and for gross misconduct you can go to the final stage immediately. The key test is what is reasonable in the circumstances.

Examples of written warning letters are set out below.

Example of a first written warning to an employee for unsatisfactory performance

Dear

This letter is to confirm the outcome of our meeting on [insert date] when you were told that your work performance was not satisfactory in the following respects [insert details of unsatisfactory work performance].

You were told at that meeting that to remedy the situation you must take the following actions: [describe actions to be taken].

You are expected to reach the standard of performance described above by [insert date], when the position will be reviewed. However, your performance will continue to be monitored until that date and we expect to see an improvement before that deadline.

If you do not reach the standard required by the date stated, further disciplinary action is likely to be taken under the company's disciplinary procedure.

In the meantime, the company will provide all necessary training and support to help you achieve the standard required, and you should ensure that you let me know of any support you feel you require.

Please let me know within five working days if you wish to appeal against this decision or if you wish to discuss any aspect of this letter.

Finally, please sign the enclosed copy of this warning and return it to me as acknowledgement of receipt.

Yours sincerely,

Example of a first written warning to an employee for misconduct

Dear

This letter is to confirm the outcome of our meeting on [insert date] when we discussed the complaint about your conduct.

You were told that, following a thorough investigation, the company had found that [insert details of complaint].

You are warned that any repetition of this misconduct, or similar misconduct, will result in further disciplinary action under the company's disciplinary procedure.

Please let me know within five working days if you wish to appeal against this decision or if you wish to discuss any aspect of this letter.

Finally, please sign the enclosed copy of this warning and return it to me as acknowledgement of receipt.

Yours sincerely,

Example of a final written warning to an employee

Dear

I write to confirm the outcome of our discussion on [insert date].

As you are aware, over the past [months/weeks] you have failed to meet the standards required by the company in the following respects: [list ways in which performance or conduct have fallen short of the required standard].

As discussed with you, we have agreed to give you until [insert date] to meet the standards required. This means that you are required to take the following actions by that date: [describe actions required].

I must warn you that, in view of previous warnings you have been given, if you fail to meet the standards required as described above by the above date, you will be dismissed.

Please let me know within five working days if you wish to appeal against this decision or if you wish to discuss any aspect of this letter.

In the meantime, would you please sign the enclosed copy and return it to me as acknowledgement of receipt.

Yours sincerely,

Other disciplinary sanctions

Other sanctions you could consider include transferring the employee to another job, demotion, non-payment of increments or bonuses, etc. However, you need to be aware that any such sanction could be a breach of the employment contract unless specifically provided for in the contract. Withholding pay or bonuses, or imposing any penalty in which the employee suffers a financial loss, could result in action by the employee under the Employment Rights Act 1996 to recover any such loss, or possibly the employee resigning and pursuing a case for constructive dismissal. This is, in effect, a unilateral repudiation of the contract by the employer.

Dismissal

The ultimate sanction is dismissal. Usually this should be with the appropriate notice, but for gross misconduct you may dismiss without giving notice or pay in lieu of notice.

Specific disciplinary situations

Failure to comply with a reasonable instruction

It is an implied term of an employee's contract that he will follow the reasonable instructions of an employer and you would therefore be justified in taking disciplinary action against anyone who failed to do so. The situation becomes more complicated if you wish to change an employee's duties or working pattern for business reasons. Although you may have no automatic contractual right to insist on any such change, if there are compelling business reasons for doing so, you may be within your rights to ask an employee to work under the new arrangements and to take disciplinary action if he fails to do so. The ultimate test is what is reasonable in the circumstances. Ideally, any such changes should be through discussion and agreement.

Breach of disciplinary rules

Disciplinary and work rules should be made known to all employees and it is completely legitimate for you to state that any breach of a particular rule could render the employee liable to dismissal. As discussed earlier it is inadvisable to state that dismissal will be automatic, as this implies that the matter has been pre-judged and that no account would be taken of any mitigating circumstances.

When considering disciplinary action for breach of any rules it is important to ensure that there is consistency. For example, if a rule has previously been ignored, it is likely to be unfair to make an example of a person by applying a disciplinary sanction automatically and without first drawing the attention of employees to the need to follow the rule in question.

Breach of health and safety regulations

Provided you take all necessary steps to alert employees to health and safety requirements, such as by placing appropriate notices near dangerous machinery, any disciplinary action for breach of health and safety rules is likely to be fair. It is important, however, that you carry out a full investigation of any alleged breach, that the employee is informed of any allegation against him and is given an opportunity to explain, and that any penalty is reasonable in the circumstances.

Drunkenness at work

Although drunkenness at work often crops up as an example of what constitutes gross misconduct, whether it is or not depends on the circumstances of the case. There are a number of factors that have to be taken into account, including for example:

- the nature of the work carried out and the degree of risk to the employee, his colleagues and others;
- whether there is a specific rule relating to drinking;
- the position and responsibilities of the employee in the organization;
- the general attitude of the organization to drinking;
- the evidence that the employee is under the influence of alcohol;
- any explanation provided by the employee about his conduct.

A common reaction by an employee accused of drunkenness is that this occurred because he was ill or on medication at the time. If this proves to be correct, following investigation, then disciplinary action may not be appropriate.

You also need to consider whether this is an isolated incident or the symptom of an underlying medical problem. If it is the latter then it may require counselling and possibly longer-term medical treatment. Any instance of drunkenness needs to be investigated carefully, taking into account the nature of the work carried out by the individual, his age, length of service, previous disciplinary record, personal circumstances, general conduct, etc.

Where drunkenness results in threatening or abusive behaviour, then a disciplinary process should take into account that behaviour. In these circumstances, and also where the employee may be working in a potentially dangerous industrial environment, it is often necessary to send the employee home on suspension.

Fighting at work

Fighting at work is frequently described in disciplinary procedures as gross misconduct. However, whether or not it is specifically mentioned, fighting would generally be regarded as very serious misconduct. You would still have to carry out an investigation, consider all the facts, give the employees concerned the opportunity to respond and to explain their actions, and finally to take action that is considered reasonable in the circumstances.

Unsatisfactory attendance

Unsatisfactory attendance can include a range of different behaviours such as:

- failure to comply with absence reporting procedures;
- reporting the wrong reasons for absence;
- being absent without authorization;
- prolonging an authorized absence without good reason;
- working while on sick or compassionate leave;
- carrying out other activities, eg participating in sports while on sick leave;
- being absent frequently, even though for genuine reasons;
- persistent lateness or generally poor timekeeping.

The procedure for dealing with an unacceptably high level of absence is set out in Chapter 6.

It is sometimes the case that an employee tries to avoid a disciplinary meeting by claiming sickness. In these circumstances you should usually rearrange the meeting to accommodate this sickness absence, but should notify the employee that the re-arranged hearing will go ahead anyway on the new date whether or not the employee can attend, and that the employee can put forward his case through a representative, or in writing, if he is unable to attend at the rescheduled time. Although it is difficult to be totally prescriptive about the actions to be taken, as this will depend on the circumstances, you cannot be expected to keep postponing hearings until the employee is available.

Many organizations treat performance issues as outside the disciplinary process and apply instead a separate performance management process. However, the same stages as outlined above will still apply and the outcomes will be the same.

Unsatisfactory performance

Disciplinary action will normally be taken because of misconduct or capability, such as failing to conform to the required standards. If you are considering taking disciplinary action because of the employee's poor performance, you should ensure that:

- the employee has been given all necessary training and instructions about the work;
- an explanation has been given of the standards required;
- the employee has been made aware of any shortcomings;
- the consequence of failing to meet the required standards has been explained;
- there is clear evidence of failure to achieve the standards required.

Before taking any disciplinary action for poor performance you must ensure that the employee has been given all necessary training and counselling and has been given an opportunity to improve. Of course, where the consequences of an error are extremely serious, there may be a need instead to take immediate action.

Criminal proceedings

If an employee has been found guilty of a criminal offence outside work and which bears no direct relationship to his work in the company, you should not treat this as an automatic reason for dismissal. There is a need to consider the impact on his work and the company before taking any decision. Equally, if a criminal case is pending, there is no reason for you to wait for the outcome before making a decision. The issue is not whether the employee is guilty of the offence he is charged with, but whether you, the employer, acted reasonably in the circumstances. This means that if you dismissed the employee in the belief that he was going to be convicted, even if no conviction resulted, a dismissal would be fair if this was considered to be a reasonable response in the circumstances.

Appeals against disciplinary action

You should provide a procedure that enables employees to appeal against any disciplinary action. The procedure should:

- specify time limits for lodging and hearing the appeal;
- provide for the appeal to be dealt with swiftly;
- if possible, provide for the appeal to be heard by a more senior manager not previously involved in the process;
- notify the appellant of the arrangements for the hearing and of his right to be accompanied;
- describe what will happen during the appeal hearing;

- give the employee an opportunity to comment on any new evidence arising before the appeal hearing.

You should write to the employee with the results of the appeal and the reason for the decision as soon as possible after the hearing.

Those hearing the appeal should consider the following questions:

- Has there been a sufficient investigation to establish the facts?
- Has the organization's own disciplinary procedure been correctly followed?
- Was the employee given sufficient information about the allegations against him?
- Was the employee given sufficient opportunity to respond to those allegations?
- Has sufficient attention been given to explanations put forward by the employee?
- Do they genuinely believe that the employee has committed the alleged misconduct?
- Can this belief be sustained on the balance of probabilities?
- Is the misconduct sufficient to justify the disciplinary penalty imposed?
- Have all mitigating circumstances been considered?
- Is the penalty imposed reasonable?

If the managers hearing the appeal can satisfy themselves on all the above issues, this will prove a strong response to any case brought against the company by the employee.

In small companies it may not be possible to find a manager who has not been previously involved, in which case the person or persons hearing the appeal should try to be as neutral as possible, or the organization could consider appointing an external arbitrator, which should be included in any agreed procedure.

Further information

ACAS Code of Practice on Disciplinary and Grievance Procedures, 2009
Employment Act 2002
Employment Act 2008
Employment Rights Act 1996
Trade Union and Labour Relations (Consolidation) Act 1992

Dealing with Grievances

13

Grievance procedure

As an employer you have a legal obligation under the Employment Rights Act 1996 to provide, in the written statement of terms and conditions of employment, details of the person to whom any employee who has a grievance should apply. A grievance procedure sets out how such an application should be made and how it will be dealt with.

Principles

The procedure should aim to settle the grievance as quickly, fairly and as near to the point of origin as possible. In practice this means that the issue should, more often than not, be settled by the employee's immediate supervisor or line manager. However, the procedure should describe what will happen if the grievance cannot be resolved at this level. Any such procedure should:

- be in writing;
- be made known to all employees;
- allow for the employee to be accompanied by a fellow employee or trade union representative, if desired;
- ensure a speedy resolution of the problem.

An example of a grievance procedure is set out below.

Example grievance procedure

Principles

1 The company realizes that there will be occasions when our employees may wish to raise formally issues or complaints about the company or other

employees. While we would hope that in most cases these could be resolved informally, we will try to deal speedily and effectively with any that remain unresolved, through the following procedure.

2   This procedure applies to all employees, but does not confer any contractual rights.

3   Any employee pursuing a grievance should continue to work normally while the grievance is being investigated. Generally the status quo will be maintained during this investigation, unless doing so could result in serious problems for the employee or the company.

4   You may be accompanied or represented by a fellow employee or a trade union representative at any stage of the procedure.

5   If your grievance relates to disciplinary action it should be raised under the company's disciplinary procedure.

6   Where a grievance is against your immediate supervisor or line manager, the matter should be raised with the next manager above that person.

7   In any collective disputes or grievances a spokesperson should be appointed to represent the group of employees affected.

Procedure

Stage 1

Any grievance should be raised initially with your immediate supervisor or line manager. The supervisor or manager should normally respond in writing within five working days.

Stage 2

If the matter is not resolved at Stage 1 or within five working days you should refer the grievance in writing to the next senior manager, who should normally arrange a meeting to consider it within five working days of your request. You should clearly set out the reason for referring the grievance to the second stage of the procedure.

Stage 3

If the matter still remains unresolved after Stage 2 you may refer the grievance in writing to [insert job title], who should normally arrange a meeting to consider it within 10 working days. You should clearly set out the reason for referring the grievance to the third stage of the procedure. The decision of [insert job title] will be given in writing and will be final.

Handling a grievance

In handling a grievance you should take the following actions:

1 Ensure that you are familiar with the procedure and that you apply it correctly.

2 Listen carefully to the points being made by the employee and try to gauge whether the specific grievance may be symptomatic of more deep-rooted problems.

3 Listen to any opposing points of view.

4 Having considered all the evidence, try to conclude whether there is an issue to be addressed.

5 Decide what action to take, trying to be fair to the individual, but without setting a precedent for the company.

6 Notify all those concerned of the decision reached, and of the appeal process.

7 Where a grievance has raised issues relating to policies, procedures or behaviour ensure that action is taken to remedy any problems.

It is common for employees who are being subjected to disciplinary action to raise a grievance as a sort of counterclaim. You should, as far as possible, treat the two issues separately, handling each under its respective procedure. If there is a disciplinary decision to dismiss the employee you should still ensure that you deal with any outstanding grievance.

It is important that you consider any written complaint made by an employee as a potential grievance. If you receive any such complaint, even in a letter of resignation, you should ask the employee if she wants it treated as Stage 1 of the grievance procedure.

Bullying and harassment

Bullying and harassment in the workplace are serious matters for the employer and you should immediately investigate any such claims made by your employees. There are complexities in investigating these kinds of issue because there is a need to consider when what might be described as a 'robust management style', such as that demonstrated by certain television chefs, tips over into overt bullying.

The Department for Business, Innovation and Skills (BIS) states that bullying includes:

- offensive or insulting behaviour by another employee that makes an individual feel threatened or taken advantage of;

- humiliation of an employee, but not necessarily on the grounds of age, sex, race, disability, sexual orientation, religion or other belief;

- less obvious ways of making an employee feel frightened or demoralized.

The kinds of actions that are usually described as bullying include where the individual is:

- constantly picked on;
- humiliated in front of colleagues;
- regularly unfairly treated;
- physically or verbally abused;
- blamed for problems caused by others;
- given too much to do so that failure is inevitable;
- regularly threatened with dismissal;
- unfairly passed over for promotion or training opportunities;
- subject to inconsistent changes in working conditions and duties;
- excluded from social events;
- subject to malicious rumours and gossip.

The Equality Act 2010 identifies three types of harassment. The first type applies to all 'protected characteristics' (ie those grounds on which people can be discriminated against) apart from pregnancy and maternity, marriage and civil partnership; involves unwanted conduct 'related to' the relevant characteristic; and which has the purpose or effect of creating an intimidating, hostile, degrading, humiliating or offensive environment for the complainant or violating the complainant's dignity.

The second type is sexual harassment, which is unwanted conduct of a sexual nature that has the same purpose or effect as the first type. The third type involves treating someone less favourably because they have submitted to or rejected sexual harassment.

In determining the effect of the unwanted conduct, courts and tribunals are required to balance competing rights on the facts of a particular case.

The Act also confirms that employers will be potentially liable for third-party harassment in respect of all the protected characteristics, ie where the employer knows that harassment by a third party has occurred on at least two previous occasions and has failed to take reasonably practicable steps to put a stop to it.

Examples of harassment include:

- embarrassing or otherwise offensive jokes;
- unwelcome physical contact or sexual advances;
- racial or sexual abuse or abuse relating to sexual orientation, religion or other belief, age or disability.

One of the main problems in dealing with claims of harassment and/or bullying is that such claims might be malicious, and they are frequently used as a defence mechanism when an employer seeks to discipline or dismiss an employee. However, you must thoroughly investigate any such claim and should:

- if possible use an impartial, trained investigator;
- consider suspension of the alleged bully or harasser on full pay;
- allow both parties to be accompanied to a hearing by a colleague or trade union officer;
- make it clear that both parties have the right of appeal.

When you are dealing with a case of bullying or harassment, decide carefully what action you are going to take. This could range from counselling or training to a disciplinary penalty. Such penalties can include a written warning, suspension, transfer or dismissal of the bully, harasser or malicious claimant. Where bullying or harassment is found to have occurred, make sure that the solution does not penalize the victim.

One of the ways of preventing bullying or harassment is to have a bullying and harassment policy that is widely publicized among staff and managers. An example of a policy of this kind is set out in Chapter 9.

Appeals against grading

You should have a separate appeal process for appeals against grading, especially where a job evaluation scheme is used. Such a procedure might need to provide for the re-evaluation of a job by a different job evaluation panel if such panels are used to establish job sizes.

Mediation

When there are internal disputes, particularly those involving groups of employees, you may wish to consider mediation (or Alternative Dispute Resolution) as an alternative to legal action. Both parties would need to agree to this approach.

Further information

Equality Act 2010
www.acas.org.uk
www.gov.uk/salve-workplace-dispute/formal-procedures

Terminating Employment

14

There are various ways that the employment relationship can come to an end, the most common being that the employee resigns, retires or is dismissed. It is critical to distinguish between a voluntary resignation and a dismissal, because it is only if there has been a dismissal that an employee can pursue a claim for unfair or wrongful dismissal, or redundancy.

Meaning of dismissal

A dismissal occurs when:

- the contract is ended by the employer with or without notice;
- a fixed-term contract expires without being renewed;
- the employee ends the contract with or without notice and is entitled to do so because of the employer's unreasonable conduct (known as 'constructive dismissal').

Dismissal with notice

When you dismiss someone that person is entitled either to the period of notice set out in the contract of employment, or to the statutory minimum period of notice set out in the Employment Rights Act 1996, whichever is the more favourable. The statutory periods of notice are:

- less than one month's employment – no statutory entitlement;
- one month to two years' employment – one week;
- two years' to 12 years' employment – one week for each complete year of employment;
- 12 years' employment or more – 12 weeks.

For senior staff the contractual periods of notice are very often much longer than the statutory rights to notice, six months being common for directors.

An exception to these notice provisions is any employees engaged for a specific task that is not expected to last more than three months, unless they have continuous employment that takes them over that limit.

When you give notice it should be in writing and should clearly state the last day of employment.

Notice by the employee

An employee is legally required to give you one week's notice after one month's service, but this does not increase with length of service, unless provided for in the contract. Subject to this statutory minimum, notice is otherwise that which is set out in the contract of employment.

While you have the right to insist that the employee gives you the full notice set out in the contract, in writing if required, the only recourse open to you if he fails to do so is to sue for breach of contract. This may not be a practical solution as you would need to establish that the business had been damaged in some way. What you cannot do, however, is to withhold pay for all or part of the notice period, as this would be an illegal deduction.

Counter notice

If an employee is dismissed with notice but gives counter notice, indicating a leaving date earlier than that proposed by you, the original notice will still stand and the employee will be treated as having been dismissed by you.

Withdrawing notice

Sometimes an employee, having resigned, has second thoughts and seeks to withdraw his notice. However, once the notice has been given you are under no obligation to allow the employee to withdraw it.

Pay during notice

You will normally have to pay an employee full salary during any notice period (subject to deduction of any sick pay, statutory sick pay or any maternity pay being received), regardless of whether it is you or the employee who gives notice.

An exception to this is where the contract of employment provides for a notice period that is at least one week longer than the statutory notice to which the employee is entitled. For example, an employee with two years' service is entitled to two weeks' statutory notice, but if the contract gives one month's notice, then there is no legal obligation to pay the full salary during the notice period, unless the contract gives a specific right to the entitlement.

However, it is unlikely that you will be able to use the above provision to avoid paying salary during the notice period because it would generally be assumed by any court that an entitlement to notice in the contract means paid notice, even where this is not specifically stated.

Pay in lieu of notice

It is common practice, when an employee leaves, for the employer not to require that person to work his full notice period but to give pay in lieu of notice. As the employee has a contractual right to work during the notice period you should ensure that a clause giving you the option of payment in lieu of notice is inserted into the employment contract. You should also include any conditions attaching to the notice period. For example, you may not wish the employee to come into the office because of the danger of gaining access to commercially sensitive information. Conditions of this kind are generally known as 'garden leave' clauses.

Other payments on termination of employment

When an employee leaves the company the payments you will normally have to make are:

- any outstanding pay up to the last day of employment;
- payment for any holiday not taken;
- any outstanding bonuses to which the employee is entitled;
- any statutory sick pay (SSP) the employee is entitled to up to the last day of employment;
- any statutory maternity pay (SMP) or statutory paternity pay (SPP) to which the employee is entitled;
- a refund of pension contributions.

You may sometimes also wish to make an ex gratia payment, commonly known as a 'golden handshake', but this is entirely optional. Sometimes these are made subject to the employee agreeing to sign what since July 2013 is known as a settlement agreement (formerly a compromise agreement – see below). If the employee was dismissed because of redundancy there might also be an entitlement to redundancy pay.

The employee has the right to retain all benefits during the notice period but these can be bought out by agreement.

Termination without notice

There may be occasions when you have to dismiss an employee without giving the full notice entitlement. This usually arises when there has been gross misconduct by the employee or where continued employment might pose a serious risk to others. In these circumstances the employee would not be entitled to any pay in lieu of notice.

Before taking such drastic action you should:

- investigate the circumstances;
- interview the employee concerned and any others who can shed light on the situation;

- notify the employee of the charge being brought against him;
- give the employee an opportunity to state his case.

If, having heard all the facts, you consider that:

- you have reasonable grounds for concluding that the employee committed the offence in question; and
- this falls within the definition of what you would regard as gross misconduct; and
- there are no mitigating circumstances;
- then you can dismiss with immediate effect. You should then send a letter confirming your decision (and giving a right of appeal).

The key points to bear in mind are whether it is reasonable to conclude that the incident in question amounts to gross misconduct and whether dismissal is the appropriate sanction in the circumstances.

Apart from dismissal for gross misconduct, termination of employment without notice is likely to be a breach of the employment contract that could allow the employee to bring a claim of wrongful (as opposed to 'unfair') dismissal.

Written reason for dismissal

You should provide a written reason for dismissal, although you are not legally required to do so unless the dismissed employee asks for one and had been continuously employed for at least two years.

Date of termination of employment

The actual date of termination of employment is important because this affects the employee's length of service and consequent entitlement to various employment rights.

Where notice has been given, the termination date will be the last day of the notice period. So, for example, if an employee has 22 months' service and is given three months' notice, this would bring the total length of service to over two years, thereby giving that person the right to bring an unfair dismissal claim if he wished to do so.

Where employment is terminated without notice, the termination date is the date on which the employee is told of the dismissal.

Avoiding unfair dismissal

For a dismissal to be fair it must be for one of five reasons, and your decision to dismiss the employee for one of those reasons must have been reasonable in the circumstances. The five potentially fair reasons for dismissing an employee are:

1 a lack of capability or qualifications for carrying out the work required;

2 unsatisfactory conduct;

3 redundancy;

4 where continued employment would break the law;

5 some other substantial reason (SOSR).

In dismissing an employee for any one of the above reasons you must also ensure that:

- you follow the ACAS Code of Practice on Disciplinary and Grievance Procedures;
- you follow your own disciplinary procedure, where applicable;
- except in the case of gross misconduct, the employee has been given an opportunity to improve;
- in the case of misconduct the employee has been given the opportunity to explain the behaviour complained of;
- any appeal by the employee has been heard.

Formerly, a potentially fair reason for dismissal was reaching retirement age. However, the abolition of the Default Retirement Age means that any decision to terminate employment that may have been based on reaching retirement age will now have to be for a different reason, usually performance.

Automatically unfair dismissal

Some reasons for dismissal are considered to be automatically unfair. These are decisions where the main reason is because of:

- pregnancy, or the taking of parental, paternity or adoption leave or time off for dependants;
- trade union membership or activities, or non-membership;
- the employee requesting a flexible working arrangement;
- the employee trying to exercise or exercising the right to be accompanied at a disciplinary or grievance hearing;
- reasons relating to jury service;
- reasons relating to the Information and Consultation of Employees Regulations 2004 for undertakings with 50 or more employees;
- failure to give correct notification of the right to continue working beyond the normal retirement age;
- the employee's duties as an employee representative in relation to redundancy consultation, business transfer, the Working Time Regulations 1998 or the Maternity and Parental Leave Regulations 1999;

- the employee's duties as a safety representative;
- an employee leaving the workplace because of some serious or imminent danger;
- an employee's responsibilities as a trustee of an occupational pension scheme;
- a protected or opting-out shop or betting office worker refusing to work on a Sunday;
- a shop or betting office worker giving or proposing to give an opting-out notice;
- the assertion of certain statutory rights, for example in relation to payment of wages and notice periods;
- the employee asserting rights under the Working Time Regulations;
- the employee making a protected disclosure under the Public Interest Disclosure Act 1998 ('whistle-blowing');
- the employee enforcing or proposing to enforce entitlement to the National Minimum Wage.

In all of the above situations there is no qualifying period of employment and no upper age limit for claiming unfair dismissal. Other reasons that are likely to make the dismissal unfair are where it:

- was for a reason that is discriminatory for one of the protected characteristics defined by the Equality Act 2010;
- was because a business transfer was the main reason;
- related to a spent conviction under the Rehabilitation of Offenders Act 1974 (see Chapter 1);
- occurred during the first 12 weeks of industrial action.

From 25 June 2013 there is no service requirement to bring a claim for unfair dismissal if the reason for that dismissal relates to poitical beliefs or affiliations. However, such a dismissal could be fair provided you have followed a correct process and can show that dismissal was reasonable in the circumstances.

Settlement agreements

When terminating employment you can ask the employee or worker to sign a settlement (formerly compromise) agreement that will prevent that person making a later claim to an employment tribunal or account. This will be legally binding provided that:

- the agreement is in writing;
- it relates to the particular complaint or dispute (which might give rise to proceedings);
- the employee has received legal advice from a relevant independent adviser;
- an insurance policy or professional indemnity covering the risk or claim is held by the independent adviser;

- the agreement identifies the adviser;
- the agreement states that it satisfies the conditions regulating settlement agreements.

A fear that many employers have when broaching the subject of a settlement agreement is the possibility of being the victim of a claim for constructive dismissal. For this reason it is desirable to be able to conduct discussions on a 'without prejudice' basis. This means that any statements made during a 'without prejudice' meeting or discussion cannot be used in a court or tribunal as evidence. This 'without prejudice' confidentiality does not, however, apply where there is no existing dispute between the parties. Section 111A of the ERA 1996 has therefore been introduced to allow greater flexibility in the use of confidential discussions as a means of ending the employment relationship. This runs alongside the 'without prejudice' principle and provides that even where no employment dispute exists, the parties may still offer and discuss a settlement agreement in the knowledge that their conversations cannot be used in any subsequent unfair dismissal claim.

There are, however, some situations in which section 111A will not apply. These include claims that:

- relate to an automatically unfair reason for dismissal such as whistle-blowing, union membership or asserting a statutory right;
- are made on grounds other than unfair dismissal, such as discrimination, harassment, victimization or other behaviour prohibited by the Equalities Act 2010;
- relate to breach of contract or wrongful dismissal.

The confidentiality provisions of section 111A are, additionally, subject to there being no 'improper behaviour' such as:

a Any form of harassment, bullying and intimidation, including through the use of offensive words or aggressive behaviour;

b Physical assault or the threat of physical assault and other criminal behaviour;

c All forms of victimization;

d Discrimination because of age, sex, race, disability, sexual orientation, religion or belief, transgender, pregnancy and maternity, and marriage or civil partnership;

e Putting undue pressure on a party, such as:

   i Not giving reasonable time for consideration;

   ii An employer saying before any form of disciplinary process has begun that if a settlement proposal is rejected then the employee will be dismissed;

   iii An employee threatening to undermine an organization's public reputation if the organization does not sign the agreement (unless there is a justifiable reason for whistle-blowing).

Wrongful dismissal

Wrongful dismissal arises when an employee has been dismissed in breach of the contract of employment. This could arise, for example, if you failed to follow the stages in a disciplinary procedure that was part of the employee's contract, or if you failed to give the employee the contractual notice to which he was entitled.

The significance of wrongful dismissal is that the employee can bring a claim to an employment tribunal or through the courts without having to have the two years' continuous employment necessary for bringing a claim of unfair dismissal.

Damages can potentially be quite high in these cases but the employee would be expected to 'mitigate his loss' by finding a new job and this would be taken into account in assessing the amount payable.

Constructive dismissal

Constructive dismissal arises when the employee resigns because he feels that he has no option but to do so due to the employer's unreasonable behaviour. Generally, for such a claim to succeed against you as an employer your behaviour would have to be so unreasonable as to fundamentally breach the contract. However, this requirement is likely to be slightly less stringent in business transfers.

To avoid potential claims for constructive dismissal you should therefore avoid actions that might be construed as destroying the employment relationship. The kinds of actions that might give rise to such claims include:

- lowering the employee's status through demotion or a pay reduction without good reason;
- displaying a lack of confidence or trust in a subordinate;
- undermining a manager's or supervisor's authority by cutting him out of the loop and dealing instead directly with his staff;
- failing to give contractually agreed pay and benefits;
- changing someone's job responsibilities without consulting him;
- changing someone's working environment by moving him to inadequate office accommodation.

Types of dismissal

You can dismiss employees on the grounds of:

- inability to do the job to the required standard;
- illness or injury leading to an unacceptably high level of absence;
- a lack of qualifications;
- misconduct;

- redundancy;
- where continued employment would break the law (for example, where a driver loses his driving licence);
- for some other substantial reason (SOSR).

Dismissal for inability to perform to the required standard

If you are considering dismissing an employee because of his inability to achieve the work standards required you need first to satisfy yourself that the individual cannot perform to the required standard. In doing so you need to ask the following questions:

- What is the standard of performance required?
- In what way does the employee fail to meet the standard?
- What evidence do you have to support this belief?
- Has the employee received all necessary training and instruction?
- Does the employee know what standard of performance is required?
- Has the employee been warned about his poor performance?
- Has the employee been given sufficient opportunity to improve?
- Have you considered transferring the employee to other work or redesigning the job?
- Has the employee been given an opportunity to put his point of view?
- Having regard to all the circumstances, is dismissal a reasonable option?

Before taking the decision to dismiss for poor performance you need to go through the following process:

1 Consider whether the employee's performance is reasonable in relation to the standards laid down for the job.
2 Consider whether there are any changes that could be made, or training that should be given, to improve performance.
3 Produce evidence in support of your contention that performance is not up to the required standard.
4 Discuss the matter with the employee, informally at first, stating what improvements are required and the likely consequences if they do not arise.
5 If the informal discussion does not produce improvement then a formal written warning may be necessary, in which you should tell the employee of the standards required, the ways in which he has fallen short of these standards, what he needs to do to remedy the situation and the likely consequences of his not doing so.
6 Following the first written warning it may be appropriate to give a final written warning, which should emphasize that if no improvement is forthcoming the result may be dismissal.

7 Dismissal is the final step if nothing else works and provided you have given every opportunity for improvement.

The process is summarized in Figure 14.1.

FIGURE 14.1 Dismissal for poor performance

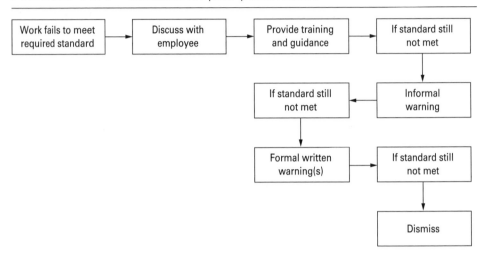

An example of the kind of letter you may need to write when dismissing for an inability to perform the job to the required standard is set out below.

Example letter terminating employment on grounds of capability

Dear

I write to confirm the outcome of our meeting on [insert date].

I regret that, because you are unable to carry out your work to the standard required by the company, we have no alternative but to terminate your employment with effect from [insert date].

As you know, we have made every effort to try to ensure that you met the standards required by providing all appropriate training and support, but without success. We have also looked into possible alternative employment in the company, but, as you know, there are currently no other jobs available appropriate to your skills and experience.

You are entitled to [insert notice entitlement] weeks' notice and [although you will not be required to attend work] you will continue to receive full pay and benefits during this period. You will also be entitled to any outstanding holiday pay up to your last day of service and I will arrange for these payments to be made to you as soon as possible.

If you disagree with this decision, or feel that you have been treated unfairly by the company, you have the right to appeal through the company's disciplinary procedure. If you wish to do so, please let me know by [insert date].

The company will be prepared to provide you with a fair and accurate reference.

I regret that we have had to take this step and would like to wish you every success in finding a new job.

Yours sincerely,

Absence through illness or injury

You need to exercise extra care when considering the dismissal of someone because of absence caused by illness or injury. It is quite legitimate to dismiss someone for such a reason if it is causing an unacceptable level of disruption to the business, but tribunals naturally tend to be more sympathetic to someone in this position than they might be to those dismissed for other reasons.

Long-term absence

The procedure to be followed in these cases is as follows:

1 Discuss the position with the employee to try to find out when he is likely to return to work.

2 If there is some doubt about the date of return, get written permission from the employee to contact his doctor for an opinion about a likely return date.

3 If the employee is unwilling for you to contact his doctor, or that doctor is unwilling to give an opinion, ask if the employee would be prepared to be examined by the company's medical adviser or other suitable specialist (see example letter below).

4 If any medical opinion confirms that the employee is unlikely to return in the near future you will need to discuss the situation with him, indicating how long you would be prepared to keep the job open but making it clear that you might have to dismiss the employee if the absence continued beyond that date.

5 Consider whether there are any conditions inherent in the job that could have contributed to the employee's illness.

6 If the employee is disabled consider if there are any reasonable adjustments that could be made to overcome the disability.

7 Consider whether there are other jobs in the company that the employee could carry out despite the illness or injury.

8 Ask yourself whether you have reached the point where you can no longer manage without the employee's job being carried out.

9 If all options have been explored and you have no alternative to dismissal, you should give the employee notice (see example letter below).

The final step is to arrange for the appropriate termination payment to be made. Generally, the employee will be entitled to full pay during the notice period, even if his entitlement to sick pay or SSP has expired. The process is summarized in Figure 14.2.

FIGURE 14.2   Dismissal following long-term ill health

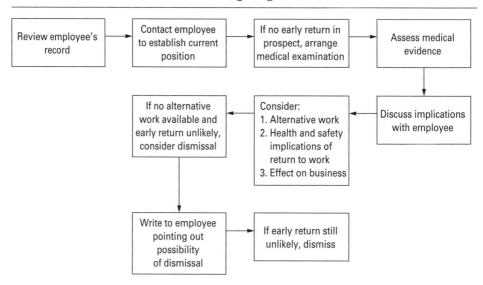

Example letter to employee on long-term absence where termination of employment is being considered

Dear

I refer to my previous letter of [insert date] on this matter.

As you know, we have, with your permission, consulted your doctor about your illness and resulting absence from work, which has now been continuous since [insert date]. However, your doctor was unable to indicate when you might be able to return to work.

You will appreciate that we are unable to keep your job open indefinitely as this causes us operational difficulties. We therefore need to know whether you can give us a definite date when you are likely to return to work. If you feel that you are unable to return to your old job, but could carry out some other job in the company, could you please let us have your suggestions about any alternative job you feel would be suited to your skills and experience. We will give any such suggestion full consideration.

If you are unable to return to work in any capacity, we will reluctantly have to consider terminating your employment. However, before we take any final decision we would like you to have a medical examination, which we will pay for, so that we can obtain a second opinion.

If you do not agree to this medical examination, could you please let us know of any reasons why you consider that we should not take steps to terminate your employment.

I enclose a stamped, addressed envelope for your reply.

Yours sincerely,

Example letter terminating employment because of employee's long-term ill health

Dear

I'm sorry to hear that your health has not improved and that you will not, therefore, be able to return to your job as [insert job title].

As you know, we have discussed this with you and although we have considered alternative work within the company, you are aware that we have been unable to find anything suitable.

We have also consulted our medical adviser about the likely prospect of a return to work, but he has confirmed that you are unlikely to be able to return to your job in the foreseeable future. In the circumstances, I regret that I have little choice but to give you notice in accordance with your contract of employment.

Your employment with the company will therefore cease on [insert date]. You will be entitled to payment for your notice period of [insert number of weeks] and we have also decided to pay you a further [insert number] weeks' pay, as an ex gratia payment in recognition of your past service with the company.

You will need to contact [insert name] to discuss any outstanding matters, such as your pension entitlement, and to get any other advice that you might require. You have the right to appeal against this decision and if you wish to do so please let me know within five working days.

I am sorry that we have had to terminate your employment with the company and I hope that your health improves in the future. If it improves sufficiently for you to return to work at any time please do not hesitate to contact me.

Yours sincerely,

Frequent short-term absences

Frequent short unplanned absences can often be more disruptive than one long-term absence. Where such absences occur, and particularly where they follow a clear pattern, such as extra days being taken after bank holidays, you will need to take action that could lead to dismissal. What constitutes an unsatisfactory level of attendance is for you to decide.

When you have an employee whose absences have reached an unacceptable level you should take the following action:

- Consider whether the absences are higher than those for comparable employees.
- Consider the reasons for the absences and the employee's overall attendance record.
- Discuss the absences with the employee, warn him that the attendance record is unacceptable, and tell him about the likely consequences if the record does not improve.
- Consider whether there may be any factors in the job that could be contributing to the absences.
- Give the employee an opportunity to improve.
- Consider whether the problem could be resolved by changing the job, or by transferring the employee to other duties.
- If the position does not improve, you will have to issue a disciplinary warning.
- If the disciplinary warning has no effect, and you have followed your disciplinary procedure, you may have no alternative but to dismiss the employee.

Dismissal for misconduct

There are a number of sanctions that might be appropriate in cases of misconduct; this depends on the seriousness of the misconduct. Some actions, such as lateness for example, should be dealt with by giving the employee the appropriate warnings under the disciplinary procedure, with dismissal being the last resort if everything else has failed. In cases of serious misconduct you may instead go straight to a final written warning and, where this misconduct falls within the definition of gross misconduct, you may be justified in summarily dismissing the individual concerned, ie dismissal without notice or payment in lieu of notice.

The kinds of actions that have been classified as gross misconduct are described in Chapter 12. Before taking the step of dismissing someone you should:

- Thoroughly investigate the circumstances.
- Give the employee an opportunity to explain his conduct.
- Consider the employee's previous record and particularly any prior disciplinary warnings.

- Ensure that the employee had been made aware that the conduct in question could lead to dismissal, or that the conduct was such that any reasonable employee might expect dismissal to result from it (you cannot be expected to spell out every possible action that might be regarded as serious misconduct).

- Consider whether, where appropriate, the employee had been given time to improve.

- Ensure that you have followed your disciplinary procedure.

If all the above conditions have been complied with, and you have reasonable grounds for believing that the employee is guilty of the conduct complained of, and that dismissal is a reasonable response in the circumstances, then you may take action to dismiss the employee.

In taking this action the key points to bear in mind are that your action must be considered reasonable and it should be consistent with penalties that may have been imposed in the past for similar offences. You must also give the employee the right to appeal against the decision.

An example letter terminating employment for misconduct is set out below.

Example letter terminating employment on grounds of misconduct

Dear

I write to confirm the outcome of our meeting held on [insert date].

I regret that it has been decided to terminate your employment with effect from [insert date] for the following reason(s): [describe reason(s) for dismissal].

You are entitled to [insert notice entitlement] weeks' notice and you will continue to receive full pay and benefits during this period. You will also be entitled to any outstanding holiday pay up to your last day of service and I will arrange for these payments to be made to you as soon as possible.

If you disagree with this decision, or feel that you have been treated unfairly by the company, you have the right to appeal through the company's disciplinary procedure. If you wish to do so, please let me know by [insert date].

The company will be prepared to provide you with a fair and accurate reference.

I regret that we have had to take this step and would like to wish you every success in finding a new job.

Yours sincerely,

Redundancy

A redundancy occurs when you dismiss someone because your requirement for the work that person was doing has ceased or reduced in that location.

Avoiding redundancies

When faced with the prospect of making staff redundant your first step should always be to consider other possible options. These might include:

- putting a freeze on recruitment;
- bringing contracted-out work back into the company;
- reducing or removing overtime working;
- reducing working hours or asking staff to work part time, or share jobs;
- work reorganization, and so forth.

Selecting staff for redundancy

The first step in any redundancy programme is usually to ask for volunteers. The problem with this is that those who volunteer may not be the ones you wish to lose, and also employees might feel that by volunteering they could be undermining their future prospects with the company. However, a voluntary redundancy programme might help to reduce the overall number who may be subject to compulsory redundancy. In seeking volunteers you should indicate that the company reserves the right not to accept any such offer if the employee in question has knowledge, skills and experience the company wishes to retain.

If compulsory redundancy is inevitable you will have to consider the selection criteria. In choosing the criteria you must ensure that they are objective and are not seen to be biased against any particular individual or group within the company.

Common redundancy criteria are a) on the basis of performance – in which case you need to ensure that any decisions can be supported by concrete evidence, such as ratings in the company's performance appraisal scheme; b) attendance or disciplinary record – which again must be supported by accurate records.

A growing trend is to carry out a skills audit to determine the company's current and future knowledge and skills requirement. This can then be used to support any decisions about redundancy. Whatever redundancy criteria are applied you must ensure that you do not select employees because of a protected characteristic as defined by the Equality Act 2010 – sex, sexual orientation, marital status, race, age, pregnancy, disability, belief, etc – or for any reasons connected with trade union membership, political beliefs or affiliations, or carrying out duties as a safety representative. Also, any selection made because the employee attempted to assert any of his legal rights is likely to be unfair.

An example letter of compulsory redundancy is set out below.

Example letter making an employee compulsorily redundant

Dear

I refer to our recent meeting when I indicated that because of a reduction in demand for the company's services I had to consider making your job redundant.

I regret that I now have to confirm that your job will become redundant with effect from [insert date].

We have fully discussed the possibility of you taking alternative employment with the company, but, as you know, there are at present no jobs available that are appropriate to your skills and experience. If this situation changes in the future we would be happy to re-employ you, should you still be available.

The redundancy payments you are entitled to are set out below:

statutory redundancy pay:	[...weeks × £ ...per week] =	£ ...
additional severance pay:	[...weeks × £ ...per week] =	£ ...
pay in lieu of notice:	[...weeks × £ ...per week] =	£ ...
outstanding holiday pay:	[...weeks × £ ...per week] =	£ ...

The company secretary will write to you separately about your pension entitlement. You have the right to appeal against this decision, and if you wish to do so I would be grateful if you would let me know within five working days.

I would like to take this opportunity to thank you for your past service with the company and to wish you every success for the future. If you wish to appeal against this selection or if you would like to discuss any aspect of this letter please do not hesitate to contact me.

Yours sincerely,

The redundancy process

Consultation with trade unions and/or employee representatives

If you are proposing to make 20 or more employees redundant you are legally required to consult any trade unions and employee representatives about ways of avoiding or reducing the redundancies, and of ameliorating the consequences. You must tell them:

- the reasons for the redundancies;
- the numbers and descriptions of jobs it is proposed to make redundant;
- the total number of employees in the company or establishment where the redundancies are occurring;

- the method of carrying out the redundancies, including selection criteria;
- how redundancy pay will be calculated;
- any proposals for reducing or avoiding the redundancies and for ameliorating the consequences.

There is also a strict timescale for consultation, depending on the numbers being made redundant, and if you intend to make 20 or more people redundant within 45 days or less you must also notify the Redundancy Payments Service. A form for this purpose can be downloaded from **http://www.bis.gov.uk/insolvency/about-us/forms/redundancy-payments-forms**. The overall process is set out in Figure 14.3.

FIGURE 14.3 The redundancy process

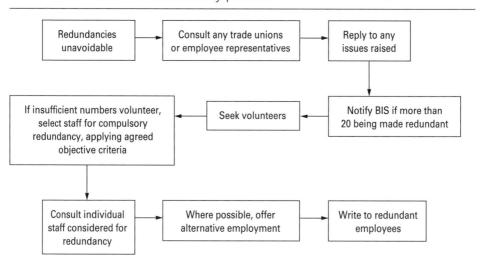

Following consultation with the employee representatives or trade unions you must also ensure that you consult with each individual that you propose to make redundant (see below).

Individual redundancy procedure

Quite apart from the rules relating to collective redundancies, there is a need to follow a definite procedure in making individual employees redundant. The process to be followed includes:

1 an individual consultation meeting with the employee to be made redundant;

2 a further meeting to hear any proposals put forward by the employee, and at which the final decision can be taken;

3 holding any appeal hearing against the redundancy.

At the initial meeting you should indicate that you are considering making the employee's job redundant and explain the reasons why this particular job is the one to be selected. You should stress that the meeting is a consultative one and that no final decision has been taken at that stage. You should give the employee a reasonable amount of time to consider his position and to make any suggestions, eg work reorganization. What is a 'reasonable' amount of time is not defined but a small employer should allow at least two weeks, and ideally four, for this consultation period.

At the second meeting you should listen to any suggestions put forward by the employee and then confirm your decision following the meeting. The employee has the right to be accompanied at this meeting by a colleague or a trade union representative. If the decision is to confirm the redundancy you need to give the employee the opportunity to appeal and then hear any appeal. Again, the employee has the right to be accompanied at the appeal hearing.

Rights of redundant employees

Any employee made redundant has a right to:

- paid time off work to look for another job if he has completed at least two years' continuous service;
- redundancy pay if he has completed at least two years' continuous service;
- the contractual or statutory notice period, or pay in lieu of notice;
- a four-week trial period (which can be extended by agreement) in a suitable alternative job without losing the right to redundancy pay if the job proves unsuitable – this can be ended by either party.

Redundancy pay is calculated on the basis of age and length of service as set out in Figure 14.4. The number of weeks' pay is multiplied by the current statutory rate, which is periodically reviewed.

If you make an offer of alternative employment you should ensure that any such offer is made in writing. An example letter is set out below.

Example letter offering alternative employment

Dear

Following our recent discussion, I write to confirm that your previous job has become redundant with effect from [insert date] but that the company is able to offer you alternative employment as [insert job title] from that date.

Your terms and conditions of employment will remain unchanged.

As explained to you, you have the right to a trial period of four weeks, beginning with the date you start the new job, for both you and the company to decide whether the job is a suitable one for you. If either party decides that the job is not suitable, this will not affect your entitlement to a redundancy payment.

I would be grateful if you would confirm your acceptance of this offer.

Yours sincerely,

FIGURE 14.4   Ready reckoner

EMPLOYMENT LEGISLATION

Ready reckoner for calculating the number of weeks' pay due

Read off your age and number of complete years' service. The table will then show how many weeks' pay you are entitled to.

If you are aged between 64 and 65, the amount due will be reduced by one twelfth for every complete month you are over 64.

Age	2	3	4	5	6	7	8	9	10	11	12	13	14	15	16	17	18	19	20
18*[1]	1																		
19	1	1½																	
20	1	1½	2																
21	1	1½	2	2½															
22	1	1½	2	2½	3														
23	1½	2	2½	3	3½	4													
24	2	2½	3	3½	4	4½	5												
25	2	3	3½	4	4½	5	5½	6											
26	2	3	4	4½	5	5½	6	6½	7										
27	2	3	4	5	5½	6	6½	7	7½	8									
28	2	3	4	5	6	6½	7	7½	8	8½	9								
29	2	3	4	5	6	7	7½	8	8½	9	9½	10							
30	2	3	4	5	6	7	8	8½	9	9½	10	10½	11						
31	2	3	4	5	6	7	8	9	9½	10	10½	11	11½	12					
32	2	3	4	5	6	7	8	9	10	10½	11	11½	12	12½	13				
33	2	3	4	5	6	7	8	9	10	11	11½	12	12½	13	13½	14			
34	2	3	4	5	6	7	8	9	10	11	12	12½	13	13½	14	14½	15		
35	2	3	4	5	6	7	8	9	10	11	12	13	13½	14	14½	15	15½	16	
36	2	3	4	5	6	7	8	9	10	11	12	13	14	14½	15	15½	16	16½	17
37	2	3	4	5	6	7	8	9	10	11	12	13	14	15	15½	16	16½	17	17½
38	2	3	4	5	6	7	8	9	10	11	12	13	14	15	16	16½	17	17½	18
39	2	3	4	5	6	7	8	9	10	11	12	13	14	15	16	17	17½	18	18½
40	2	3	4	5	6	7	8	9	10	11	12	13	14	15	16	17	18	18½	19
41	2	3	4	5	6	7	8	9	10	11	12	13	14	15	16	17	18	19	19½
42	2½	3½	4½	5½	6½	7½	8½	9½	10½	11½	12½	13½	14½	15½	16½	17½	18½	19½	20½
43	3	4	5	6	7	8	9	10	11	12	13	14	15	16	17	18	19	20	21
44	3	4½	5½	6½	7½	8½	9½	10½	11½	12½	13½	14½	15½	16½	17½	18½	19½	20½	21½
45	3	4½	6	7	8	9	10	11	12	13	14	15	16	17	18	19	20	21	22
46	3	4½	6	7½	8½	9½	10½	11½	12½	13½	14½	15½	16½	17½	18½	19½	20½	21½	22½
47	3	4½	6	7½	9	10	11	12	13	14	15	16	17	18	19	20	21	22	23
48	3	4½	6	7½	9	10½	11½	12½	13½	14½	15½	16½	17½	18½	19½	20½	21½	22½	23½
49	3	4½	6	7½	9	10½	12	13	14	15	16	17	18	19	20	21	22	23	24
50	3	4½	6	7½	9	10½	12	13½	14½	15½	16½	17½	18½	19½	20½	21½	22½	23½	24½
51	3	4½	6	7½	9	10½	12	13½	15	16	17	18	19	20	21	22	23	24	25
52	3	4½	6	7½	9	10½	12	13½	15	16½	17½	18½	19½	20½	21½	22½	23½	24½	25½
53	3	4½	6	7½	9	10½	12	13½	15	16½	18	19	20	21	22	23	24	25	26
54	3	4½	6	7½	9	10½	12	13½	15	16½	18	19½	20½	21½	22½	23½	24½	25½	26½
55	3	4½	6	7½	9	10½	12	13½	15	16½	18	19½	21	22	23	24	25	26	27
56	3	4½	6	7½	9	10½	12	13½	15	16½	18	19½	21	22½	23½	24½	25½	26½	27½
57	3	4½	6	7½	9	10½	12	13½	15	16½	18	19½	21	22½	24	25	26	27	28
58	3	4½	6	7½	9	10½	12	13½	15	16½	18	19½	21	22½	24	25½	26½	27½	28½
59	3	4½	6	7½	9	10½	12	13½	15	16½	18	19½	21	22½	24	25½	27	28	29
60	3	4½	6	7½	9	10½	12	13½	15	16½	18	19½	21	22½	24	25½	27	28½	29½
61*[2]	3	4½	6	7½	9	10½	12	13½	15	16½	18	19½	21	22½	24	25½	27	28½	30

18* [1] – It is possible that an individual could start to build up continuous service before age 16, but this is likely to be rare, and therefore we have started this Table from age 18.

61* [2] – The same figures should be used when calculating the redundancy payment for a person aged 61 and above.

Redundancy policy

You may wish to introduce a redundancy policy; an example is set out below.

Example redundancy policy

Introduction

The aim of this policy is to clarify what procedures will be followed in the event of redundancies becoming unavoidable in the company. Every effort will be made to ensure that redundancies will be avoided, but we have to accept that there could be circumstances beyond the company's control that could result in a reduced demand for our services.

Avoidance of redundancies

In the event of a reduction in demand serious enough to require a commensurate reduction in working hours, our first step will be to consider organizational ways of adjusting to the reduction. This will include:

reducing costs where possible;

cutting back on overtime;

reducing the number of short-term temporary or agency staff;

bringing work in-house, rather than using contractors, where this is possible;

redesigning jobs and reorganizing work;

asking for volunteers to work part-time or job-share;

considering any other proposals put forward.

If we are unable to achieve the required savings by reorganizing we would ask for volunteers for redundancy. However, the company reserves the right to refuse to agree to make someone redundant if it is not in our interests to do so.

Consultation

In the event of compulsory redundancies being unavoidable the company will consult trade union and employee representatives about:

redundancies proposed;

reasons for the proposals;

number and descriptions of employees who it is proposed to make redundant;

total number of employees of that type employed in the company;

proposed method of selecting the employees for redundancy;

how the redundancies will be carried out;

how any redundancy payments will be calculated.

The consultation will be carried out for the purpose of considering ways of:

avoiding the dismissals;

reducing the number of employees to be dismissed; and

mitigating the consequences of the dismissals.

In addition to any collective discussions, any individual employee whose job is considered for redundancy will also be consulted to consider alternative suggestions.

Selection of staff for redundancy

The criteria for the selection of staff to be made redundant will be discussed as part of the consultation process.

We will ensure that any criteria selected are fair and objective.

Any employee selected for redundancy will be notified in writing, following individual consultation.

Notice period

The employee's contractual or statutory period of notice, whichever is the greater, will apply.

Redundancy pay

Redundancy pay will be calculated in accordance with the relevant statutory provisions, which are based on the employee's age, length of continuous employment, and the current statutory weekly rate or the actual weekly wage.

Right of appeal

Any employee who feels that the selection criteria were unfair or incorrectly applied can appeal to the Managing Director. Any such appeal must be made in writing within 10 working days of receiving the redundancy notification. The Managing Director will arrange an interview within five days with the employee, who has the right to be accompanied by a trade union representative or colleague. The Managing Director will give a decision on the issue within 10 working days of the interview.

Time off to seek alternative employment

Any employee made redundant will be considered for other suitable jobs in the company. If no such jobs are available, appropriate time off will be given to look for alternative employment.

Dismissal for Some Other Substantial Reason (SOSR)

It is potentially fair to dismiss an employee on the grounds of 'some other substantial reason of a kind such as to justify the dismissal of an employee holding the position which the employee held'. The heading includes those reasons that don't fall neatly into one of the other headings. Examples of reasons for dismissal that have been held to come under the SOSR heading include:

- a necessary business re-organization that is not a statutory redundancy;
- the expiry of a fixed-term contract without renewal;
- pressure from a key customer, client or third party where there is no suitable alternative employment;
- dismissal of the temporary replacement for an employee absent due to maternity leave;
- dismissal of the temporary replacement for an employee suspended on medical grounds;
- serious personality clashes or a complete breakdown in the working relationship between employees.

Giving references

You are not legally required to give a reference, although it is likely to be illegal if you withhold a reference for someone because of having previously taken legal action against you.

Any reference you do give must be fair and accurate, otherwise you could be liable to an action for defamation or negligence.

To avoid any possible legal action employers often opt to give a neutral reference, which merely states the facts about the job held by the employee but avoids any judgements about the employee's performance or personality.

Employees do not have an automatic right to see any reference you give, but under the Data Protection Act 1998 they do have access to any references given to you by another employer. However, you can refuse to give access if doing so would give information about another person who could be identified as the source of the information. Information about a third party cannot be disclosed unless that person has consented to the disclosure. Therefore, if you do not want a reference you give to be disclosed you should state that the reference is given in confidence.

The key points concerning references are:

- There is no legal obligation to provide a reference apart from jobs subject to FCA (Financial Conduct Authority) rules.
- Most employers provide references for reasons of reciprocity and because not to do so could be to the detriment of the employee.
- When references are given it is important that they are accurate, as otherwise legal action could be taken against the giver; the recipient of an inaccurate

reference could also have a claim for any loss incurred through acting on that reference.

- Givers of references are not liable for any inaccurate statements if made in good faith.

- There are a number of ways in which the subject of a reference may gain access to it, and under the provisions of the Data Protection Act 1998 there is a right to such access – you should therefore work on the assumption that the reference may be seen by the person to whom it refers.

- You should be wary of giving a good reference to an unsatisfactory employee who is dismissed, as this could severely weaken your case if that person brings a charge of unfair dismissal; similarly, misleading a prospective employer could leave you open to a claim from that employer.

- References may be obtained in writing or by telephone, but a written note should be kept of any telephone reference.

Exit interviews

When an employee resigns you might find it useful to discuss the reasons for his departure. This may not only help to correct any perceived deficiencies, but can sometimes have the effect of persuading the employee not to leave, by addressing his concerns. The main drawback is that you cannot be sure that the reasons given for leaving are the true ones. Often, if an employee has decided to leave anyway he may see little point in criticizing the company or its management and possibly jeopardizing the content of any reference or future relationships.

Examples of the kinds of questions that you might want to ask at an exit interview are:

- Why are you leaving the company?
- Which company are you going to?
- What sort of job are you going to do?
- What advantages does the new job offer over your old one?
- How will your reward package differ from your old one?
- Was your job with us what you expected?
- Could your qualifications, experience and skills have been better used?
- Did you receive all the support you required?
- Did you get all the training you needed?
- How did you view your prospects in the company?
- What did you think of the working environment?
- Are there any changes that we should make to our employment practices?
- Are there any other issues you think we should know about?

Further information

Data Protection Act 1998
Disability Discrimination Act 1995
Employment Rights Act 1996
Enterprise and Regulatory Reform Act 2013 (Commencement No. 2) Order 2013
Equality Act 2010
Maternity and Parental Leave Regulations 1999
National Minimum Wage Regulations 1999
Public Interest Disclosure Act 1998
Rehabilitation of Offenders Act 1974
Settlement Agreements: A Guide, ACAS 2013
Settlement Agreements Code of Practice 4, ACAS July 2013
The Redundancy Payments Scheme – A guide for employees, employers and others, PL808, BERR (now BIS)
Trade Union and Labour Relations Consolidation Act 1992
Working Time Regulations 1998
www.bis.gov.uk/insolvency

Dealing with Tribunal Cases

15

Following the introduction of tribunal fees in July 2013 the total number of employment tribunal cases received from August 2013 (after fees were introduced) until the end of March 2014 was 16,206 compared to 39,567 in the same 8 month period the previous year, a drop of 59 per cent. The statistics for April 2014 to June 2014 show a continuation of this trend with total claims lodged of 4245 compared to 13,899 in the same quarter the previous year, although this has been affected by the introduction of Early Conciliation which requires ACAS to be notified of any dispute before a claim can now be lodged. Individuals who could previously immediately lodge a claim now usually have to wait up to one month until ACAS agree that they can do so.

Below is a list of the average awards for unfair dismissal and discrimination claims:

Unfair dismissal	£11,813
Race discrimination	£11,203
Sex discrimination	£14,336
Disability discrimination	£14,502
Religious discrimination	£8,131
Sexual orientation discrimination	£8,701
Age discrimination	£18,801

In total there were 889 costs awards compared to 651 for the previous year, of which 647 were made in favour of respondents. The median award was £1,000 compared with £1,842 for the previous year.

Fees for lodging a claim are either £160 or £250 on issue of the claim and either £250 or £950 for a hearing, the precise figure depending on the type of claim. To bring a case to the Employment Appeal Tribunal would cost £400 plus £1,200 if the case goes to a full hearing. Some applicants may be able to apply for remission of these charges.

The role of employment tribunals

Employment tribunals are legally constituted bodies set up to hear complaints about matters connected with employment. They are like informal courts with three members, including a legally qualified employment judge. The rules governing their procedure are set out in the Employment Tribunals (Constitution and Rules of Procedure) Regulations 2013.

How a claim arises

Any employee wishing to make a claim to an employment tribunal must do so within three months of the date of termination of employment, or of the event to which the complaint relates. The applicant has to complete a form ET1, which sets out the grounds of the complaint and this is sent to the employer. A change introduced by the 2013 Regulations is that the claimant must now specify the amount of compensation to be claimed and how it is calculated. This can be changed during the case but the aim is to make the claimant think about her claim so that unrealistic expectations can be identified and responded to.

New rules have been introduced to try and weed out those claims that should not proceed because of some fundamental problem and any claim will be rejected if not made on the new ET1 form, omits the name and address of the claimant(s) and respondent, and is not accompanied by the correct fee (or remission application).

If you, as an employer, receive a form ET1 you will need to respond by completing form ET3, generally within 28 days, a process known as 'entering an appearance'. This will be rejected if it is not on the new ET3 form, does not set out the respondent's full name and address, or does not state whether the respondent wishes to resist any part of the claim or is not received within the time limit.

After both the ET1 and ET3 have been received an employment tribunal judge will decide if a claim should be struck out because it has no reasonable chance of success. A tribunal can also ask for a deposit of up to £1,000 to be paid if it is considered that any part of a claim has little prospect of success. It is hoped that this will discourage applicants from including everything they can think of and focus instead on a specific allegation.

The tribunal may order a preliminary hearing to consider the merits of the case and any issues arising from it including the possibility of settling the matter through alternative dispute resolution.

How to defend a claim

The process for defending a claim is as follows:

- You will receive a copy of the employee's claim, which will set out the grounds of her complaint in form ET1.
- You should read the form carefully to ensure that all the details are correct.

- You should set out the grounds for resisting the claim and address any errors in the employee's application.
- If insufficient information has been provided by the applicant for you to be clear about the exact nature of the claim you can ask the local tribunal office for a delay in responding – entering an appearance – until you have received further and better particulars.
- The defence you put forward will depend of course on the nature of the claim.
- Following the receipt of the ET1 you are likely to be contacted by a conciliation officer of ACAS, whose role is to try to negotiate a settlement between the parties.

Preparing for a tribunal hearing

You should be notified about a tribunal hearing 14 days in advance. When preparing for a hearing you should:

- Make sure that your witnesses are able to attend the hearing.
- Brief any witnesses to ensure that they are aware of what they may be asked and are clear about their responses.
- Arrange your documents into a bundle and number them consecutively.
- Send large bundles of documents to the tribunal office well in advance to give everyone time to read them.
- Prepare thoroughly and try to anticipate likely questions.
- Consider whether you need to be represented at the tribunal.

Procedure at the hearing

On the day of the hearing you should:

1 Arrive early and let the receptionist know who is attending the hearing.
2 Contact the other party in case there is the possibility of a last-minute settlement.
3 Confirm with your witnesses the tribunal procedure and the evidence they are to give.

The procedure at the hearing is to be determined by the tribunal but is likely to be as follows:

1 The party with the burden of proof will be asked to present their case.
2 The other party will then be asked to present her case.
3 Witnesses will next be questioned by both parties and tribunal members.
4 After the presentation of the evidence both parties will have the opportunity to make a closing statement.
5 The tribunal will then make a decision on the evidence presented.

Compensation for unfair dismissal

Tribunals can award:

- Reinstatement or re-engagement.
- A minimum basic award calculated on a similar basis as the redundancy payment subject to a maximum of 30 weeks' pay at the current statutory rate (£464 per week in 2014).
- A compensatory award designed to compensate for loss of earnings up to a maximum of £76,574 in 2014 (reviewed annually) or 12 months' pay if lower. This limit may be disregarded in certain cases, such as those relating to discrimination or where the dismissal relates to health and safety or whistle-blowing issues.

Unreasonable behaviour

- A tribunal can take into account the unreasonable behaviour of a party's representative when awarding costs against that party.
- The tribunal has to consider an award of costs where proceedings that have no reasonable prospect of success have been pursued.

Reconsideration of a tribunal's decision

You can apply for a tribunal to reconsider a decision within 14 days of receiving the written decision. An employment judge will consider whether there is any prospect of the original decision being changed or revoked.

It is up to the employment judge to decide whether to allow any such reconsideration. An appeal to the Employment Appeal Tribunal can take place on a point of law.

Further information

Copies of both the ET1 and ET3 forms can be downloaded from:
   www.employmenttribunals.gov.uk under 'Forms & Guidance'
Employment Tribunals Act 1996
Employment Tribunal enquiry line, Tel: 0845 795 9775
http://www.justice.gov.uk/downloads/tribunals/employment/et-fees-factsheet.pdf
The Employment Tribunals (Constitution and Rules of Procedure) Regulations 2013
www.legislation.gov.uk

Ensuring the Health, Safety and Welfare of Employees

16

General responsibility

Duties of employers to employees

As an employer you have a general responsibility to ensure the health and safety of your employees. This requirement is given legal force through the Health and Safety at Work, etc Act 1974. This requires that you must take all reasonably practicable steps to provide:

- a safe working environment, including safe access to and from your premises;
- a safe system of work;
- safe tools, appliances and equipment;
- protection from hazards;
- any necessary training and instruction to your staff.

In addition, if you employ five or more people you must:

- publish a written health and safety policy (see example below);
- form a safety committee if asked to do so in writing by at least two safety representatives;
- consult all employees on health and safety matters.

Duty to the general public

In addition to your duties to employees, you also have a duty to ensure the health and safety of any visitors to your premises.

Duties of employees

At work your employees have a duty to take reasonable care of their own health and safety at work and of other people who may be affected by their acts or omissions, and to cooperate with you and others to ensure that your legal obligations are met.

Enforcement of the Health and Safety at Work, etc Act 1974

The Health and Safety at Work, etc Act is enforced by inspectors appointed by the Health and Safety Executive. They have the power to:

- enter and inspect premises;
- collect information, including measurements, photographs, recordings and so forth;
- take samples;
- issue prohibition notices that have the effect of immediately halting the machinery or process in question;
- issue improvement notices requiring you to remedy specific defects;
- bring proceedings before a magistrates' court.

In practice an inspector will not institute criminal proceedings unless you have persistently flouted the law or the breach is a very serious one.

Safety representatives

Safety representatives can be appointed by recognized independent trade unions and, where appointed, you have a duty to consult them on safety issues.

Any safety representative should, as far as is reasonably practicable, have been employed continuously for two years or more, or have at least two years' experience in a similar environment. It is common for unions to appoint shop stewards as safety representatives, but this can lead to a conflict of interest where, for example, the shop steward has to represent employees who have been accused of breaching safety procedures. However, you have no choice but to accept the union's nominated representative.

The role of a safety representative is to:

- investigate potential hazards and dangerous occurrences at work and examine the causes of accidents;
- investigate complaints by any employee represented about that employee's health, safety or welfare;
- make representations about general health, safety and welfare matters;
- carry out inspections;
- represent employees in consultations with the Health and Safety Executive;

- receive information from inspectors;
- attend meetings of safety committees.

You must give all reasonable assistance and facilities to enable safety inspections to take place.

In addition, the Health and Safety (Consultation with Employees) Regulations 1996 require you to consult employees, where there are no recognized trade unions, on a range of health and safety issues that are likely to affect employees. Consultation can be with the employees directly or with elected 'representatives of employee safety' (RoES).

Whether you deal with safety representatives appointed by recognized independent trade unions or with RoES elected by employees, you must let them have reasonable paid time off to carry out their functions and to receive training.

Protection for health and safety representatives

You may not dismiss, or take action short of dismissal (such as downgrading, or disciplinary action) against safety representatives and employees for taking what may be regarded as appropriate action in relation to health and safety issues. This protection is for:

- any employee to whom you give specific health and safety responsibilities;
- a recognized workers' representative on health and safety matters or a member of a safety committee;
- any employee who draws your attention to circumstances connected with his work that he believes to be harmful or potentially harmful (generally this will apply only where there is no appointed safety representative);
- any employee who leaves or proposes to leave his place of work because he reasonably believes that there is a serious and imminent danger that he could not have been expected to avert, and who refuses to return to the place of work while the danger persists;
- any employee who, in dangerous circumstances, takes or proposes to take appropriate steps to protect himself or other people from danger.

Whether or not any action you take against an employee is justified will depend on the circumstances. If the employee is negligent and you can demonstrate that the action you took would have been taken by any reasonable employer in the same circumstances, the protection will not apply to the employee. If the employee considers that the action is not justified, he may complain to an employment tribunal, regardless of his length of service.

Safety committees

Safety representatives can require you to set up a safety committee and this must be done within three months of receiving a written request from two or more safety representatives. Before setting up the safety committee, however, you should consult both the safety representatives and any recognized trade union.

Membership

Where a safety committee is set up you can decide the membership, although it clearly makes sense to have regard to the views of the trade union representatives. The relationship of the safety committee to other committees, and the general working arrangements, will depend on how your company is organized. For example, where you have a number of different plants or workplaces it might be necessary to have separate committees at each of these, perhaps with a coordinating committee at the group or company level.

The membership of the committee should be limited to a reasonable size with an equal number of management and employees' representatives.

Management representatives should include those who have the necessary knowledge and experience to provide accurate information on technical issues relating to health and safety, and should include not just line managers, but also functional specialists such as engineers. They should have the necessary authority to be able to make decisions. Other specialists may be co-opted onto the committee or can be asked to attend meetings in relation to items about which they have particular knowledge.

Role and objectives

The main role of the safety committee is to keep under review health and safety measures taken by the company. Specific functions are likely to include:

- the study of accidents and notifiable diseases, statistics and trends, to enable reports and recommendations to be made to the company's management;
- examination of safety audits, to report on problems and recommend any necessary changes;
- the consideration of reports and information provided by health and safety inspectors;
- the consideration of reports from safety representatives;
- assistance in the development of work safety rules and safe systems of work;
- monitoring the effectiveness of safety training for employees;
- monitoring the effectiveness of health and safety communication in the workplace;
- providing a link with the various government inspectorates and agencies.

Management of health and safety

The Management of Health and Safety at Work Regulations 1999 require you to:

- Assess the risk to health and safety of your employees and anyone else affected by your work activities, and if you have more than five employees, to record any significant findings.
- Make arrangements for putting into practice the preventive and protective measures arising from the risk assessments, and to put these in writing if you have more than five employees.
- Carry out health and safety surveillance of employees where appropriate.
- Appoint competent persons to carry out health and safety measures, preferably from within your company.
- Arrange any necessary contacts with emergency services.
- Provide information and training to employees.
- Cooperate with other occupants of your premises to coordinate safety measures.
- Ensure that temporary employees are also given the appropriate information.

First aid

You are required to make first aid arrangements for your employees. The extent of these facilities will depend on the:

- number of employees;
- type of work carried out;
- size of the working premises and the location of employees;
- location of the working premises.

The number of first aid staff to be provided will depend on all of the above factors, plus whether there is shift working, and the distance from medical services. As a general rule there should be one first aider for every 50 to 100 employees. Where hazards are greater there should be one for every 50 employees and at least one for 20 or more employees. If you feel that there is no need for a first aider you should appoint someone to take action in the event of an injury or illness.

Provision of sanitary facilities

The HSE has provided guidance on the provision of sanitary facilities, which should include:

- enough toilets and washbasins for those expected to use them – people should not have to queue for long periods to go to the toilet;

- where possible, separate facilities for men and women – failing that, rooms with lockable doors;
- clean facilities – to help achieve this walls and floors should preferably be tiled (or covered in suitable waterproof material) to make them easier to clean;
- a supply of toilet paper and, for female employees, a means of disposing of sanitary dressings;
- facilities that are well lit and ventilated;
- facilities with hot and cold running water;
- enough soap or other washing agents;
- a basin large enough to wash hands and forearms if necessary;
- a means for drying hands, eg paper towels or a hot air dryer; and
- showers where necessary, eg for particularly dirty work.

Reporting of injuries, diseases and dangerous occurrences

The Reporting of Injuries, Diseases and Dangerous Occurrences Regulations 2013 (RIDDOR) require you to report to the HSE any of the following types of incident:

- a death at work or within one year as a result of an injury or condition incurred at work;
- certain specified injuries such as fractures, amputation, loss of sight, electric shock, loss of consciousness, poisoning, injury caused by violence at work and so forth;
- lost time where the person is unfit for work for more than seven consecutive days excluding the day of the accident (accidents resulting in a worker being incapacitated for more than three days must be recorded, but not reported);
- any of the dangerous occurrences specified in the Regulations, including those relating to lifting machinery, pressure systems, dangerous substances, breathing apparatus, explosives and so forth;
- where a person suffers from any of the diseases listed and works in one of the specified activities.

Generally, these must be reported immediately, followed by a written report within seven days.

Health and safety policy

If you have more than five employees you are required to have a health and safety policy, which would normally be incorporated into the staff handbook. An example policy is set out below.

Example health and safety policy

It is the company's policy to establish and maintain safe and healthy working conditions for all staff in accordance with current health and safety legislation.

It is also your responsibility, along with all of our employees, to take reasonable care to ensure the health, safety and welfare of yourself, your colleagues and any visitors to our premises. You should cooperate with any measures introduced to promote health and safety and should bring to the attention of the appropriate supervisor or line manager anything which you feel is, or may become, a safety hazard.

Any infringement of the health and safety policy and rules could lead to disciplinary action and, in certain circumstances, to criminal proceedings.

The director of operations is the main person responsible for ensuring the overall health and safety of our premises.

Fire and bomb alerts

Instructions on what to do in the event of the fire alarm sounding or a bomb alert, and the instructions for evacuating the building, are displayed throughout the building. You should make sure that you have read and understood these instructions and know the location of all emergency exits. In the event of an alarm you should leave the building immediately without attempting to retrieve papers, files, personal possessions and so forth.

Security

You are issued with instructions relating to security and the wearing of security passes on joining the company. These must be complied with at all times. In the interests of security the company reserves the right to search staff and their baggage on entering or leaving the premises.

First aid

Some members of staff are trained in first aid and their names are displayed on the notice board. First-aid boxes are located at [insert location(s)].

Accidents

Any accident or injury on our premises must be reported to your line manager immediately, so that the matter can be properly investigated, recorded and, if appropriate, reported to the proper authorities.

Risk assessments

The company will carry out regular risk assessments relating to the work environment and the equipment used to ensure that these pose no health hazards. Any concerns you might have in this respect should be reported to your line manager.

Smoking at work

Smoking is banned in public places and offices. A policy document on smoking is set out in Chapter 9.

Health and safety regulations

Some of the main health and safety regulations you may need to be aware of, depending on the nature of your business, are as follows:

Safety Representatives and Safety Committees Regulations 1977

Control of Asbestos at Work Regulations 1987

Control of Lead at Work Regulations 1998

Noise at Work Regulations 1989

Control of Substances Hazardous to Health Regulations (CoSHH) 2002

Electricity at Work Regulations 1989

Personal Protective Equipment at Work Regulations 1992

Manual Handling Operations Regulations 1992

Health and Safety (Display Screen Equipment) Regulations 1992

Provision and use of Work Equipment Regulations 1998

Supply of Machinery (Safety) Regulations 1998

Workplace (Health, Safety and Welfare) Regulations 1992

Chemicals (Hazard Information & Packaging for Supply) Regulations 1996

Fire Precautions (Workplace) Regulations 1997

Lifting Operations and Lifting Equipment Regulations 1998

Construction (Design and Management) Regulations 1994

Confined Spaces Regulations 1987

Pressure Systems and Transportable Gas Containers Regulations 1989

Health and Safety (Safety Signs and Signals) Regulations 1996

Highly Flammable Liquids and Liquefied Petroleum Gases Regulations 1972

The Corporate Manslaughter and Corporate Homicide Act 2007

This Act came into force on 6 April 2008 and sets out an offence leading to conviction of an organization where a gross failure in the way activities were managed or organized results in a person's death.

Official sentencing guidelines on corporate manslaughter and health and safety offences causing death were published by the Sentencing Guidelines Council in February 2010. These set out in detail the factors a court should take into account in passing sentence under the Act, including, for example 'whether the fine will have the effect of putting the defendant out of business'. One company that was prosecuted under the Health and Safety legislation after a worker was killed as a result of a fall from faulty scaffolding was fined only £1 (but over £13,000 in costs) because the judge took into account the fact that any significant fine would cause the company to go out of business.

Further information

Health and Safety at Work, etc Act 1974
Health and Safety (Consultation with Employees) Regulations 1996
Leading Health and Safety at Work Guidelines: Leadership actions for directors and board members, IoD, HSE, www.iod.com/hsguide
Management of Health and Safety at Work Regulations 1999
Stranks, J (2007) *Health and Safety at Work*, revised 8th edn, Kogan Page, London
The Corporate Manslaughter and Corporate Homicide Act 2007

Working with Trade Unions

17

The majority of small and medium-sized businesses in the United Kingdom do not have trade unions and this chapter will not therefore apply to them. However, where trade unions do exist, and particularly where they are recognized by the employer, they do make a difference to the way in which the company is run.

The degree of difference between an organization with a union or unions and one without depends on the attitude of management and whether or not there is union recognition. The key difference in a company where unions are recognized is that changes to terms and conditions of employment, and perhaps to working methods and arrangements, will be discussed and negotiated collectively with those unions, rather than with individual employees or their non-union representatives.

The rest of this chapter highlights some of the other key implications for employers and managers.

The role of a trade union

The primary role of a trade union is to protect the interests of its members. This entails negotiating the best possible deals in terms of pay, conditions of service and working arrangements generally. Many unions also have political objectives but these are generally a secondary consideration.

Recognizing a trade union

Why recognize a trade union?

If you have not previously recognized a union the thought of having to consult one and possibly negotiate with it on a range of issues can be alarming. However, there are a number of advantages:

- it can provide a focal point for consultation and communication;
- it can help to convince the employees of the need for change or for new ways of working;
- the involvement of a union in the change process can help to legitimize the actions of management in the eyes of the workforce;
- it can improve communications between management and the workforce;
- if you wish to introduce changes to working practices, or contract terms, you need only reach agreement with the elected representatives and not with every individual employee, provided they are all members of the union.

The right of recognition

You can voluntarily agree to recognize a trade union. However, following the Employment Relations Act 1999, if you have 21 or more workers you are legally required to recognize an independent trade union (or unions) for a group of workers (described as a 'bargaining unit') if a majority of the workforce vote for such recognition. A 'majority' in this case means a simple majority of those voting and at least 40 per cent in that bargaining unit.

The meaning of a bargaining unit

Any group or groups of workers at a particular workplace can constitute a 'bargaining unit'. This is one of the issues that you will need to resolve in discussion with the union.

The meaning of union independence

Many trade union rights depend on the trade union being recognized as independent – not under the control of the employer. Being independent has the advantage that the right not to be dismissed or suffer action short of dismissal on the grounds of trade union membership or activities only applies where the union is independent. Also, only an independent union can negotiate away the right to strike in a collective agreement.

If an independent union is recognized by you it then acquires additional rights. These are:

- the right to information for collective bargaining purposes;
- the right (in certain circumstances) to be consulted about proposed collective redundancies and transfers;
- the right to paid time off for union officials and for unpaid time off for union members to carry out trade union activities;
- the right to be consulted on health and safety matters.

Recognition procedure

An application by a union for recognition must satisfy the following criteria:

- the request must be received by the employer;
- the trade union must be independent and have a certificate to that effect;
- the employer must have at least 21 workers on the day the request is received or have employed an average of at least 21 workers in the 13 weeks preceding the date of the request;
- the request must be in writing, identify the union(s) involved and state that it is a request under the provisions of schedule 1 of the Trade Union and Labour Relations (Consolidation) Act 1992.

If you accept the union's request and agree with the identification of the bargaining unit within 10 working days of receiving the request from the union, the union becomes recognized for collective bargaining purposes and no further action is required. If, however, you wish to negotiate there is a procedure to be followed, which is summarized in Figure 17.1.

Voluntary recognition

If you are considering the voluntary recognition of a union you should take into account:

- the degree of support for the union among the workforce;
- the ability of the union to represent those employees effectively;
- whether any other union is recognized for the workforce in question;
- the costs and benefits to you as employer;
- the status and reputation of the union;
- the effects of union recognition on existing collective agreements and other terms and conditions of employment.

Action to be taken on receiving a request for recognition

When a request for recognition is received you have to consider:

- whether to recognize that union;
- whether to enter into a single-union agreement;
- the issues for which recognition should be given and whether they should be limited to specific issues such as disciplinary and grievance procedures;
- whether recognition is in the interests of the company and workforce;
- whether recognition has been given to any other union(s) representing any of those workers.

FIGURE 17.1 Union recognition process (simplified)

The scope and content of any recognition agreement

Once a union has been recognized a recognition agreement will need to be drawn up. The agreement provides a framework for collective bargaining and sets out those issues about which bargaining will take place. The agreement should include:

- the names of the parties to the agreement;
- the workers covered by the agreement;
- the purposes for which the trade union is recognized;
- the number of shop stewards the organization is prepared to deal with and the process for their election;
- the facilities that they will be given;
- the way in which the agreement will operate;
- provisions for terminating the agreement.

You should try to get a single-union agreement as this is likely to simplify administration, save time and money, and reduce the potential for inter-union disputes.

De-recognizing a trade union

Once a recognition agreement has been entered into you cannot end it within three years of the agreement being made. After that period you can end the agreement with or without the consent of the union. On the other hand, the union can end the agreement at any time with or without your consent.

You can withdraw from recognition agreements if the number of workers falls below the minimum required number of 21 in any 13-week period. To withdraw from the agreement in these circumstances you must give a notice to this effect to the union(s) involved and notify the Central Arbitration Committee (CAC). The information given must:

- identify the bargaining arrangements;
- set out the 13-week period;
- state the date on which notice is given;
- be given within a period of five working days following the 13-week period;
- state that you and any associated employer employed fewer than 21 workers on average during that 13-week period;
- state the date on which the bargaining arrangements are to cease – this must be at least 35 working days after the date of the notice.

Employees' union rights

Trade union membership

All employees have the right either to belong to, or refuse to belong to, a trade union.

You must not penalize or in any other way discourage trade union membership, for example by failing to provide training or promotion opportunities, by selecting union members first in the event of redundancy and so forth. Similarly, it is unlawful to dismiss someone either because she is a member of a union or because she refuses to join one.

Where an employee feels that she has been penalized for belonging to a trade union she can bring a complaint to an employment tribunal. The onus is then on the employer to prove that the behaviour complained of, or the penalty imposed, is not because of the employee's membership or non-membership of a trade union.

Time off rights for trade union officers and members

Both members and officials of recognized independent trade unions have the right to a reasonable amount of time off from work to take part in various trade union duties and activities. Trade union officials have the right to paid time off to carry out trade union duties and to undertake training.

Any official should be paid at the normal rate, just as if she had not had any time off or, where earnings are variable such as in piece work, at the average hourly rate.

Local trade union representatives or shop stewards

Role

Most trade unions have local unpaid representatives, commonly known as shop stewards, although there are a number of other descriptions. The role of these representatives will vary according to the organization but is likely to include some or all of the following:

- representing their members locally, particularly at grievance and disciplinary hearings;
- recruiting new members to the union;
- collecting trade union dues in the absence of any check-off agreement;
- acting as a conduit of information between the union and its members;
- representing the views of the local members to the full-time trade union officer;
- consulting with the management;
- negotiating certain issues at a local level, although the extent and range of this will depend on the structure of the union;
- safeguarding employees' health and safety in the workplace, where the steward is also the safety representative.

Appointment of shop stewards

You should agree the appointment of shop stewards with the union and you should reserve the right to impose conditions or veto particular appointments. The kinds of conditions that it would be reasonable to impose are those relating to the employee's length of service, experience of the jobs being represented, disciplinary record, attendance and so forth. There should also be an agreement about the number of shop stewards.

Facilities for shop stewards

The facilities you will normally be expected to give to shop stewards include:

- reasonable time off with pay to carry out trade union duties such as attending meetings and representing employees;

- reasonable time off with pay to receive training in trade union duties;
- office facilities.

Working with shop stewards

The nature of the working relationship with shop stewards will often depend more on the personalities involved than on any organizational factors. If you or your management experience difficulty in working with any particular local representative the matter should be raised with the full-time union officer at the next higher tier in the union, before taking action such as withdrawing time-off facilities. Generally the union will be interested in maintaining good relations, so will try to resolve any problems.

When working with shop stewards or any other trade union representatives on a day-to-day basis it is wise to confirm any agreement in writing (unless it is 'off the record'). Any such letter should also relate to one subject only, so if several subjects are discussed there will need to be several letters. This is to avoid any possibility of ambiguity, or of certain points being accidentally or deliberately overlooked.

Providing information to trade unions

You are legally required to disclose to representatives of recognized independent trade unions information that they might need for collective bargaining, and to maintain good industrial relations.

Although the information to be given is not specified in the legislation, it is likely to cover at least the following:

- pay and benefits;
- conditions of service and employment policies;
- manpower data;
- performance, productivity and efficiency data;
- financial data.

The above is the kind of information that should be disclosed, according to an ACAS Code of Practice; it is, therefore, advisory rather than obligatory. Listed, recognized unions also have the statutory right to information relating to redundancies, transfers of undertakings (mergers and takeovers), occupational pensions and the company's policy on training.

Restrictions on disclosure

You can refuse to disclose information that:

- would be against the interests of national security;
- cannot be disclosed because doing so would be illegal;

- has been given to you in confidence;
- relates specifically to an individual and she has not consented to its disclosure;
- would cause substantial damage to your business;
- has been obtained by you to bring, or to defend against, any legal proceedings.

The Information and Consultation Regulations 2004

The Information and Consultation Regulations give employees the right to be informed about an undertaking's economic situation, informed and consulted about employment prospects, and informed and consulted about decisions likely to lead to substantial changes in work organization or contractual relations, including redundancies and transfers. It applies to undertakings employing 50 or more people. The number of employees in an undertaking is averaged out over a 12-month period.

You are free to agree different procedures to those set out in the Regulations and can meet your obligations through existing agreements. You may also withhold information where disclosure would seriously harm the undertaking or be prejudicial to it. Alternatively, you can require that the information be kept confidential by any employee representatives to whom it is disclosed.

The requirement to inform and consult employees is triggered either by a formal request from employees for an information and consultation (I&C) agreement, or it can be initiated by the employer. An employee request to negotiate an agreement must be made by at least 10 per cent of the employees in the undertaking, subject to a minimum of 15 employees and a maximum of 2,500. Where you have a pre-existing agreement you can ballot the workforce to ascertain whether it endorses the request by employees, provided that fewer than 40 per cent of your employees make the request.

Handling disputes

A trade dispute is any dispute about work issues either between you and your workers, or between different groups of workers.

Industrial action

Industrial action includes:

- strikes;
- a ban on overtime;
- working to rule;

- refusal to undertake voluntary or non-contractual activities;
- withdrawing cooperation from the employer, for example by not sitting on joint committees;
- refusal to work at a location or operate certain plant or equipment or processes.

There is no right to strike in UK employment law but there is immunity from civil liability for actions in tort provided certain conditions are met.

Legal immunity of unions

A trade union will only be immune from legal action where:

- there is a trade dispute and the action is called wholly or mainly in support of that dispute;
- the trade union has held a properly conducted secret ballot;
- the trade union has given notice of official industrial action to employers likely to be affected;
- the action is not secondary action (action against another employer who is not the main party to the dispute);
- the action is not intended to promote union closed shop practices or to prevent employers using non-union firms as suppliers;
- the action is not in support of any employee dismissed while taking unofficial industrial action;
- the action does not involve unlawful picketing.

Dismissing employees for taking unofficial industrial action

You can dismiss all or some of your employees if they take unofficial action and can re-engage some or none of them without facing claims for unfair dismissal.

Picketing

Although the official reason for picketing is to give information, the real aims of picketing are to:

- try to persuade others to join the strike;
- prevent goods or supplies from reaching the employer; and
- ensure that those already on strike do not return.

Picketing is only lawful if it is:

- undertaken in relation to a trade dispute;
- carried out by a person attending near her own place of work, or a trade union official accompanying a member;

- for the purpose of peacefully obtaining or communicating information or peacefully persuading a person to work or not to work;
- an unemployed person picketing by or near her last place of work in relation to a trade dispute connected with the dismissal;
- a person who does not have a fixed place of work, or for whom it is not practicable to picket at her place of work, who may picket at any premises of her employer from which her work is administered.

You can sue any pickets not complying with these rules, take out an injunction to stop any unlawful picketing and start an action for damages.

There is no statutory limit on the number of pickets.

Handling industrial action

How you respond to any industrial action will depend on the nature and scale of that action. However, there are a number of responses that might generally apply in a range of situations. These are:

- Consider voluntary conciliation, possibly through ACAS, or through an independent arbitrator.
- Take no action and continue to pay the employees normally, if it is felt that the business can be continued without too much disruption during the dispute.
- Where there is a breach of contract consider taking individual disciplinary action against those taking part in the action.
- Where any actions are unofficial and do not have immunity, seek a court injunction.
- Use any agreed collective disputes procedure to settle the dispute.
- Call upon support from the relevant employer's association or ACAS.
- Consider writing to any employees taking part, threatening to suspend them, possibly even terminating their employment if the industrial action persists.
- Where industrial action takes the form of non-performance of certain activities notify the employees that they will only be paid for those activities they do undertake.
- If the industrial action is unofficial, consider dismissing those taking part.
- Consider withholding all or part of the pay of any employee taking part in a strike or other industrial action.
- Refuse to let employees work normally unless they sign an undertaking not to take part in industrial action.
- Close down the place of work and reopen it after a period of, say, three months, selectively re-engaging dismissed employees.
- Terminate existing contracts and offer new ones calculated on the basis of the work the employees are prepared to do.

- Consider notifying the union and the individuals involved in the action that you will be seeking to make deductions from employees' wages to make up for lost revenue arising from the industrial action.

Further information

Cushway, B (2000) *Working with Unions – The new skills required to deal with union recognition*, Pearson Education, London
Employment Relations Act 1999
The Information and Consultation Regulations 2004
Trade Union and Labour Relations (Consolidation) Act 1992

INDEX

NB: Page locators in *italics* indicate figures or tables

INDEX OF ADVERTISERS